The Newlywed Home

The Newlywed Home

A COUPLE'S GUIDE *to* SETTING UP HOUSE *with* STYLE

Anush J. Benliyan

ARTISAN | NEW YORK

Text copyright © 2025 by Anush J. Benliyan
Hand-lettering © 2025 by Abraham Lule
Table setting illustrations © 2025 by Natalie Hubbert
Illustrations on pages 172–173 © 2025 NinjaStudio/Shutterstock, Inc.
For photography credits, turn to page 216, which functions as
an extension of this page.

Hachette Book Group supports the right to free expression and the value of copyright. The purpose of copyright is to encourage writers and artists to produce the creative works that enrich our culture.

The scanning, uploading, and distribution of this book without permission is a theft of the author's intellectual property. If you would like permission to use material from the book (other than for review purposes), please contact permissions@hbgusa.com. Thank you for your support of the author's rights.

Library of Congress Cataloging-in-Publication Data is on file.

ISBN 978-1-64829-218-7

Design by Suet Chong

Artisan books may be purchased in bulk for business, educational, or promotional use. For information, please contact your local bookseller or the Hachette Book Group Special Markets Department at special.markets@hbgusa.com.

The publisher is not responsible for websites (or their content) that are not owned by the publisher.

The Hachette Speakers Bureau provides a wide range of authors for speaking events. To find out more, go to hachettespeakersbureau.com or email HachetteSpeakers@hbgusa.com.

Published by Artisan,
an imprint of Workman Publishing,
a division of Hachette Book Group, Inc.
1290 Avenue of the Americas
New York, NY 10104
artisanbooks.com

The Artisan name and logo are registered trademarks of
Hachette Book Group, Inc.

Printed in China (TLF) on responsibly sourced paper
First printing, September 2025

10 9 8 7 6 5 4 3 2 1

For Ash,
my love.

And Roman,
our everything.

CONTENTS

Introduction
Honey, We're Home
9

First Impressions
THE ENTRYWAY
17

Comfort Zone
THE LIVING ROOM
37

No Reservations
THE KITCHEN
65

Get Together
THE DINING ROOM
91

Pillow Talk
THE BEDROOM
121

Vanity Fair
THE BATHROOM

147

Love Interests
THE "BONUS" ROOM

165

Sun-Kissed
OUTDOOR SPACES

181

To Have and to Hold Onto
MERGING, EDITING, AND ORGANIZING

203

Wedding Registry Checklist 210

Resources 212

Photography Credits 216

Acknowledgments 218

Index 220

INTRODUCTION

Honey, We're Home

There is a subtle yet significant distinction between moving in with a romantic partner and creating a home with a life partner. The difference lies in the sincerity and purpose of both parties as they intentionally make space for each other, joyously celebrate each other's identities, actively honor the love they share, and discover commonalities (and make compromises) when it comes to style, comfort, and daily habits.

Establishing a family residence is a huge, beautiful step between committed companions, and it marks the beginning of a lifetime spent calling the same place home. As such, your shared abode should feel like exactly that: home for both of you individually and as a couple. Whether you're already cohabitating or are moving in together only after the wedding, when you make this new commitment to set down roots, it's the perfect opportunity to do so in style. Realizing a dream home that's mature, aesthetically pleasing, comfortable, and representative of a union requires a lot of care and collaboration. My hope is that this book will be your trusted sidekick as you merge your lives in a meaningful way and will accompany you at every stage of the process, from ideating to organizing to adding the finishing touches. It is intended to help you navigate and conquer such challenges as merging and curating belongings, designing functional spaces that serve you both, and setting the stage for self-care, intimacy, entertaining, recreation, and an overall well-rounded homelife.

As a lifestyle and design journalist, I've had the great privilege of being invited into the homes of folks from myriad walks of life, among them renowned artists, architects, actors, musicians, chefs, and entrepreneurs. Through my interviews, I've been able to take a peek into the private lives of creative couples and their expressive, unique homes. I've also had the honor of picking the brains of some of the world's leading interior designers, learning about their philosophies, processes, and inspirations. These special encounters have taught me that authenticity, above all, is the secret to an undeniably charming, one-of-a-kind home that not only supports one's lifestyle but also enriches it.

Given my background, when I moved in with my now husband, I felt confident and clear about the direction for our shared home. I had packed up my life and moved numerous times before, and in each case was able to settle myself into a new phase with ease. I quickly realized, however, that this was unlike starting afresh on my own. It seems like a no-brainer in retrospect, but grasping that my partner was coming to our new house with his own expectations and belongings—many, many belongings—was tougher for me than I'd like to admit. I've always been someone who cares deeply about my surroundings, holding the belief that the spaces in which we exist have the power to alter our well-being, so the thought of losing control of my habitat shook me a bit. Unbeknownst to me then, my partner felt the same. This cheerful new beginning soon morphed into a minefield of quarrels and stress, layered with an overwhelming number of questions to ask, decisions to make, and compromises to reach.

Thankfully, it didn't take us long to understand that the only road to success was a two-way street. We had always referred to ourselves as teammates, calling on each other through thick and thin, and overcoming this hurdle was no different. After all, our endgame was the same: an attractive home that made us feel relaxed and contented; where we could both see ourselves represented as individuals and continue to nurture our relationship. We would take on the design of our home as a united front, one step at a time, and embrace the project as a wonderful opportunity to learn more about each other and grow closer.

That fruitful experience produced our enchanting newlywed home, which we still reminisce about today, and laid the groundwork for this book. Room by room, each chapter will walk you through the deliberations you should address as a duo in order to reach the practical—and stylish—solutions that are right for you and your space. You will find guidelines for picking big-ticket items so you can spend wisely, and strategies to make informed decisions based on the priorities and preferences you share. You'll also learn tips on what to register for, suggestions for ways to level up your living quarters, and at-home date night ideas.

Above all, my goal with this volume is to get you, as a pair, on the same page—in every sense of the expression. To that end, throughout the book you'll find guided conversations intended to foster the healthy discourse needed to lay the foundation for your newlywed home. Some of these dialogues are complicated, some are deep, some are breezy, some are sweet. And by having them, you can nip potential disagreements about matters like privacy in the bud, establish boundaries, open up the channels for creative flow, and ultimately achieve a more balanced and peaceful home. I encourage you to revisit these conversations anytime you need to realign your expectations in the future.

As you read this book, design your home, and, frankly, take life on together hereafter, you will inevitably face conundrums and disagreements. In these instances, I have found that two things are key: keeping your lines of communication open, and never losing sight of the love and respect you have for each other. Practice active listening without interrupting, take turns sharing perspectives, and be as open as you can be to what your partner has to say.

Our homes are incredibly personal, and there are no one-size-fits-all answers. That is why I am not here to tell you what to do but rather to guide you as a couple toward discovering what is right for you. As you create your happy place, my hope is that you will feel empowered and excited to tell your love story through your interiors, that you will enjoy the process, and that when all is said and done, you will come to realize that your home is not your abode but the person with whom you share it.

SWEET
   TALK

SETTING THE TONE FOR YOUR HOME

In order to collaborate creatively and uncover your blended idea of home, you will need to be honest and open-minded with each other at every step of the process, including at the very start. Here are a few questions to ask each other to spark inspiration and get the ball rolling on this new endeavor. As you dig deeper and share your thoughts, know that there are no right or wrong answers, and that by staying true to yourselves, you will create an authentic aesthetic that, like your relationship, will stand the test of time.

Which residence from your past felt most like "home"?

It could be your childhood home, or your grandparents' house, or that of a friend. Once you identify it, reflect on it: Try to pinpoint what gave you that sense of warm, cozy comfort. Did you love sitting in the window alcove soaking up the morning sunshine? Sleeping in until noon in the delectably cushy bed? Or having lively family dinners around the large dining table? Together with your partner, unpack those settings and brainstorm what aspects of each you can incorporate into your new dwelling.

What about creating a home together are you most looking forward to?

Perhaps it's designing the bedroom of your dreams, with a king-size bed and a perfectly plush mattress, or finally having a backyard so you can dine and entertain alfresco. Figuring out what about your new shared space you are each most excited for will help you set your priorities and plan your agenda and expenditures effectively.

How would you describe your ideal home in just three words?

Defining and visualizing your goals can be a helpful practice, so take time to ponder what the perfect dwelling with your partner would look like for you and pinpoint the words that best encapsulate it. Whether they describe a design style or a feeling, your words, combined with those of your partner, will paint a picture of your collective philosophy and can serve as the bedrock for your home project. If along the way you feel as though you're veering off course, return to these six words to re-center yourselves on your objectives.

Discovering a Shared Vision

Merging your styles into one cohesive home can be a challenge, but with both parties up to it, the creative process of uncovering your shared design identity will be a fulfilling and worthwhile experience. One engaging way to start is by constructing your own mood boards for your new home.

First, independently find images that speak to you and create a physical or digital collage to represent your styles and goals. The images can include interior design photographs, furniture and product ads, movie stills, artworks, quotes—anything that represents your idea of home. As you browse around, check in with yourselves to ask whether you are being inspired or influenced. Design trends are inevitable and not necessarily taboo—if you really love something, don't worry about whether it's trendy or not; trust your gut. But you still want to discern if something is authentic to you or if your interest is based on short-term commercial hype.

Once you're both satisfied with your assemblages, show each other your mood boards. Compare them side by side and find the ties that bind. Think of this step as creating a Venn diagram of your aesthetics and ideas about comfort, allowing you to reveal the stylistic middle ground that will become the foundation of your home. Then merge your compatible ideas—anything that would fall in the intersection of your Venn diagram—into a new visual layout to use as your master blueprint. If you see that there is a clear common denominator like a design style or color scheme, your path will be more straightforward, but if you have very different points of view, you will need to collaborate more closely to mix and match your preferences until they make sense to you. Maybe that looks like traditional furniture paired with ultramodern art; muted textiles set against dramatic wallpaper; or a blend of two design styles in a carefully curated color palette. Get creative and stay open-minded about what you can accomplish, and if what you're imagining is something you haven't seen before, take it as a testament to your originality as a couple. After all, true style tends to come not from adhering to one boilerplate look but rather from layering different yet complementary visuals.

Naturally, there will still need to be compromises on both sides, so be prepared to let go of ideas if they do not mesh well with your partner's or serve your shared vision. And if you ever feel totally stuck, go out into the world. Browse the home goods stores, hotels, and restaurants you are most drawn to and have productive discourse about what you like and don't like until you find pieces that inspire you both, then take it from there.

First Impressions

THE ENTRYWAY

When you think back to the first time you saw your partner, there are likely some details you can still see perfectly in your mind's eye. The way they had styled their hair, the book they were reading, the color of the sweater they had on . . . Over time, you've gotten to know them inside out, but that first impression will always carry a lot of weight. Sure, you might forget the particulars of your conversation or what you ordered to drink, but those little things that first caught your attention will stay with you forever.

Much like that meaningful imprint left by your initial encounter with your spouse, your entryway has the power to make a lasting impression. It is your guests' first glimpse of your space and will serve as a hint to what's inside and the people who call it home. More important, though, the entryway is what will greet *you* every time you step inside your home, day in and day out. Just as a heartfelt welcome from your beloved can reset your mood, a beautiful, comforting entryway—whether it's a grand foyer or a makeshift corner of your living room—can feel like a warm, soothing embrace. Your goal here will be to create a space that speaks to the two of you, puts you at ease, and sincerely invites visitors in.

There are a few core elements that make up an entry: a tabletop and/or wall space that can serve as a "drop zone"; additional storage solutions for coats, shoes, and other grab-and-go items; and some décor and art. Said parameters are simple yet so broad that no two entryways need look identical. Embrace the what-ifs and out-of-the-box suggestions that arise from your creative collaboration. Maybe you'll choose to include a vibrant accent wall, a unique piece of art that sparks conversation, or a box of Cuban cigars that takes center stage. If it makes a statement that you both love (and thus feels authentic to your relationship) and fits cohesively with your home's design sensibility, go for it. Trust each other and your instincts and you will no doubt create an eloquent entryway vignette that is truly one-of-a-kind—and makes a first impression worthy of a second date.

SWEET TALK

ESTABLISHING THE "HOUSE RULES"

Starting afresh together means being able to institute your own traditions and policies in your new home. This can be a relief for some—finally being able to live a certain way—but it can also be a source of contention if you and your spouse are not of the same mind on one or more matters. Most daily practices will emerge over time (how you set the thermostat, say, or load the dishwasher), but others that may seem small at face value can grow into bigger issues if not handled early on, and with care.

Take the matter of being a shoes-on or shoes-off household. If you find yourselves divided on this or a similar issue, there will need to be a calm, productive debate where you unpack your reasoning, weigh the pros and cons of your respective points of view, and move forward as a team to reach a joint decision you both feel satisfied with. Below is an example of how this sort of conversation may take shape. As you have these discussions and weigh the scales, remember to always do so with compassion and respect, focus on the ideas that connect you to help you get unstuck, and know that at the end of the day, you both just want what's best for each other.

How was this issue handled when you were growing up?

We are all informed by our past, so talk to each other about your upbringings and how those experiences shaped your points of view. Did your family home have a no-shoes rule and you just can't imagine it any other way, or did you consequently grow up dreaming of having the freedom to choose otherwise? Is it something that is a commonplace practice in your culture—like a sign of respect—and thus something you want to protect? Or perhaps you've always lived in a shoes-on household and have no idea how the opposite would work. Walk each other through your histories as they relate to this issue to get a better understanding of where you both are coming from.

What is the worst-case scenario for you?

If you are both wary of the other's proposed custom, explain what is causing your apprehension. If you've never had to take your shoes off when you enter your home, are you dubious about the logistics and convenience of this practice, wondering how you would accommodate shoes in the entryway and how it would make your guests feel? On the flip side, if you're accustomed to taking your shoes off when you enter your home, perhaps you are concerned that leaving shoes on will necessitate doing a deep clean of the floors more frequently. Hash out your reservations and talk through what you imagine your recommended lifestyle would actually look like.

How can we meet in the middle?

With your perspectives of the past and projections of the future, you can now focus on the present and decide what will work best for your household. As you reach this agreement, you will both have to compromise, so lay out the specifics of how you will address the concerns of the person who "lost" the dispute. For instance, if you choose to have a shoes-on household, devise a housekeeping game plan that appeases the partner more concerned about cleanliness. On the other hand, if you decide that your home is a shoe-free zone, you will need to pick a storage solution for footwear—see page 28 for some ideas.

A Warm Welcome

The composition of an entryway need not be complicated. So long as your grab-and-go storage needs are addressed (see page 26), you really need only one or two pieces of furniture to establish the space. What's most important is that your chosen design is comfortably functional for everyday use (doubling as storage if needed, especially for entryways without built-in closets) and visually in conversation with the rest of your home.

    Naturally, your selection will be contingent on the kind of entryway you are working with, as you'll want to avoid anything that obstructs the pathway and forces you to detour. An entry hall, be it long or short, will have limited floor space, so steer toward narrow furnishings, like a console table, bench, or hall tree, that can be placed against the wall. An extra-wide hall can feature furniture against both walls, like a sideboard and a bench that face each other. A roomy foyer, meanwhile, can accommodate a range of bigger silhouettes, including larger consoles (great for tucking baskets or stools underneath), armoires, chests, and cabinets. On the flip side, compact entryways can do well with a simple demilune table, ladder shelf, corner cubby, or petite console or cabinet. For especially tight spaces, rather than sacrificing much-needed floor space, create a floating entryway with one or more hanging wall shelves. (See page 24 for more on how to transform a liminal space into an entry.)

    As you figure out your setup, there are a couple of things to keep in mind. First, any entryway will greatly profit from a tabletop surface on which you can display catchall trays, lamps, and décor (see page 27 for styling tips), and where you can briefly set things (such as your coffee-shop latte) down as you enter your home. This doesn't have to be in the form of a literal table, though—the flat top of a cabinet, a bench, or a shelf can fit the bill. Second, seating, though optional, can be a welcome addition, especially for shoes-off households. An ottoman or accent chair on either side of your console table, or a cushioned storage bench, can provide a moment of rest and double as a temporary landing spot for purses, shopping bags, and coats. With these touchstones in place, combined with your understanding of your unique storage needs and floor plan, you can feel free to defy convention and incorporate an eclectic piece into your layout, like an upright piano, the top of which can function as a counter, or a vintage telephone table (also called a gossip bench), which combines a seat and a shelf.

An entryway mirror allows you to do a final check before you leave the house and makes the area appear more spacious.

First Impressions

Making an Entrance

Some homes lack a defined entryway, instead featuring front doors that open directly into living quarters. However, the benefits of an entryway are undeniable, and in such cases, you can still reap them by tactically manipulating your floor plan and taking advantage of practical décor pieces to carve out a faux entryway. These are a few tricks and strategies you can adopt to achieve the illusion and make the transition from outside in smoother.

Maximize Wall Space

Mount hooks and shelves on the wall perpendicular to or on either side of the front door. Add framed artworks and a mirror to keep the storage fixtures from appearing isolated in the room.

Divide the Room

Separate the front door area from your living room with a partition. A multifunctional piece of furniture, such as a low cubby unit or storage bench, can act as a pony wall (aka a half or short wall, which stands between 3 and 4 feet / 0.9 and 1.2 m tall). For a more distinct division, use a tall room divider like an étagère or a privacy screen.

Forge a Footpath

Floor coverings will go a long way in directing traffic (and protecting your floors). A runner can escort you from the front door, while an area rug in your living room can define the seating area. Choose a style with grip or use a rug pad to keep the rug in place (and prevent slips or trips), and if possible, opt for a material that can be spot-cleaned or machine washed for easy maintenance.

Use Furniture to Your Advantage

You can also define the traffic flow by having your living room furniture multitask—such as by using the back of your living room sofa to guide your path. This alone will promote an entryway effect, but if space allows, you can reinforce the illusion by using a slim console table, placed flush against the sofa back, to serve as both an entry table and a sofa table.

Everything in Its Place

You want your entryway to look appealing and introduce your sense of style, but ultimately, this transitory space is the gateway between your home and the outside world, and as such, it has practical responsibilities as well. Most notably, you will need it to incorporate reliable storage solutions for your belongings—from your house keys to your coats—and because daily life differs from household to household and individual to individual, those solutions will need to accommodate both you and your partner.

Rather than discounting each other's needs or trying to change each other's habits, work as a team to organize and optimize your entryway to cater to both of you, even if you have vastly different routines. To figure out what works for you both, you'll have to be honest about your tendencies when it comes to keeping things neat. Some folks, for instance, plop everything down the second they walk into their home. In those cases, you can employ a large, well-designed container, like a woven storage basket, to serve as a receptacle for the miscellany until you're ready to put it all away.

To avoid clutter, everything should have a designated place—particularly because of the area's high level of foot traffic and public-facing nature. Here are some beautiful solutions for a few common practical needs.

Keys and Personal Items

A place to toss your house keys, car keys, and key fobs, as well as garage and gate remotes, is a must. You might opt for a small wall-mounted key rack, on which you can each have your designated spot. Stow keys that aren't in everyday use in a drawer or cabinet so as not to get them mixed up with the others. Alternatively, there are myriad options for tabletop catchalls, like decorative trays and bowls, so your prospects for finding one that you both appreciate are promising. (A tray can also be a convenient home for sunglasses, wallets, loose change, watches, pens, lip balms, receipts, and other things you might keep in your pockets.)

Mail

You've got mail. Now what? Many folks prefer to keep their incoming and outgoing paper mail in the entryway, and there are numerous purpose-made options for this, including mail sorters, baskets, and bins (all of which are available in wall-mounted or tabletop versions). Alternatively, you can repurpose design-forward trays, shallow bowls, or trinket boxes for your mail. Come up with a sorting system that works for you both, like assigning a designated inbox for each of you, or a special container for bills to be paid. Perhaps one person is in charge of getting and separating the mail, while the other is responsible for all outgoing letters and bills. If you find yourselves needing to send mail often, a quaint writing desk or secretary stocked with stationery, pens, and stamps could be a beautiful and useful addition to the entryway.

Apparel and Accessories

Climate will largely dictate what you need in your entryway. In locations with milder weather, wall hooks or a coatrack could be sufficient for light jackets and accessories—just make sure to pick a substantial rack with a heavy base to avoid toppling. Alternatively, a mudroom-style hall tree can be a neat, relaxed solution. If you need to store bulky coats, oversize scarves, and heavy boots, a closet in or near the entry is ideal; if that's not available, consider an armoire or tall storage cabinet for winter layers. If rain is regularly in the forecast, including an umbrella stand, be it a wall-mounted one or a large floor vase, adds old-world charm. (Muddy shoes and wellies can rest on a rubber, metal, or wooden boot tray set just outside, by the front door.)

Shoes

If you decide that your home is a shoe-free zone, you will need a storage solution for footwear you take off and put on at the door, because, of course, a pile of shoes out in the open is not ideal. Cubbies and racks, though convenient options, can render your entryway into a shoe closet, especially if you have many pairs to accommodate. Instead, opt for an alternative that offers more concealment, such as a storage bench or a cabinet with flip drawers or hinged doors. If you plan to provide guests with (washable) slippers, either display the guest slippers neatly in a small basket (great for those who have people over regularly) or store them in the closet or cabinet nearest the front door.

The Newlywed Home

Pet Accoutrements

In the case that you're both obsessed with your pup and don't mind having their accoutrements on view, create a dog-walking station to keep everything within reach by using a wall-mounted shelf with hooks or a peg rail. You can even amp it up with a little portrait of your pooch hanging above the rack, or opt for a novelty leash hook in their likeness. If you prefer a more discreet storage solution, a designated basket or bin will do the trick. (This equestrian couple's entryway even served as a mini tack room, with separate shelves and brackets for helmets and riding boots.)

Extracurricular Equipment

Grab-and-go goodies for your fitness regime and/or hobbies like yoga and golf could live in the entryway for convenience, especially if your partner shares these hobbies. Same goes if you regularly ride a bike, skateboard, scooter, or other micromobility vehicle. For larger items, consider using wall-mounted racks specially designed for them to allow them pride of place in your entrance, and to ensure that they're easy to access as you head out of the house. You could even feature them as part of a gallery wall with other pieces like artworks or shelves. If the hobby accessories are small enough, you can use an oversize basket to store, say, a pair of yoga mats or tennis racquets.

But if the hobby is a passion for only one of you, or the vehicle is more an occasional mode of transportation than a key part of your lifestyle, your best bet is to store these items (especially unsightly ones, like a gym bag, or bulky ones, like a set of golf clubs or a surfboard) in a storage closet nearby or in a garage, if available.

Be Our Guest

The wedding guest book is an enduring tradition that many couples still embrace as a way to document the well-wishes and memories of their invitees on the big day. But why should the loving sentiments stop at your nuptials? Incorporating the guest-book concept into your entryway not only creates a fun feature for your visitors to engage with as they come and go but also provides you with an everlasting keepsake that will serve as a time capsule of these precious, ever-fleeting newlywed years.

You can stick to the classic, simple approach of a bound book—a hefty hardcover or a handstitched leather notebook, for example—that sits open alongside a pen on your entryway credenza. If you want to encourage more prose, stick to a lined journal. Choose an unlined book to inspire artistic expression.

Alternatively, consider a clever twist that mirrors your spirit as a couple—much like the wedding guest book has evolved over time to take many creative shapes and forms. For literary sorts, a typewriter will add a delightful vintage touch to your entryway tableau. Keep a typewriter ribbon and a sheet of paper inserted. Once the page is full of typed messages, replace it with a fresh sheet; eventually, say after five years, you can bind all the completed pages together or store them in a memento box. A Polaroid camera is another retro piece that can look charming in the foyer while also producing one-of-a-kind photographs that you will cherish for decades. Have guests sign their pictures with a short message before you either stow them for safekeeping or showcase them on a bulletin board hanging in the entryway. For a more private exchange, you can put a spin on "a message in a bottle" by employing a handsome centerpiece jug or vase and having guests jot notes onto precut strips of paper before rolling them up and dropping them in.

Make an occasion out of it by reading through the messages together every so often—from simple greetings and "I was here" declarations to heartfelt notes of affection and silly inside jokes, the messages will serve as an opportunity to reflect on the love and joy that surround your relationship.

Tokens of Love

Another wedding custom you can repurpose for homelife is the party favor—a little piece of your story for loved ones to take home with them. Useful mementos that speak to your lifestyle or interests as a couple can be customized with, say, your new address or your married monogram, and prettily presented in a decorative bowl in the entryway for guests to snag as they exit your home, be it after a housewarming party or a casual weeknight hang. Think bespoke matchboxes you designed together in the style of the bar where you first met, or postcards collected from your shared travels around the globe. For the latter, you can either write sweet thank-you notes for your guests to read, or you can keep the postcards blank and stamped for your friends and family to write to *you* instead.

DATE NIGHT

MEET CUTE

Cohabitation often leads to predictability, but contrary to how it sounds, that's actually a wonderful thing. Routines and rituals are essential for cultivating a sense of comfort and safety at home. However, there might be moments when you miss the novelty of dating life—the sense of the unexpected that gave you butterflies in those early days of going out. If you both love the element of surprise but feel as though it's starting to fade from your rapport, here's an idea to help you reintroduce it to your relationship: the mystery box, a special letter box for exchanging sweet tokens of affection with your love.

All you need to get started is a small lidded decorative box or chest. Retailers and vintage markets are full of options in a variety of materials, among them carved wood, inlaid tile, woven rattan, sleek marble, and many more, so you are sure to find one that fits in well in your entryway, where this box will live.

When one of you feels inclined, plant a little something inside for your partner to discover. Maybe it's a note specifying a dress code and time to meet in the entryway before you head to a secret date-night location, or a weather report and calendar dates to block out for a romantic getaway at an undisclosed destination. Try to embrace the spirit of mystery and keep the details under wraps, but be mindful of your partner's schedule and preferences as you make arrangements. Keep the lid of the box open or ajar, and on the occasion that you put something inside, close the lid to signify to your partner that there's something for them within, waiting to be discovered.

And not every surprise in the box has to be an elaborately planned or pricey outing. Thoughtful little things like a "just because" love note or a small confection picked up during an errand can be just as powerful in brightening your partner's day and reminding them that they're on your mind.

Display of Affection

Entryways are rooms in and of themselves that deserve to be appointed with care and attention. As a high-traffic area, the entryway should remain orderly and clear of unnecessary knickknacks, so keep your selections streamlined—you need only a few items to create a vignette that pulls the area together. And the good news is that you don't necessarily need to go shopping for all new objets d'art.

Begin by asking yourselves what you want to see when you first walk through the door. Then comb through your home and find things that speak to this description. Avoid nonspecific, mass-produced pieces, like a bowl of decorative nothings, and instead include items that not only make you smile as you pass but will also spark dialogues with your guests as they arrive and depart. (After all, the entryway is not just your entrance, it's your exit, too, so your home's first impressions are also their last.) Narrow down your selections to a few pieces that are unified in theme, then use a console or other tabletop as your "canvas" and arrange them in a way that balances scale. A whimsical statuette here, a terrarium there; a duo of vases here, an accent lamp there.

Finally, adorn the walls with a captivating mirror, unique sconces, and artworks, and use throw pillows to cozy up any lonely seats. Play around with the arrangement until you both feel that it gets the right message across.

A modest arrangement of hand-selected vintage and personal pieces—each tied to your narrative—can take your entryway from a bland utilitarian space to a genuine expression of character.

REGISTER THIS

Get up close and personal with your entryway details.

Picture frames: Three tabletop frames, in complementary finishes but different sizes.

Personalized stationery: A set of fifty note cards with your new family name and/or address.

Custom artwork: A portrait of your home by a commissioned artist.

Passing Fancy

A note on hallways and staircases: Similar to the entryway, these transitional spaces should be uncluttered and streamlined for ease of access. But having to accommodate heavy foot traffic does not mean keeping these areas entirely bare. No part of the home should feel like it was neglected or came together as an afterthought, and these passageways are no exception. They should be atmospheric and contain captivating details in case you or anyone else happens to dawdle there.

Fight the urge to furnish hallways (unless you have an exceptionally palatial corridor) and instead add a simple personal touch here and there for a subtle, eloquent effect on passersby, which can help create cohesion between the rooms that the hallway connects. Think wall art—from paintings and photographs to fabric wall hangings—and lighting features like sconces or wall-mounted candleholders, all available in plenty of design styles (contemporary, industrial, traditional, and beyond). Adding texture to the walls in the form of ornamental paneling, plaster, or wallpaper can also make a huge impact without obstructing the walkway.

If your front door opens onto a staircase, embrace it as the focal point. For a traditional look, consider adding a carpet runner and rods on the steps. Use the wall space to visually lead climbers up the stairs by displaying ascending artworks or photographs. Alternatively, one oversize tapestry or print on the staircase wall can make a bolder statement and catch the eye from the doorway. If your staircase has a turn—whether angled or curved—or a spandrel underneath, don't allow the extra ground-level area to become dead space. Think about tucking in some seating to create a nook for lounging, reading, drawing, or meditating. A cushioned bench, chaise, tête-à-tête, or chair and a half with comfy pillows can be the perfect perch for quiet moments of leisure.

You can mix things up on your stairway gallery wall, both in terms of the frames you use and the images they hold. A medley of family portraits, limited-edition prints, and sketches can help highlight this oft-overlooked area of the home.

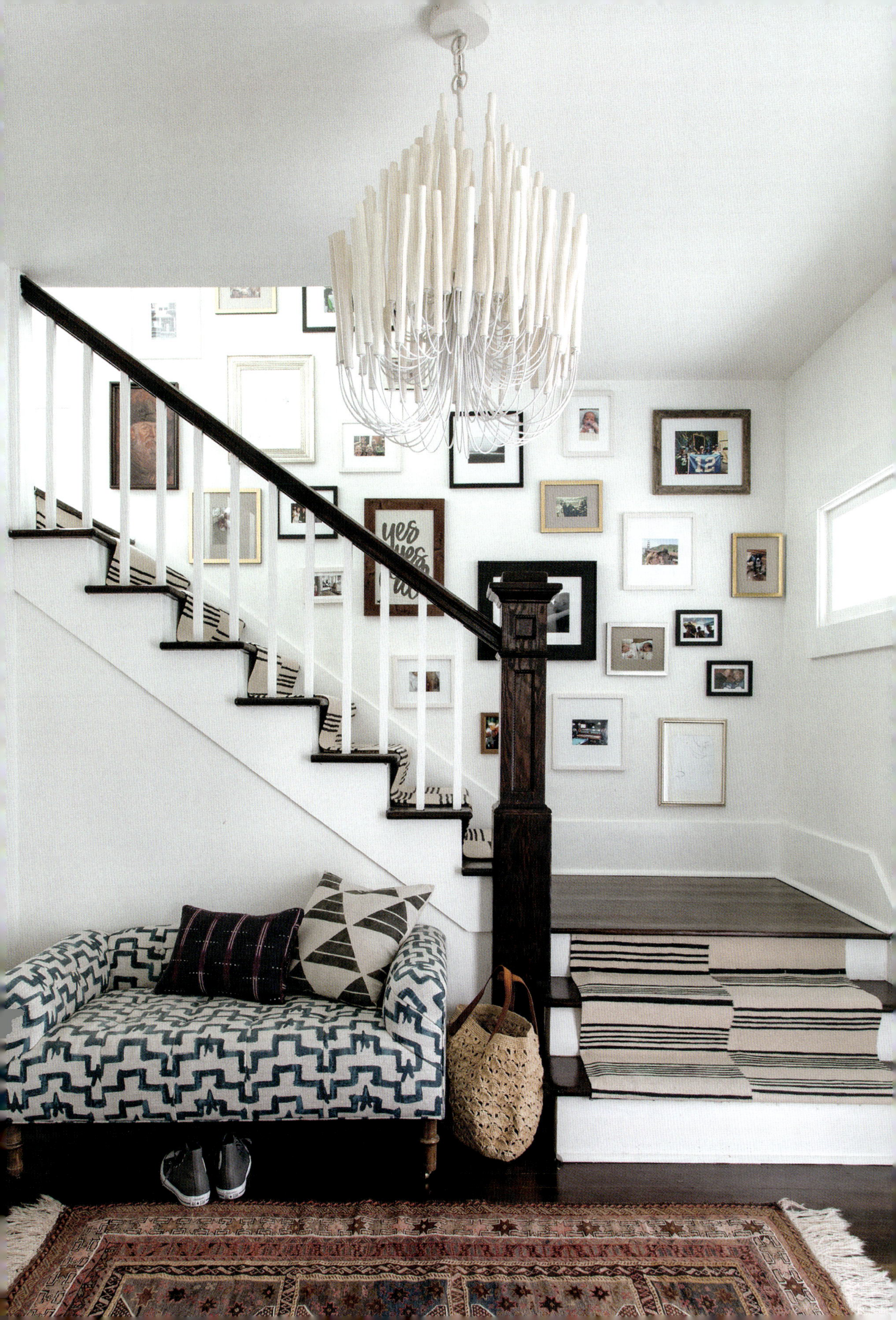

Comfort Zone

THE LIVING ROOM

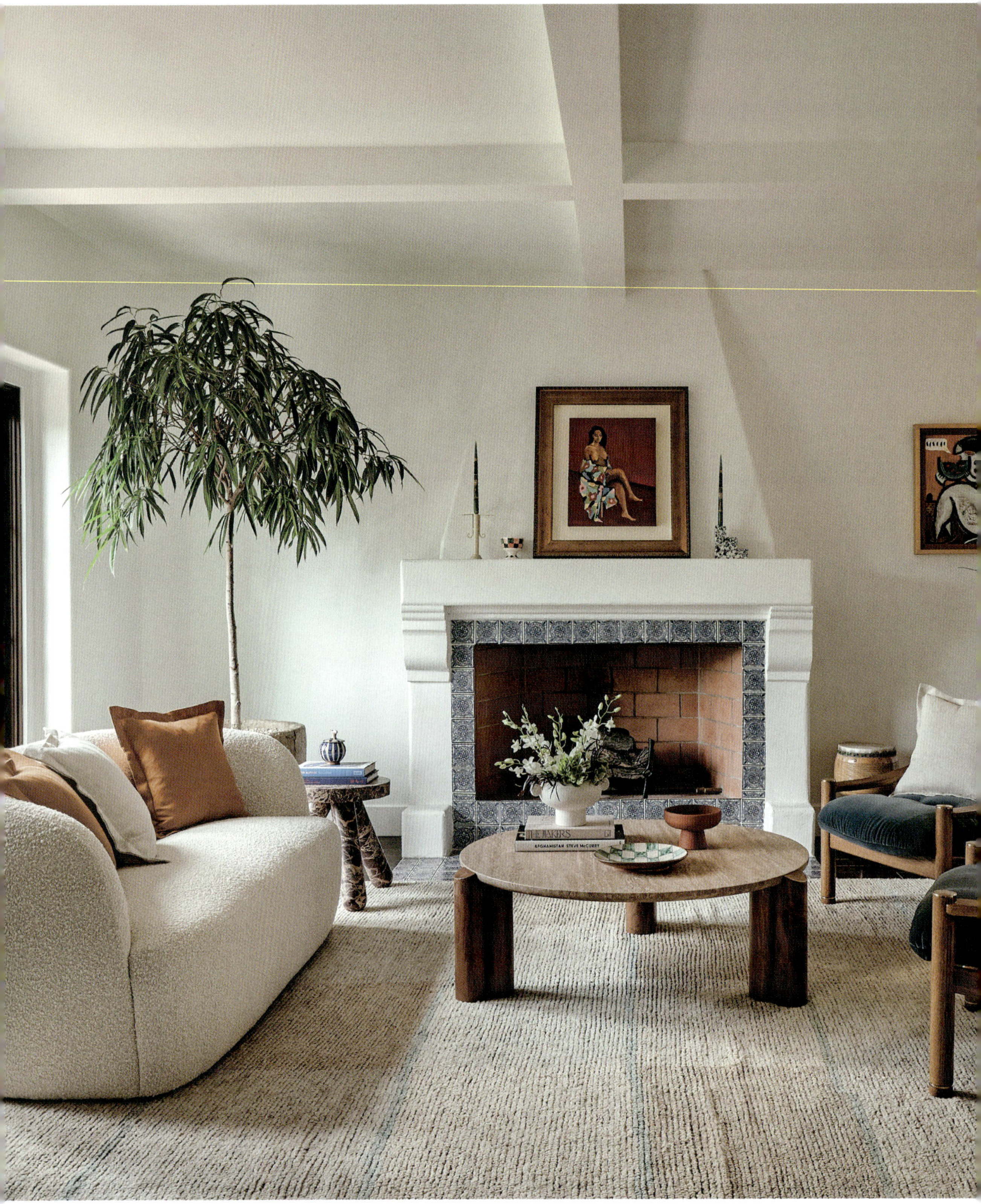
AFGHANISTAN STEVE McCURRY

It might not seem like it, but the living room is easily the most complex space in the home. Historically known as "the drawing room," this was where you welcomed visitors and displayed your most impressive possessions (you know, to show off), but with the emergence of twentieth-century in-home technologies like radio and television, it evolved to be less about entertaining and more about being entertained. (Think the nuclear family huddled around a modest TV set.) Today, the role of the living room falls somewhere between those archetypes—and somewhere between formal and informal—functioning as both a receiving room for guests and, more important, a nest for lovebirds.

In many ways it's the hub of the home, where various aspects of domestic life meet, and at its heart is leisure. It's typically a designated work-free zone where you can cozy up with your partner; engage in intimate conversation or sit in comfortable silence, have a movie date night, or catch up on some reading. In other words, simply unwind. But here's where it gets complicated: While the living room is by nature a very private space, it still needs to function as a public one. Whether you're having hors d'oeuvres before a dinner party or hosting a game night with friends, you will find yourselves at some point or another entertaining guests there, so it should be welcoming and proudly represent your personalities and love story. The good news is that it's a fantastic canvas for decoration and flair, including conversation pieces and objects with rich stories attached to them. The key lies in finding the balance between inviting, expressive, and relaxing.

Comfort Zone

SWEET TALK

HOW YOU'LL BE LIVING IN YOUR LIVING ROOM

A well-designed living room is one that successfully marries form and function and becomes a cornerstone of your homelife. With so many functions and dualities to address and incorporate, it can be the most challenging space to pin down together, but rest assured, once you nail it (and you will), the rest of the home will be a breeze.

In order to get there, you must first recognize how it can best serve you and lay the foundation accordingly. It might be tempting to immediately furnish it with attractive pieces, but by not evaluating the core role it will play in your day-to-days beforehand, you run the risk of having a living room that is not compatible with your lifestyles. So before you start making décor choices and purchasing furniture, answer the questions (opposite), which will help reveal what sort of layout—seating arrangements and focal points—will best meet your needs.

As you come up with your ideal configuration, remember to work with, not against, the architecture and dimensions of your room—adjusting your layout to include more or fewer pieces to fill and balance out the space. Those with a very tight area to work with, for instance, might have to edit down their concept, whereas those with open floor plans will need to be mindful of setting perimeters. Trust your eyes and intuition—and each other—as you work out what will be most convenient and comfortable for you.

What do you see as the main function of your living room?

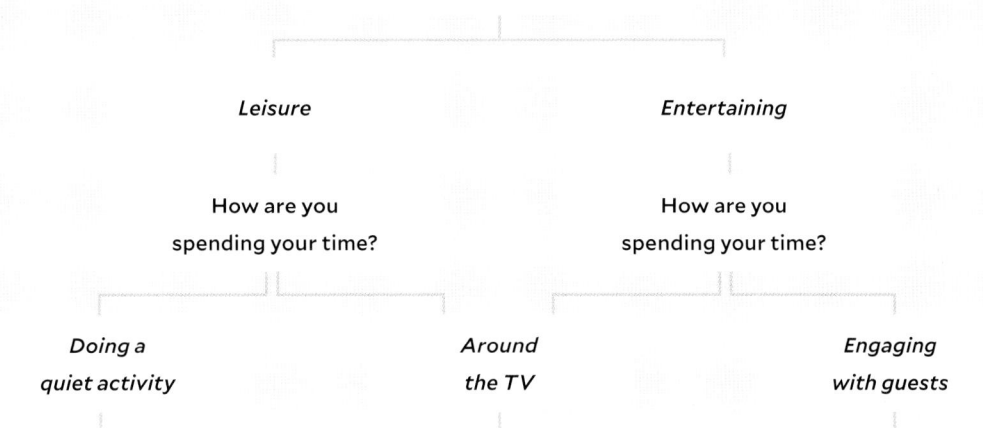

Leisure

How are you spending your time?

Doing a quiet activity

If your idea of downtime is doing low-key activities like reading, crocheting, or browsing on your phone, create your own comfy corners of the living room by choosing furniture that encourages your favorite pastimes. Add a chair and a half here, an oversize chaise there—or a plush sofa, the ends of which you each stake claim to. If watching television is not part of your routine but is something you like to do once in a while—or, say, if one of you likes to watch and the other doesn't—a discreet TV, perhaps hidden in a cabinet or behind a sliding panel, is a happy medium. Anchor the room around a coffee table and use side tables for your respective nooks.

Around the TV

If watching television is part of your nightly unwinding routine or hosting movie nights for friends and family is your claim to fame, make the TV the focal point of your living room, organizing your furniture to face the screen. If the room's framework allows it, an oversize sectional can be a cozy option, while a loveseat and pair of ottomans is a great (and charming) alternative for couples if space is tight. For optimal comfort, aim for a viewing angle of about 15 degrees, and look up the recommended seating distance for your television's size and resolution.

Entertaining

How are you spending your time?

Engaging with guests

Arrange your furniture in a way that enables face time and fosters conversation—and is party-game-friendly. Some options include parallel sofas flanking a coffee table, a pair of armchairs in front of a fireplace or window, or a combination thereof. You can have as many seats as your space can accommodate—surrounding your coffee table on two, three, or even four sides with them—so long as you keep about 3 feet (1 m) of walking space between large furniture pieces. Offer guests enough surfaces to rest a drink or plate on by including end tables on both sides of a sofa and one between armchairs.

Comfort Zone

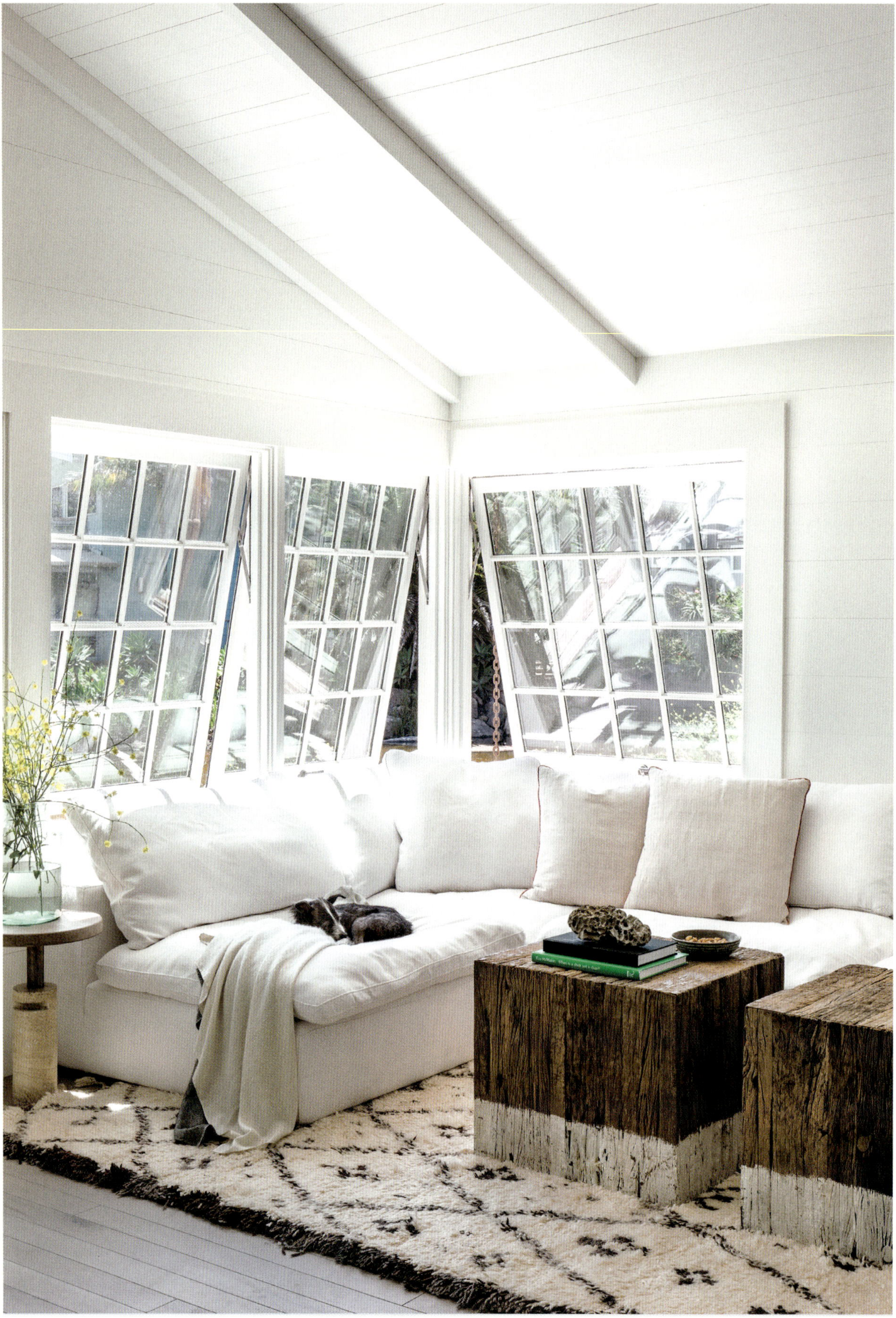

MAIN SQUEEZE

THE COUCH

It all starts with the couch. This single purchase will establish the baseline of your home's comfort level and will be instrumental in setting the tone of your design identity. So be prepared to set aside a substantial portion of your budget for this vital piece of furniture, as it's not only the key decision for the living room but also one of the most important investments for your home overall.

When it comes to couches, there is way more than meets the eye, so if possible, avoid ordering online. You want to sit on the furniture together, get cozy, and take notes so you can share your thoughts with each other and compare different models. Make a date out of furniture store and showroom hopping, perhaps planning it around a lunch in the area, and enjoy the process as you find the right fit. A quality sofa can last up to fifteen years if you take good care of it (i.e., vacuuming, fluffing, and rotating cushions regularly), so it's best to not rush this decision. Below are the core features to consider as you shop for this investment piece.

Size

Grab a measuring tape and take down the dimensions of your living room to confirm what your space will be able to accommodate. According to a principle called the two-thirds rule, your sofa should be about two-thirds the length of the parallel wall, whether it's flush to the wall or floating. (This rule also applies to additional pieces in the room in relation to the furnishings they are in front of; for instance, the coffee table should be two-thirds the length of the sofa.) A standard three-seater sofa is 90 inches (229 cm) long, whereas sectionals are closer to 100 inches (254 cm) and loveseats 60 inches (152 cm). Sofa depths will typically land between 35 and 40 inches (89 and 102 cm). To help you visualize the different options in your space as you make your calculations, you can use blue painter's tape to trace the measurements of a would-be couch on the floor to get a feel for the amount of space it would take up, and examine the surrounding free space that's left for side tables, floor lamps, and most important, walkways (you want to aim for about 3 feet/1 m of clearance).

Style

While comfort is of utmost importance, the visual significance of a sofa in a design scheme cannot be stressed enough. Get acquainted with the standard styles typically on offer to help you narrow down which type of sofa would best match your personal and overall home vibes. These include the tufted chesterfield, low-profile mid-century, versatile Lawson, and classic English roll arm designs.

CHESTERFIELD

MID-CENTURY

MODERN LAWSON

ENGLISH ROLL ARM

Another factor to mull over is the seats of the couch—a bench seat versus two seat cushions versus three seat cushions. If you tend to stick to one side of the couch, a bench seat might slope over time, whereas if you plan on regularly having company sit together on the couch, the separate cushions might not be as comfortable for those stuck sitting between the seats. Additionally, consider the height of the styles in question. If you and your partner have a significant height difference, you might need to compromise here. A low-profile sofa might be an ergonomic nightmare for a tall individual. And if you anticipate hosting overnight guests in the living room, a sleeper sofa can be a fantastic option—look for one whose mattress has a quilted cover and frame features wooden slats for a more comfortable sleep.

If you're opting for a sectional sofa, you'll likely be choosing between two main configurations: an L-shape, which is most common and perfect for corners, and a U-shape, which is great for large living rooms. Variations in designs are many; some feature chaises and/or ottomans for lounging, for example, while others have sofa seats all around. As you evaluate which shape would fit best in your home, consider also whether you want a fixed design or a modular one, which is made up of separate, rearrangeable pieces, allowing you, for instance, to flip the chaise of an L-shaped sofa to the other end.

Composition

While feather down is soft and can give you that "sitting on a cloud" feeling, it requires more upkeep, like frequent fluffing. Foam is the most popular option and great for those who like a firmer seat, but note that the cushions will soften over time. Hybrids featuring spring coils or fiberfill—as well as down-foam hybrids—can help address more nuanced tastes. For the frame, your best bet for longevity is a high-quality hardwood frame made of maple, walnut, or teak.

Fabric

Options range from velvet and leather to linen and wool blends. If you have pets or children (or plan to in the next decade), performance fabric might be right for you, as it's developed to withstand wear and tear. Leather tends to have a more masculine vibe, whereas slipcovers can lean more feminine. Consider maintenance and cleaning methods when making your decision.

Made for Each Other

If you find that between you and your partner, you have a very specific list of requirements and your ideal sofa combination is not for sale, a custom piece may be the way to go. You can personalize every element, from the frame to the fabric to the filling. If you are really having a hard time finding or customizing a sofa that meets both of your needs, or your preferences are on opposite ends of the spectrum (say, one person likes firm and sturdy while the other favors ultrasoft and fluffy), consider two mismatched oversize armchairs (or chairs and a half) in a unifying style, with a side table between them. Sure, it's an unconventional option for a couple, but who's to say you can't still snuggle up on one seat if you're feeling flirty?

On the (Coffee) Table

A low-lying table is an essential element of the living room, both in function and design. A coffee table (typically round or oval) or cocktail table (usually square or rectangular) does more than just hold your remote controls and beverages. It also operates as a focal point, one that can influence the design identity of the room, so consider curating a decorative still life to help this centralizing piece of furniture reach its potential.

Based on the shape of your coffee table, divide the surface area with imaginary lines to delineate the section(s) you can decorate. Circular, square, and oval tables can be split into four, while rectangular tables can be split into three or six.

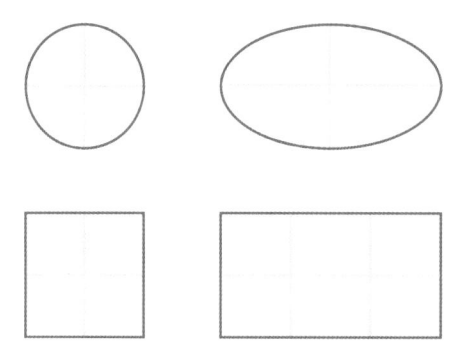

Now decide with your partner if you will need lots of free table space for everyday use or prefer that your table serve more as eye candy (or, alternatively, if you want a minimalist or maximalist arrangement). This will determine if your décor will live on the point of intersection of the dividing lines (less styling) or within a quadrant (more styling). A square table, for example, can have a centerpiece or four groupings of objects.

When choosing items for a grouping, use varying heights to keep it interesting to the eye. A trio of candlesticks, for instance, can comprise one tall, one short, and one medium-height candlestick. You can use trays to hold assemblages—an option that also makes it easier to clear the table if you need to set up a board game or bowls of snacks when company is over. Bigger, singular décor items like vases or sculptures can also work well instead of a grouping.

And remember, your arrangement need not be permanent—you can change it as you please. So as you use the room over time, if you find that the styling is not convenient or pleasing for one or both of you, make tweaks and modifications until you both agree it's just right.

Coffee-table books and magazines are always a lovely touch. Stack a few volumes with similar dimensions, using the largest at the base, and if you please, top it off with a trinket dish or box, candle, or small curio.

46   The Newlywed Home

AKILA BERJAOUI

OTTOLENGHI SIMPLE

THE ALCHEMY OF THINGS
KAREN McCARTNEY

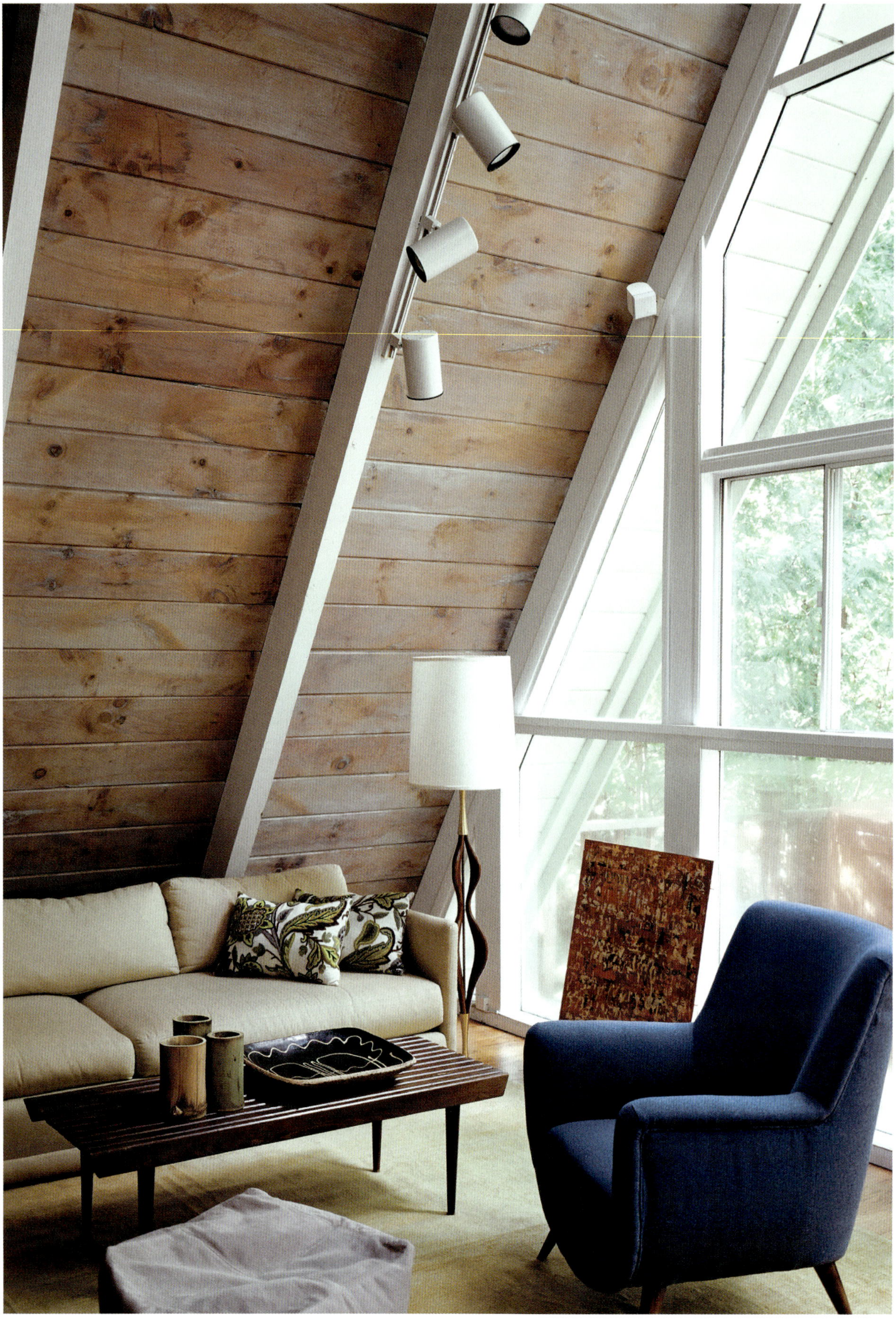

Light of My Life

Layered lighting from multiple sources is the secret to giving flexibility to a multipurpose area like the living room. You want a range of options to choose from to create different atmospheres for different occasions, be it a romantic evening in or a boisterous watch party. Generally speaking, there are three categories of light sources: ambient (illuminating the whole room), accent (illuminating an object), and task (illuminating an area). Incorporating the appropriate fixtures and lamps across these categories will allow you to adjust the vibe of the room as you need to. Here are some pointers on customizing your lighting scheme.

Soft white bulbs should be used throughout for a warm, relaxing atmosphere. Look for bulbs with a color temperature between 2700 and 3000 kelvins (K).

A ceiling light fixture, whether suspended or flush mounted, can make a striking design impact but should be used with caution, as overhead lighting can be unflattering. If you have tall ceilings, a pendant light or chandelier hung above the coffee table—with at least 7 feet (2.1 m) of clearance between the floor and the bottom of the light fixture—is a solid choice for a sitting room. If you don't have the height, flush mount lights are preferred.

A dimmer is a great, easy addition for ceiling lights, including recessed lighting, to give you the flexibility to control how much light fills the room. (Just make sure to use dimmable bulbs.)

Sconces can serve as quaint accent lighting and are a great space-saving option, particularly on either side of a couch centered against a wall.

Table and floor lamps are tried-and-true options, able to provide ambient, accent, and task lighting depending on their placement. A table lamp by an armchair can transform a corner into a reading nook, for instance, while a pair of floor lamps flanking a large sofa can provide laid-back lighting for a friendly gathering.

Dimmable track lights with adjustable heads are a great versatile inclusion, as they are able to serve as both ambient and accent lighting. Combine them with a seat-side floor lamp to round out a living room lightscape.

Read the Room

Open shelving in the living room, be it built in or freestanding, offers an opportunity to merge your stories into one curated, public-facing display. Here a shared collection can become both a proud declaration of who you are to visitors and a means of surrounding yourselves with things you both share a passion for. And what better example of such a display than a joint library?

To blend your respective book collections, begin by sifting through all the volumes together. This can be a rewarding experience in and of itself, full of discovery and insightful conversations—both about literature and personal

If your shared book collection amounts to a particularly grand display, consider incorporating a sliding bookshelf ladder for practicality and a dash of charm.

50   The Newlywed Home

stories. During the process, if you find that you each have a copy of the same book, you can either choose to keep the one that is in better condition or has more sentimental value, or hold on to the pair and display them side by side if you're both very attached to your copies. (See page 206 for more on editing and merging your belongings.)

With your library selections finalized, you'll need to decide on an organizational system that you both find intuitive and manageable. You can arrange books by genre and then alphabetically by author or title, or in a less traditional manner, like by color-coding (though the latter is more difficult to navigate). If you don't have enough books to fully populate the shelves, separate the tomes into subcategories and use decorative objects, framed photographs, art pieces, and bookends to fill in empty spaces. Bookcase lights and under-cabinet light bars can be used to further highlight the collection.

In the end, your new married library will be an apt metaphor for what it means to blend two identities in one dynamic, significant, and cohesive space. The books that you each read throughout your lives, that helped shape you into who you are today, will now live together on one shelf in this new chapter of your relationship. And who knows? You might even reach for a book to read that you would otherwise never have crossed paths with.

REGISTER THIS

Bookish accessories that will have you saying *Tome sweet tome*.

Coffee-table books: A mix of titles that speak to both partners' curiosities, be they film, fashion, travel, photography, history, or architecture.

Bookends: A supportive set in a weighty material like marble, cement, agate, bronze, or iron.

Reading lamp: A floor lamp that will double as task lighting and décor.

CARLOS MOTA
SAFARI STYLE
FEDERICO FORQUET
CHATEAU DE HAROUE
THE WORLD OF MURIEL BRANDOLINI
ADVENTURES IN EDEN
PERSIAN NIGHTS
JOHN STEFANIDIS LIVING BY DESIGN
Ephraim STÅHL
GOTLÄNDSKA RUM
Svenska interiörer
BACON
CARLOS MOTA
CARLOS MOTA

Cabinet of Curiosities

When it comes to extra living room storage, a hutch, curio cabinet, or low bookshelf can not only add practicality but also be an ever-changing reflection of you as a couple. Use drawers and non-glass-front cabinets to stow away occasionally needed goods like board games, seasonal blankets, photo albums, electronics, and spare candles. Allow yourselves a junk drawer for miscellaneous small items that inevitably accumulate, like loose change or takeout menus—just remember to clean it out every few months.

Meanwhile, use open shelves or glass-front cabinets as a rotating exhibit where you can showcase everything from family heirlooms to collectibles to objets d'art you recently fell in love with. It's an especially nice spot to display mementos from your relationship. These might include a collection of ticket stubs from past dates in a handsome shadow box, a piece of stoneware you crafted together at a pottery class, souvenirs from your travels, or framed wedding photographs.

You can update what's on display in your hutch or cabinet seasonally or dress it up for the holidays. This is also a good home for those wedding gifts from loved ones that you don't necessarily want to keep on display at all times (you know, that bauble or handicraft you didn't register for)—just show an item off when they come to visit and rotate it out when you're ready to switch up the presentation.

To help achieve harmony between what might seem like a hodgepodge of items, remember: Less is more. Don't overcrowd the shelves—everything can have its moment in the spotlight at some point or another. One option for unifying everything is staying within a color family, like earth or jewel tones. Play around with different depths and heights when arranging the pieces. And if it's starting to feel a little stuffy, add an organic element, such as a bouquet of fresh-cut flowers, to breathe new life into your display. Then step back and take in your masterpiece.

Those with a bohemian bent can fill their living room shelves with books, art, vessels, and novelty objects from different eras and origins and still achieve harmony through an eclectic theme.

Hearth and Soul

A fireplace can warm up a home—both literally and figuratively—and for those lucky enough to have one in their living room, there are plenty of opportunities for sprucing it up to complement your interiors. A word to the wise: Before you go ahead with styling, consult with a certified chimney specialist to inspect, evaluate, and prep your system, as well as advise you on safe practices.

 Once you have the green light to use the fireplace, pick out some alluring accessories that will get you fired up about it. Both a fireback and screen can offer needed protection while giving the fireplace a major cosmetic revamp—whether understated or dramatic. A unique log grate or pair of andirons can catch the eye, while a well-designed tool set can stand proud as its own piece of art. Other additions to consider for the hearth extension (the area of the floor that extends from the fireplace) include a fire-resistant basket full of logs or an oversize art piece, such as a floor vase or sculpture.

 Naturally, the mantelshelf is what will be at the forefront of your mind when decorating the fireplace, and here you can be more lighthearted in your approach, as you can always switch things up, be it for the holidays or simply on a lark. As you pick your décor—ceramics, clocks, picture frames, candelabras, or what have you—be mindful of balance, placing objects of similar heights at either end of the shelf.

 As for the space above the mantelpiece, a classic choice is hanging a centered mirror or portrait and flanking it with sconces. For a more impermanent option, lean a couple of overlapping framed artworks against the wall. Hanging a TV above a mantel is notoriously a design faux pas, primarily because of the high viewing angle it causes and the potential for damage to electronics from heat and smoke. However, if you both agree that that's the best setup for your home and you take the proper precautions (like installing a heat shield and/or a full-motion TV mount), you can confidently follow your own inclination.

 By appointing the fireplace area with love and tying it into your living room as a whole, you will welcome countless cozy evenings spent curled up together there—hot toddies optional.

> If your fireplace is deemed unusable, you can still celebrate it as a focal point. For a classic look, consider refreshing the interior with flat black paint and styling the recess with decorative logs on a grate.

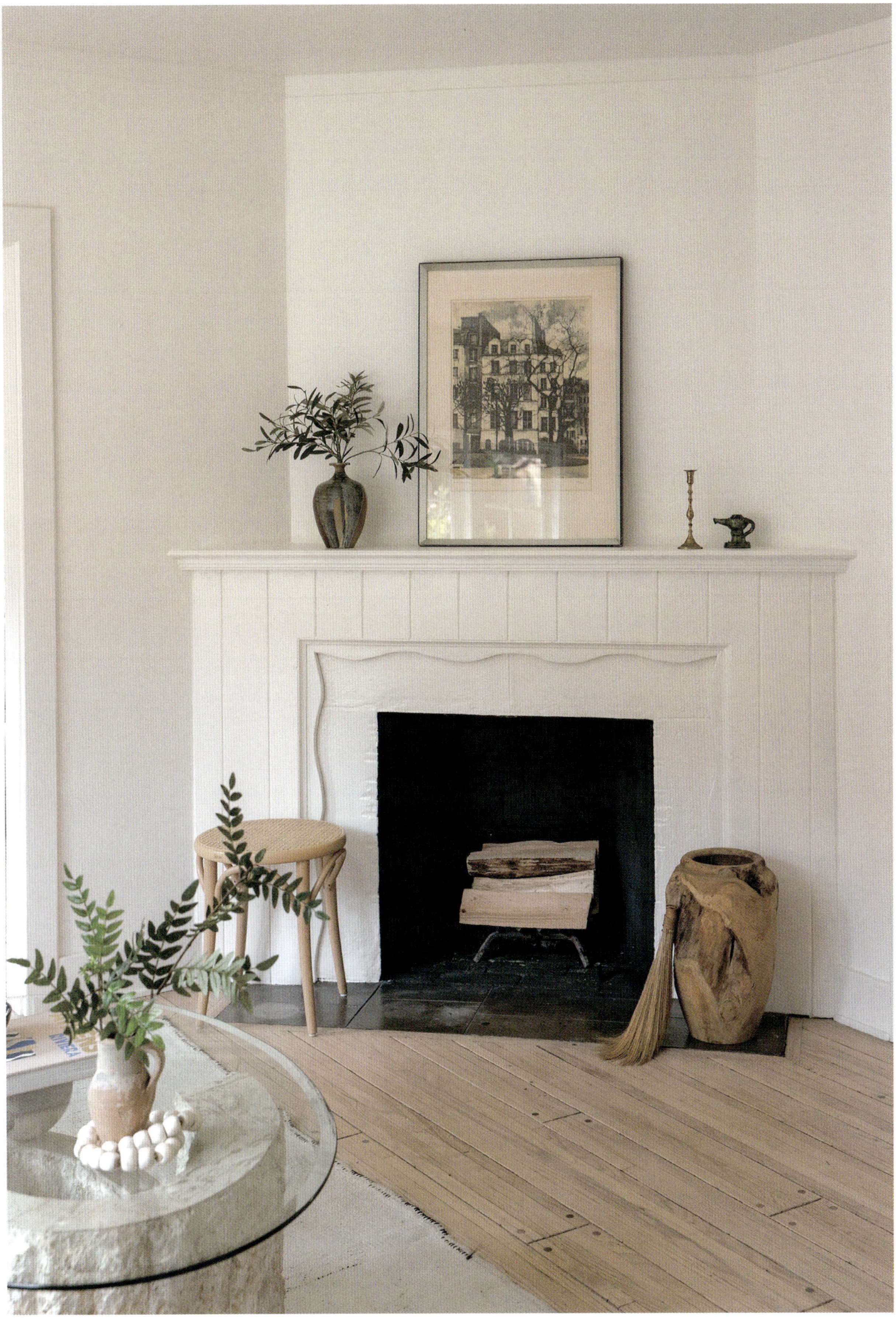

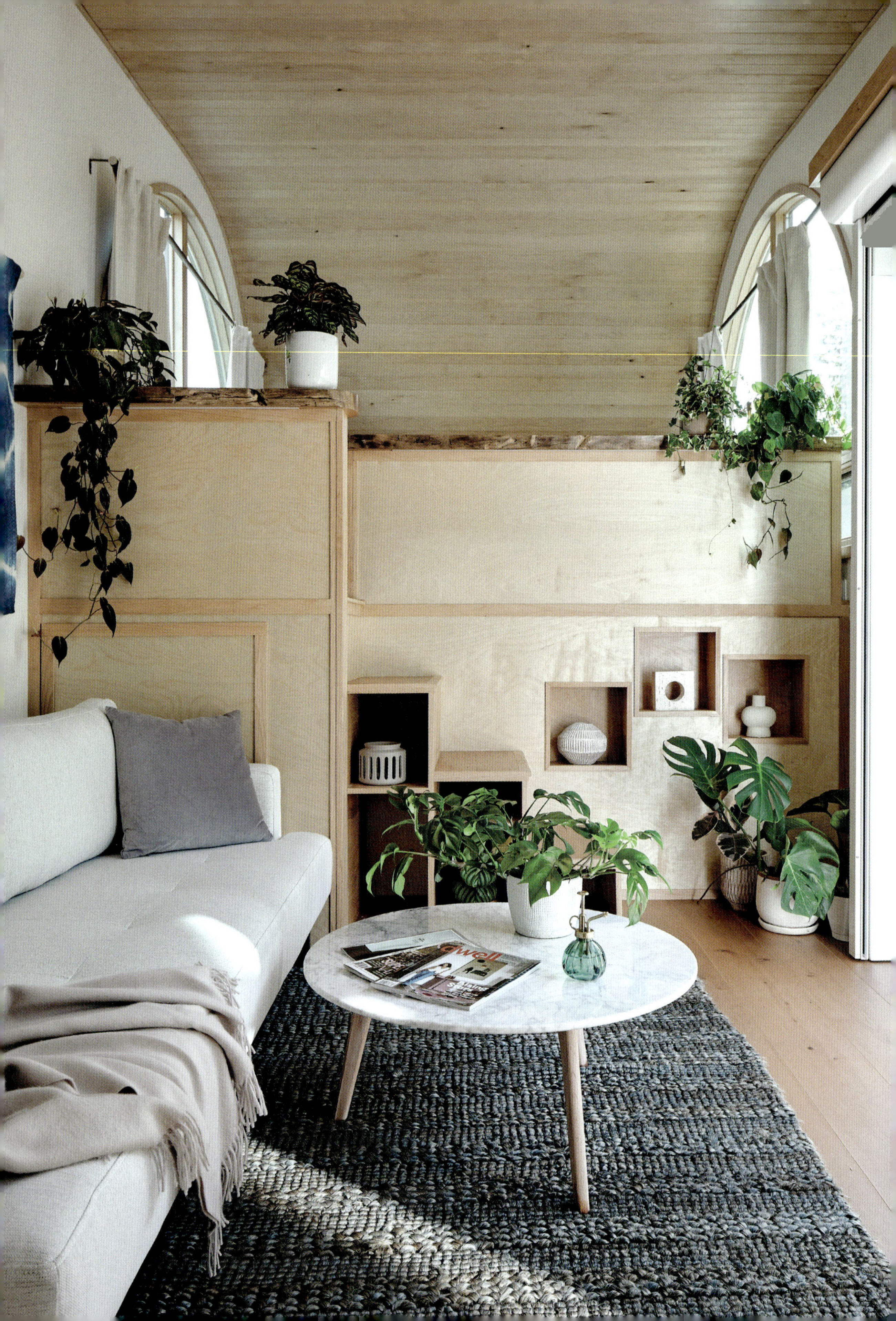

A New Leaf

Natural elements go a long way in brightening up and harmonizing the flow of a space. This sense of balance is extra welcome in the living room—and easily achieved with a peppering of curated greenery. Houseplants are fantastic for filling out stark corners and crannies of a room. If you have any specific spots that you'd like to introduce plants to, finding and understanding your room's natural light and orientation is the first order of business. (A simple cheat sheet: South-facing windows provide bright light; east- and west-facing windows provide medium light; and north-facing windows provide low light.)

With thousands of varieties on offer, choosing a houseplant can feel daunting, especially if horticulture is not your niche. As a couple, you may be self-confessed plant people or notorious black thumbs—or a combination of the two. Regardless, the right plant for you is out there. You'll just have to exercise some due diligence before you find "the one," factoring in the plant's temperature preferences, watering and grooming needs, and light tolerance, as well as your levels of commitment to the care of the plants. (Turn the page for some trusted plant suggestions.) Next on the itinerary is a trip to your local nursery with your partner to peruse what is in stock. Consult with an on-site specialist who can guide you to the plants that fit your criteria and give you the rundown on how to care for them. And remember: You don't have to rush out and break the bank with scads of plants all at once. Even just one plant can make a big impact in the design of a room.

Now with your plants selected, choose the right vessels to integrate them into your living room with style. Indoor planters come in an incredible array of designs, colors, polishes, and materials—from lightweight fiberglass to handcrafted ceramics—so take your time finding the best ones for your space. Decide together if you'd like the planters to pop or blend in with the rest of your furniture. (Note: Many specimen plants are wow factors in and of themselves and don't need to compete with a busy pot.) Play with dimension via hanging pots (great for plants with trailing vines), footed planters, or plant stands and pedestals, the latter two of which can help a smaller plant achieve the same lush effect as a tall showcase plant or indoor tree. And for those who are wary of getting their gardening gloves out, you needn't be daunted: Plopping a plastic nursery pot with drainage holes directly into your decorative cachepot is perfectly fine.

Beyond beautification, bringing the outdoors in can help make your home healthier by improving air quality (many plants have air-purifying properties), and if you and your partner are both game, the act of nurturing and grooming your houseplants can become a shared love and a reason for you to slow down together once in a while. When you work as a team to help your houseplants thrive, your relationship will likely thrive, too.

> You may choose to have a collection of one-off pots or to keep things uniform by getting kindred designs in monochromatic tones—just be sure that you choose the right size for each plant.

Garden Variety

From hardy to fussy, popular to exotic, here are some interior designer–loved houseplants for varying light conditions and care levels.

1. **Fiddle-leaf fig**
   This attention-grabbing large ficus is much loved but infamously a diva. Let it dry out between waterings (but never overwater it) and avoid repotting or moving it often to keep it happy.

2. **Monstera**
   With large, fenestrated leaves that are leathery to the touch, this handsome tropical plant is relatively easygoing and makes its presence well known.

3. **Aloe vera**
   This versatile succulent can go a couple of weeks without water, and its sap can be used topically to soothe skin.

4. **Maidenhair fern**
   A common houseplant during the Victorian era, this delicate, classic fern loves ample warmth, humidity, and attention.

5. **English ivy**
   This evergreen is a romantic trailing vine that prefers damp soil and good drainage.

6. **Rubber plant**
   With its beloved thick glossy leaves and resilient nature, this ficus is a showstopper in any home.

7. **Calathea**
   With hypnotic patterned leaves, this tropical plant is an attention-grabber for more reasons than one. It requires consistent high humidity and watering and careful monitoring, and it prefers distilled or filtered water.

8. **Peace lily**
   This shiny-leafed plant can produce white flowers—though, despite the name, they're not actually lilies. Try to keep the soil consistently moist.

9. **Dracaena**
   A forgiving evergreen, this shrub featuring sharp foliage makes an edgy design statement.

BRIGHT
LIGHT

1

2

3

HIGH
MAINTENANCE

4

5

6

LOW
MAINTENANCE

7

8

9

LOW
LIGHT

Comfort Zone 59

DATE NIGHT

NOSTALGIA THEATER

You've poured your vino, made some popcorn, and nestled together under a throw blanket, and then one of you asks: *What should we watch tonight?* This seemingly straightforward question can stop a romantic night in its tracks as you scroll through options and take turns vetoing each other's suggestions. Before you know it, the bottle is almost empty, the popcorn is down to the kernels, and you haven't even hit Play yet. For occasions such as these, a fun solution is what we'll call "Nostalgia Theater."

Take a few minutes to separately jot down your favorite childhood movies on strips of paper. They don't have to be *good* movies—just a mix of obscure and popular films that you grew up watching and loved as a kid and teen (and perhaps haven't seen since). To keep it fair, decide on a set number, like ten per person. When you're done, fold up each strip and toss it in a lidded jar (preferably one with an eye-catching design that won't look out of place in the living room), shake the jar, and pick a movie to watch that night. Keep the jar handy for the next time you're between series.

Two rules that you should implement: no do-overs—you *have* to watch the movie that was picked—and no judging (though light teasing is allowed, if that's part of your rapport). The person whose suggestion is chosen can take a moment to preface their pick, recounting their memories of watching the movie, what it meant to them, where they were when they first saw it, and so forth. Then settle in and enjoy the show. Even if the movie is a flop and you're both laughing through the entire thing, one of you will be flooded with memories and nostalgia, while the other will get a precious peek into their partner's childhood and perhaps uncover a new side to their spouse.

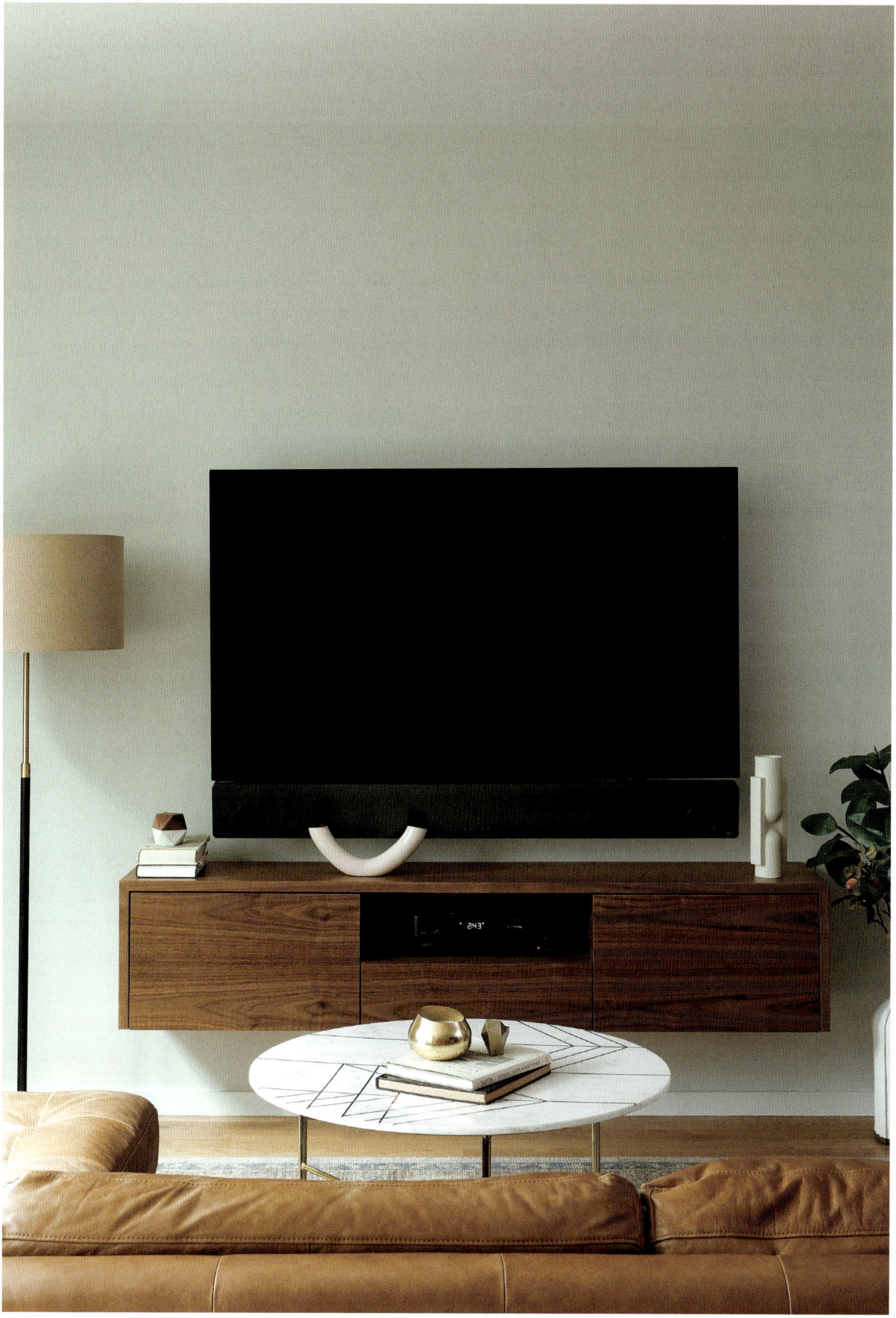

True Colors

Your living room has the potential to be an ultimate expression of character and warmth, and a surefire way of creating depth is through curated layers of color and texture. To get going, you will need to pick a color palette for the room to ensure that the space will be well-balanced. A simple route is the tried-and-true 60-30-10 ratio: Have a dominant color cover 60 percent of the space, a secondary color take up 30 percent of the space, and an accent color make the remaining 10 percent pop. Each hue can be a color *family* instead of an exact shade—like neutrals, whites, blues, pinks, or greens—and if you're having trouble identifying a trio of compatible hues, reference a color wheel. On the wheel, complementary colors (for a bolder palette) are evenly spaced from each other and analogous colors (for a subtler palette) are right next to each other.

Adhering to these colorway rules, you can fill up the room—starting with your dominant features, then secondary elements, and finally accents—with a dynamic mix of textiles and materials. Here are some ideas for each tier of your living room color palette.

Dominant: The room's color family will be introduced via your wall treatment (paint, wallpaper, and/or finishes) and substantial furnishings (like the sofa and shelving), as well as flooring. Adding a large area rug is a great way to cement your dominant hue—and, for what it's worth, improve the room's acoustics by absorbing sound. Just aim to have at least the front legs (if not all four legs) of your sofa and any chairs sit atop the rug.

Secondary: Now it's time to add some depth to the space with a coordinating color. Avenues include accent furniture such as your coffee table and side tables, poufs and footstools, and an armchair or two. Window treatments like curtains or drapes are another means for incorporating this second shade (see page 133 for tips on hanging curtains).

Accent: To round out the space, add the finishing touches—and get playful—with your third, supporting color. This can be in the form of artworks on the wall, tabletop décor, throw blankets and pillows on the sofa, lampshades, planters, and small details like curtain tassels.

To achieve a polished, bespoke color scheme—like this complementary palette of blues and oranges—consider having your sofas, chairs, ottomans, pillows, and other pieces reupholstered in harmonious quality fabrics of your choice.

62 The Newlywed Home

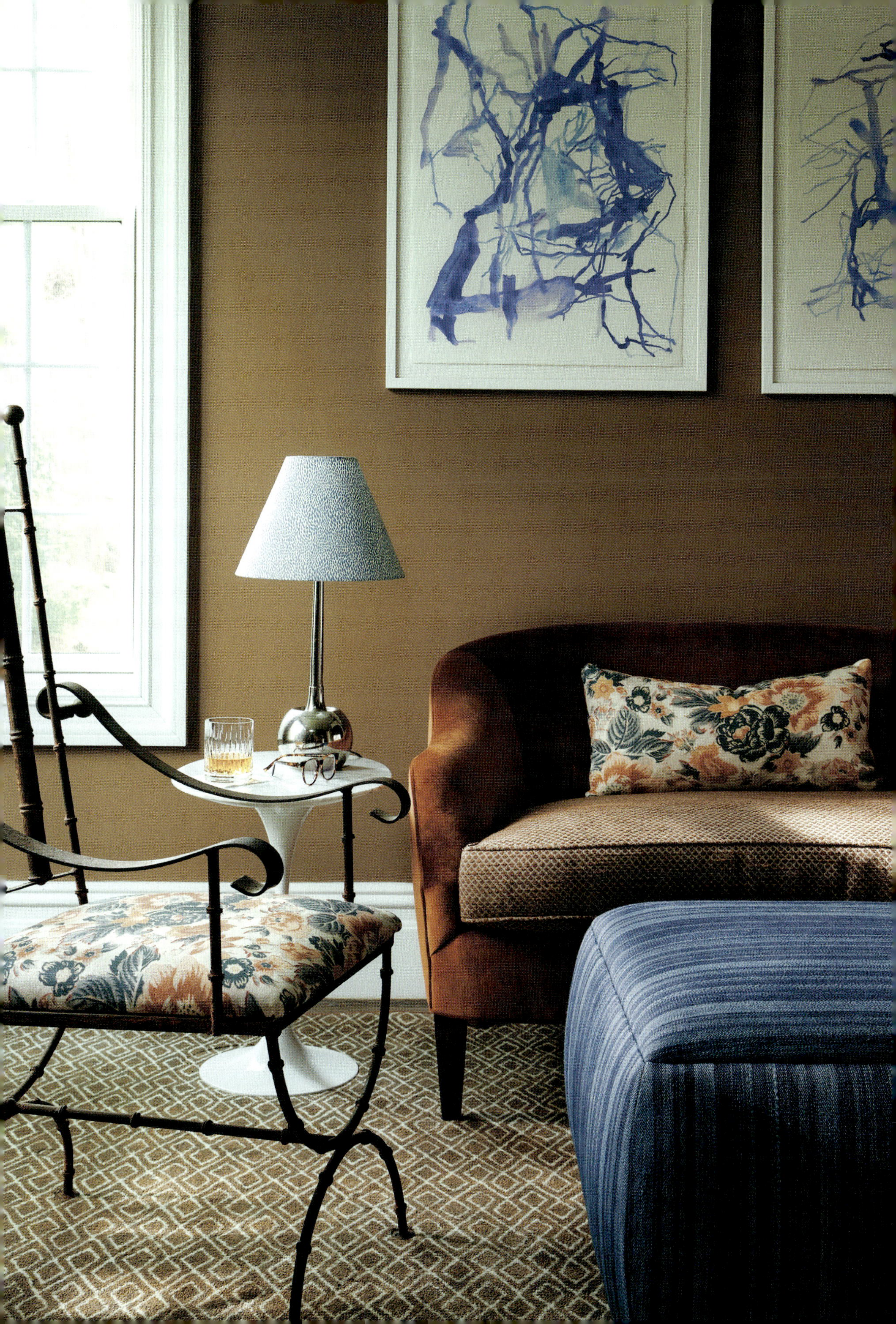

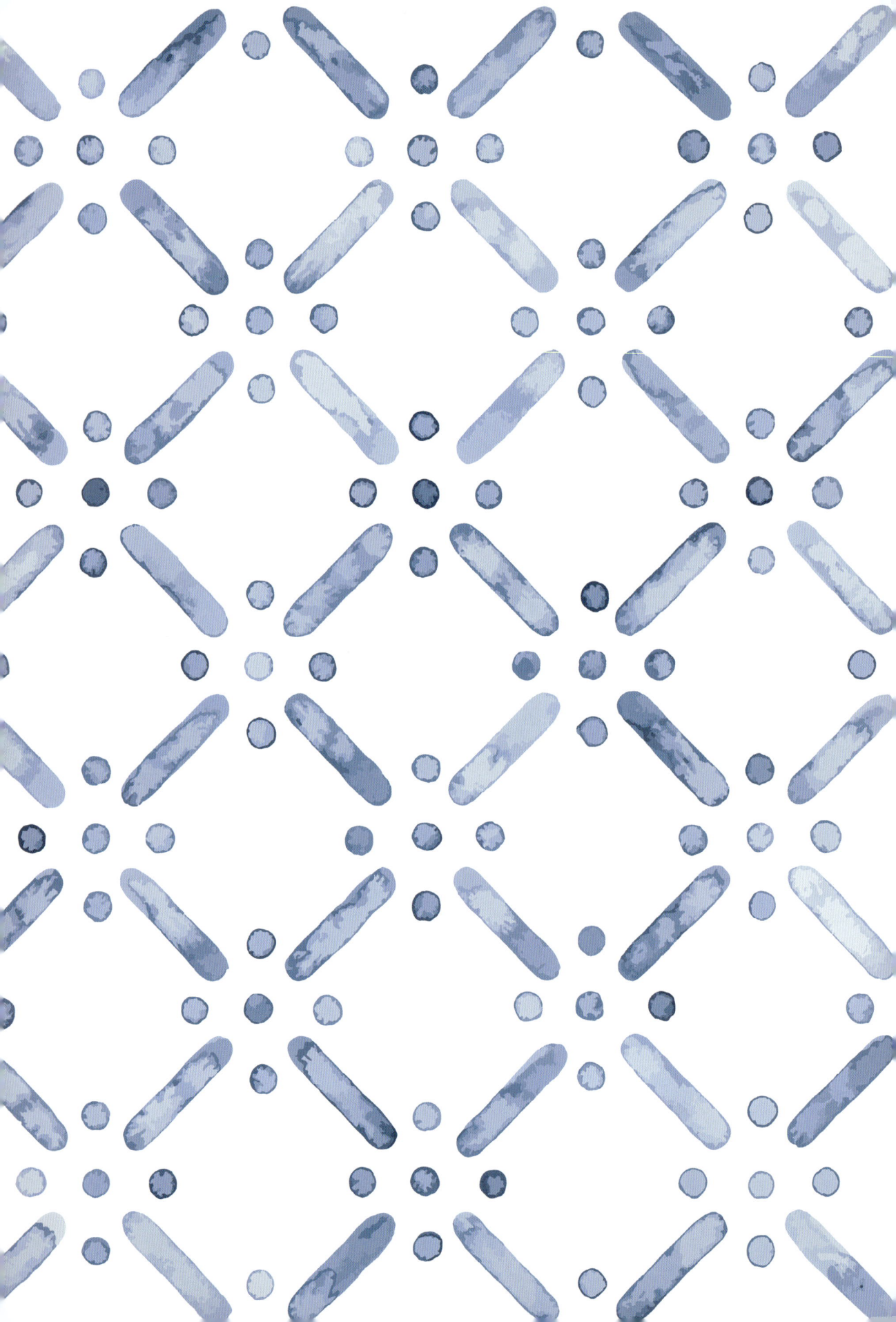

No Reservations

THE KITCHEN

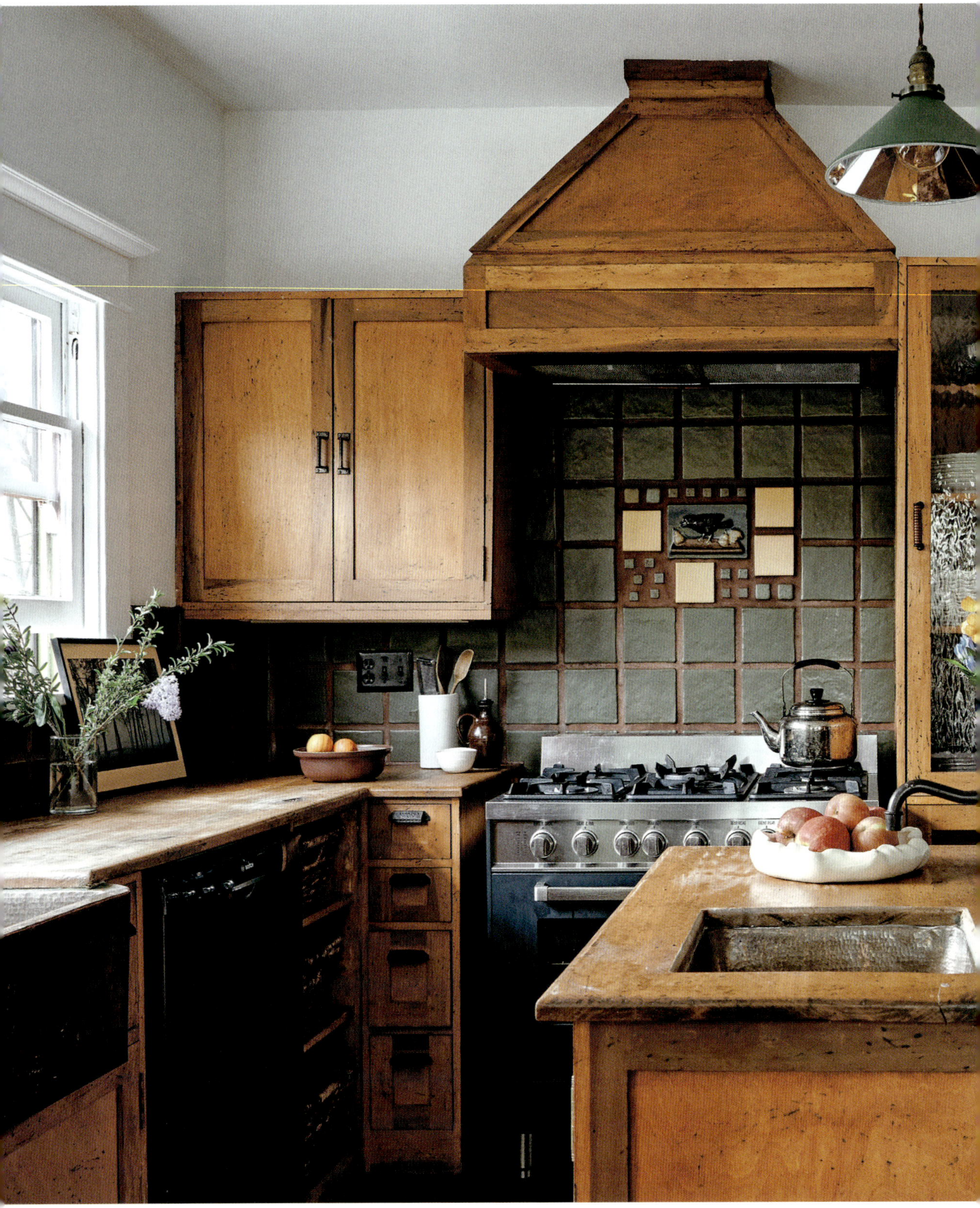

The word "companion" comes from the Old French *compaignon,* meaning "one with whom you break bread." There's something so beautiful and comforting about that notion that perhaps sharing food with and feeding loved ones is embedded deeply in us—human instinct.

It's fair to assert that food is a fundamental aspect of any romantic relationship, from sharing a meal on your first date to learning each other's preferences to the comfort foods you both crave and the dishes you make for and with each other. In fact, cooking together can be key to intimacy in a partnership. It can foster and improve communication and, in time, strengthen your bond. Plus, there's always room for flirtation as you cook side by side—or for heating things up in the kitchen, if you will. As we prepare and partake in food together, we commune, make memories, and deepen emotional connections.

Which brings us to the kitchen. We've all heard the saying that "the kitchen is the heart of the home," and this is especially true for couples. It is the most used space—occupied morning, noon, and night—and the area that, like it or not, requires the most upkeep. It is where we naturally congregate with visiting family and friends, where we find ourselves having both important and humdrum conversations, and where we unreservedly coexist. If our homes are a reflection of who we are, then our kitchens are an honest reflection of how we live.

For newlyweds, the kitchen's function in everyday life is particularly important. It is here that you will nourish and fuel each other's bodies and souls, express yourselves both verbally and creatively, and ultimately connect on a profound level. From the morning brews you sip together—be it in silence or over a chat—to the dishes you wash hip to hip at the sink, it's the intimacy that's concealed in the day-to-day activities of this humble room that you will cherish for decades to come. So take care as you appoint your kitchen, for it will be the backdrop to many of your fondest married memories.

No Reservations

SWEET TALK

FINDING YOUR KITCHEN STYLE

The ideal kitchen is welcoming and attractive, of course, but it must also be organized, convenient, and easy to clean, because it is, first and foremost, a working room. The key lies in finding the right balance between beauty and functionality, and where your combined style and needs meet on that spectrum. Having a pristine, picture-perfect kitchen might be a dream come true for some, but for others, function trumps form in this room. Whatever your style preferences, the challenge (and reward) comes from actually figuring out what daily life in the kitchen will look like and how the space will accommodate both partners' needs in a way that promotes productivity, ease, comfort, and joy while still looking the part. For many, the answers will reveal themselves over time, through the process of using the space together for weeks or months, and that's totally normal—encouraged, even. After all, the kitchen is an especially organic, ever-evolving space that will adapt to life in all its new phases. But what you *can* do ahead of time is find common ground and address your expectations by simply talking through these fundamental matters with your partner in order to set the stage for success.

To start, take some time to understand what your natural propensities are, which general style you are inclined to, and where your styles align. This short quiz can get the conversation going by helping you home in on whether your shared kitchen style (or middle ground) is maximalist, minimalist, or somewhere in between. Take turns quizzing each other and jotting down your answers, then use the key to tally up your respective points. Next, add your two totals together for your final number and check your result for some ideas on what you can implement in your joint kitchen. And a word of advice: Accept the outcome not as gospel for what you should do but as a guide to where your tendencies lie and what concepts to explore, then take it from there.

1. **When you have coffee or tea, you tend to ...**
   A. Search for the mug that fits your current mood.
   B. Use whatever mug you happen to grab.
   C. Always use the same mug.

2. **The refrigerator door should be ...**
   A. A collage of magnets, cards, and photos.
   B. The place for important memos and lists.
   C. Totally bare.

3. **When it comes to spices, you ...**
   A. Showcase your collection.
   B. Display only the salt and pepper.
   C. Keep them all in a cupboard or drawer.

4. **How often do you shop for new kitchen items?**
   A. Every couple of weeks.
   B. Every couple of months.
   C. Once in a blue moon.

5. **If you purchased a new set of flatware, you'd likely ...**
   A. Keep your old set in use to have more options.
   B. Keep your old set but stow it away.
   C. Get rid of the old set.

6. **What best describes your dream kitchen?**
   A. Decorated and full of character.
   B. Cozy and quaint.
   C. Serene and clean.

KEY:
A = 2 points
B = 1 point
C = 0 points

RESULTS:
17 to 24 points: MAXIMALIST
9 to 16 points: HYBRID
0 to 8 points: MINIMALIST

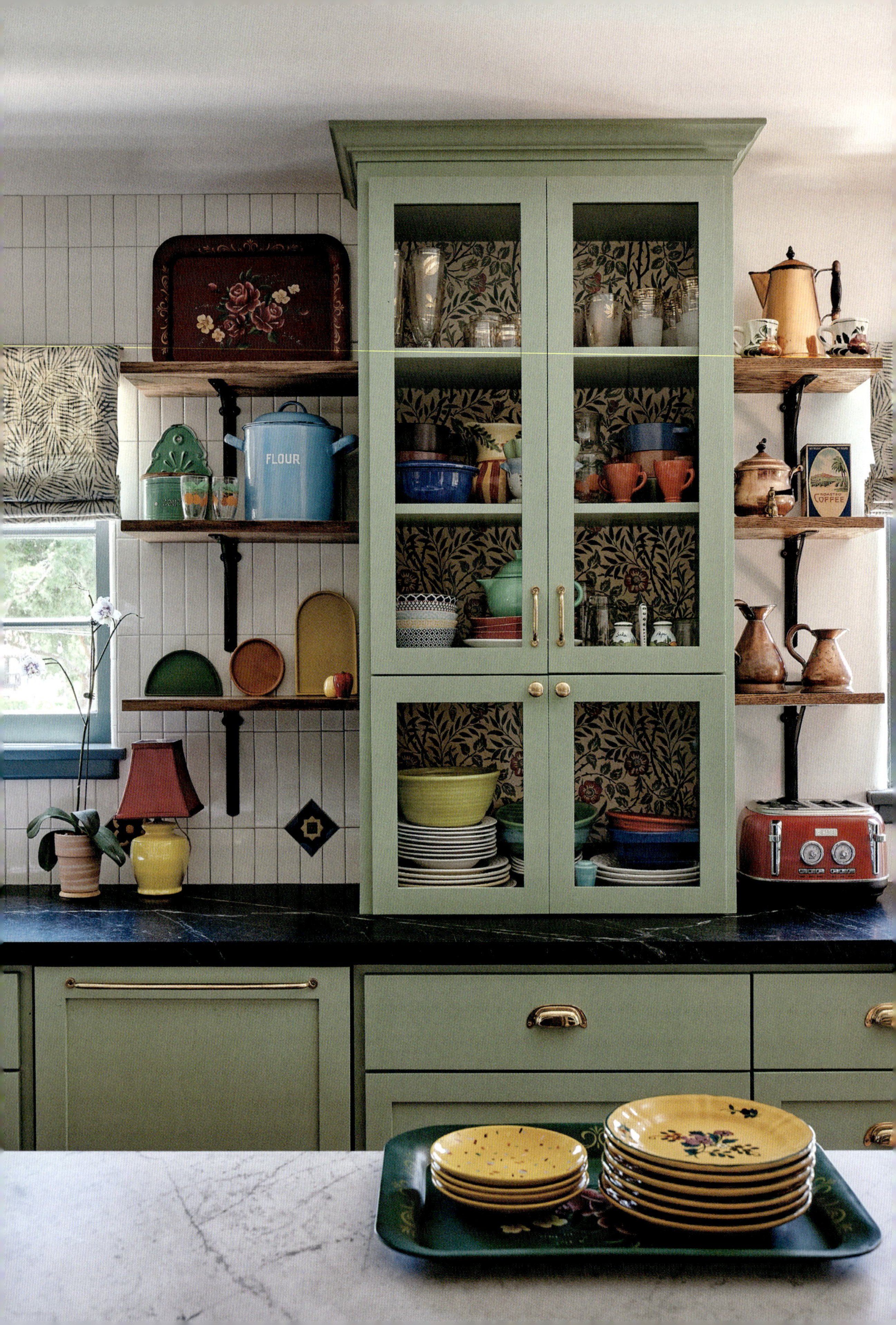
FLOUR
COFFEE

The Maximalist Kitchen

Don't confuse maximalism with clutter. A maximalist kitchen is one that is decorated and full of life but still well organized and sensible. Here practicality meets playfulness, allowing for more creativity and coloring outside the lines, so to speak, through mixed textures and hues. Embrace the lived-in, homey approach, and have fun with your decorations and cooking accessories—but be careful not to overcrowd surfaces or lose sight of functionality.

If you're both maximalists and one or both of you love to cook, transform your kitchen into a home chef's haven. Keep your arsenal of utensils on display and easily accessible in open crocks, grouping like items (all wooden spoons in one vessel, for example). For extra flair, repurpose your favorite water pitchers or sturdy, embellished vases as crocks. Keep spices at the ready in either a rotating spice rack on the counter or on a ledge shelf. Use a wall-mounted or pendant pot rack to hang cookware (but stick to one or two metals and/or color families for displayed pots and pans). To balance things out, opt for closed cabinets that can neatly keep your other cookware and accoutrements concealed.

If you're both maximalists and neither of you likes to cook, create a feast for the eyes by decorating the counters, shelves, and even the space above the cabinetry with beloved belongings and artworks. Lean framed paintings or photography prints against the backsplash, or create a collage on a floating shelf. Add a refreshing natural element with lush bouquets of cut flowers or foraged oversize leafy branches in a statement vase, or make a lasting impression with a sizable tabletop planter.

Contrasting materials, such as copper and enamel, can harmoniously coexist when grouped respectively. More fragile pieces, including ceramics and glassware, can be exhibited behind glass doors. For more depth, paint your cabinet exteriors and wallpaper the interiors.

The Minimalist Kitchen

Clean and simple, a minimalist kitchen is a no-fuss zone that can be simultaneously high functioning and serene. The resulting space is tidy, highly organized, and easy on the eyes, often favoring a more contemporary aesthetic. Heads up, though: If you are tight on square footage, this approach might prove to be more challenging, depending on how much storage space and/or kitchenware you have.

If you're both minimalists and one or both of you love to cook, you're going to want to invest in a few high-quality, multifunctional tools that you can easily tuck away. Work together to create an organizational system that allows for all of your kitchen accoutrements to be discreetly stowed, neatly exhibiting just a few everyday essentials. Your system should be carefully considered and user-friendly, but not so complicated that you and/or your partner have a hard time maintaining it. Consider using open shelving to display select dishware or dry goods decanted in cohesive containers. Decorative touches can range from one-off ceramics to statement-making pendant lights. Amplify the simplicity by sticking to a color scheme, but don't feel obligated to choose muted or neutral tones if that is not your taste.

If you're both minimalists and neither of you likes to cook, you can really go all in on a totally sleek look—bare countertops welcome! Consider concealing appliances and installing electrical outlets inside certain drawers or counter-height cabinets to create stations for gadgets and electronics. If you'd like a touch of décor, opt for singular pieces like a grounding sculpture or a large fruit bowl centerpiece.

———— Handleless (push-to-pull) cabinets, particularly those free of beveled designs, can further streamline a minimalist kitchen's bare effect. You can offset the simplicity of the flat panel façades by opting for a scene-stealing color for the cabinetry.

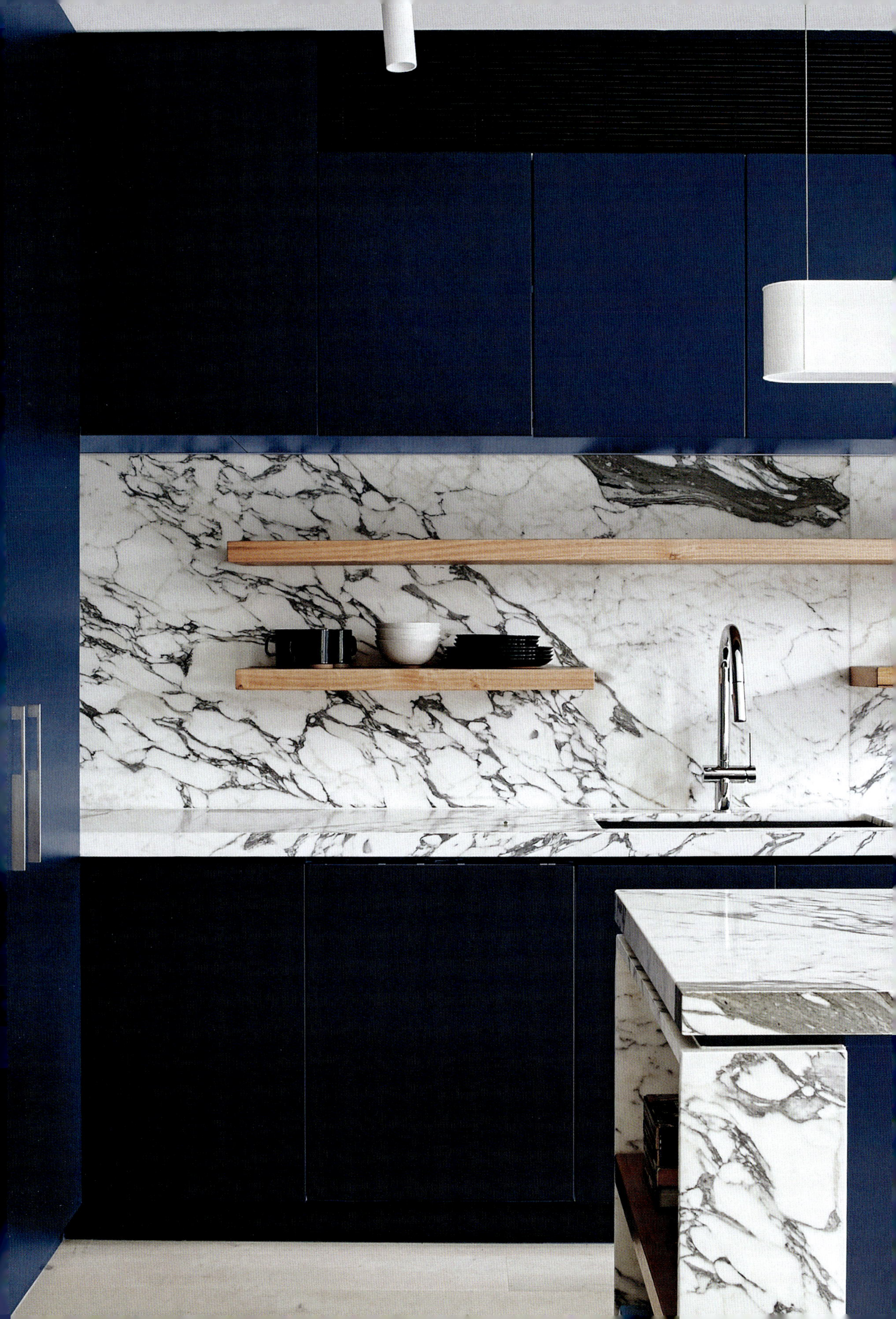

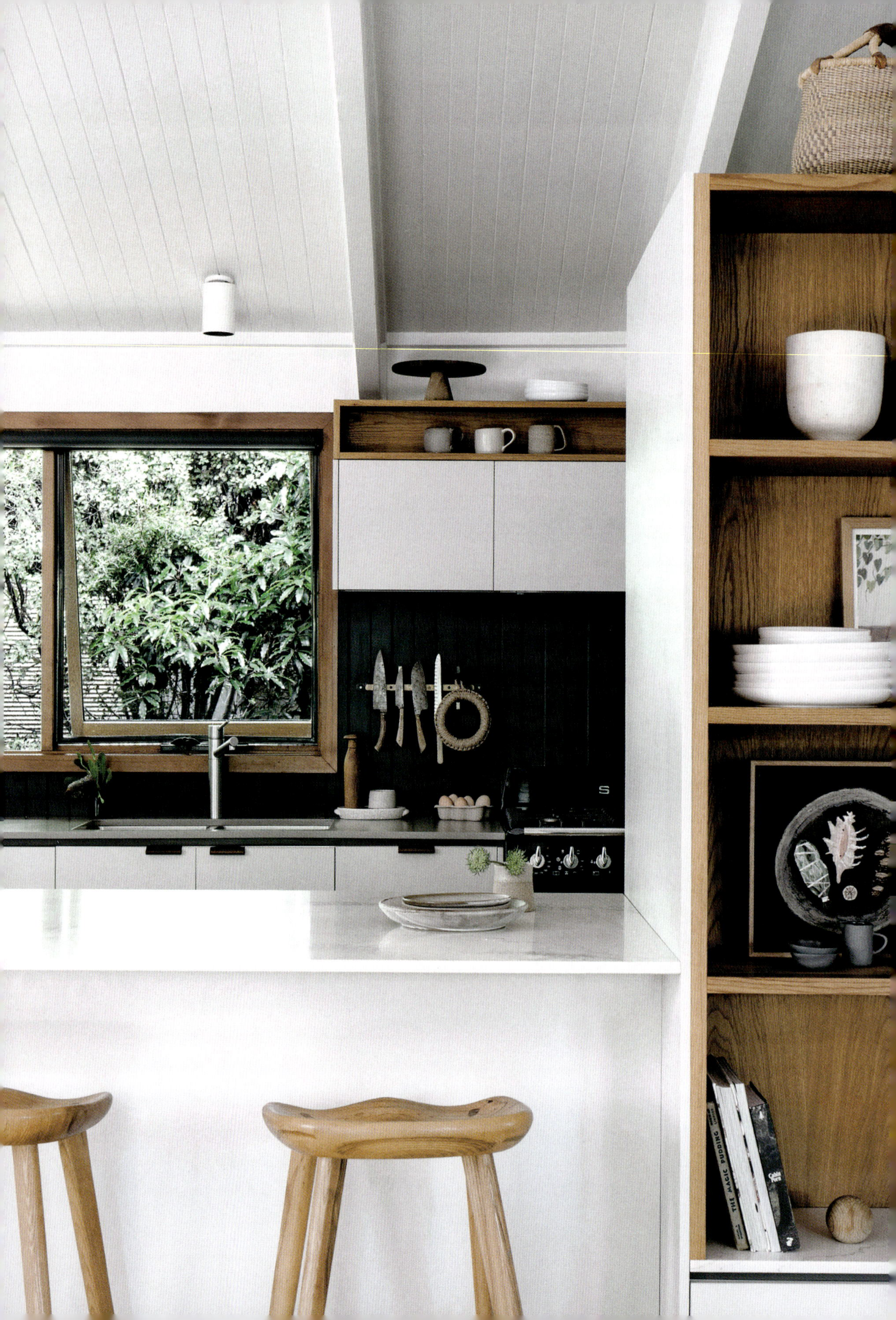
THE MAGIC PUDDING

The Hybrid Kitchen

Maximal minimalism, minimal maximalism—whatever you call it, if you land somewhere in the middle (which the majority of couples do), you like a bit of both worlds. You can comfortably pick and choose the elements from each end of the spectrum that most speak to you to create a handsome but unintimidating kitchen.

If you're a hybrid couple and one or both of you love to cook, optimize your kitchen for gastronomy. Give the most utilized utensils pride of place on your counters in open crocks and racks so they're always at hand, and stash the others in nearby cupboards and drawers. Trays and turntables are a great way to corral groupings of those and other trappings (like oils and spices) while conserving space. Consider accessorizing with dual-purpose accents like live herb plants in eye-catching planters, which can function as both décor and ingredients. If your layout allows, a narrow wooden worktable—either against a wall or in lieu of an island—can be a charming addition and make for convenient cooking à deux.

If you're a hybrid couple and neither of you likes to cook, you can settle for a few versatile small appliances, like a toaster oven or air fryer, and focus more on the aesthetics. Set the tone of the kitchen with a handful of decorations, from carefully styled rustic wooden cutting boards to a hook rack highlighting your mug collection to a quirky countertop task lamp. Mix and match other ideas from the maximalist and minimalist categories that work well with your lifestyle, and when in doubt, channel your favorite homewares shop or cooking show to inspire your vision.

Ensure everyday cooking essentials are easy to access with convenient kitchen accessories such as magnetic knife bars and salt cellars. Use open shelving to display a curation of coordinating tableware, and stow bolder designs behind cabinet doors.

Good as New

The kitchen is often the first room that couples choose to renovate, and for good reason. For starters, it is typically the most high-traffic area of the home. Here, unlike in other rooms that you can simply refurnish, wear and tear might look like cracked tiles or delaminating cabinetry, the replacing of which could be a big undertaking. Plus, with the permanence of a kitchen's fittings and the rapid rise and fall of trends, it's easy for this space to feel outdated.

But if you're not ready to bring in the demolition crew, consider making some less involved kitchen updates to hold you over. Major appliances, including refrigerators, dishwashers, and freestanding electric ranges, that are faulty or timeworn can be replaced. Other intermediate interventions include painting cabinetry in a new hue (with a semigloss or satin finish paint); refinishing the kitchen sink; giving your backsplash a fresh look via peel-and-stick tiles; and changing the countertops with new laminate, butcher block, or other screw-in alternatives. Though you may need to get a professional to help with these projects (depending on your DIY skills), just one or two of the updates can terrifically revamp your kitchen.

If even these options require more time or money than you care to invest, fret not. You can still give your kitchen a second wind with the right accents. First, swap out the hardware: Cabinet knobs and drawer pulls, the kitchen faucet and side spray, and light fixtures have a lot of influence on the overall look of a kitchen. Then, bring in textiles: A new runner and window treatments—even dish towels hanging from your appliance pulls—can make a noticeable difference. And lastly, upgrade the items displayed on the countertops, from the small appliances to the tabletop decorations. These tweaks will give your kitchen a strong sense of personality and instantly usher it into a new era.

TO REMODEL OR NOT TO REMODEL

A kitchen that is fully customized to your taste and lifestyle is likely at the top of your wish list, but is it the right time to go forward with this major to-do? There are a number of potentially deal-breaking factors to consider before you invest your time and money into a renovation. Here are five questions to ask yourselves—and talk through together—as you determine whether it's time to pull the trigger on a new kitchen.

How long do you plan to live in the home?
If you're staying put indefinitely, it's certainly worth investing in renovations, but if you think a move may be on the horizon in the next few years, you may want to consider starting with lower-cost upgrades (such as those noted opposite) so that you aren't spending money you won't necessarily recoup when it's time to leave.

When was the kitchen built or last remodeled?
The average lifespan of a kitchen is ten to fifteen years. If your kitchen is older than that, chances are it feels out of date, and/or shows considerable signs of wear (damaged appliances, cabinetry, and tiles, for instance).

Do you have the funds?
A full kitchen renovation can cost anywhere from $20,000 to $70,000.

How much time can you devote to this project?
It can take anywhere from two to four (or more) months to complete a kitchen renovation, during which time you will need to focus lots of attention on making decisions.

Can you bear not having a kitchen for a while?
Or possibly evacuating your home for the time it takes to renovate the kitchen? Besides the fact that your kitchen will be out of order, construction brings with it a slew of other major disruptions, including air and noise pollution, which you'll need to either tolerate or escape.

Going Gourmet

Every hardworking home chef deserves an arsenal of quality cookware and tools, which can turn any old kitchen into a high-functioning cookery. Don't mistake a wide range of kitchen equipment for an oversupply of it, though. You might have already accumulated a ton of gadgets and gizmos, especially between the two of you (see page 206 for information on how to handle duplicate items), but by choosing your core items judiciously and learning how to use and care for them properly, you will be well equipped to make everything from perfect scrambled eggs to a complicated cassoulet—and you won't have to worry about repurchasing items every few years. Here are the foundational pieces worth investing in, and some useful intel to help you make your choices.

Knives

First up are your knives—arguably the most essential cooking tools of all. A great set can make food prep exponentially easier and more enjoyable. A standard knife block will include a serrated bread knife, which, as its name suggests, is used for cutting bread and other baked goods; a sharp-tipped boning knife for handling meat; a compact paring knife for detailed fruit and vegetable prep; and the star player of any set—or kitchen, for that matter—the multifunctional chef's knife. With its wide, subtly curved, and pointed blade, this versatile tool is capable of singlehandedly taking on the majority of all knifing tasks.

You may choose to buy a readymade knife set if you please, but for a more bespoke cooking experience, elect to pick out individual knives and build your own perfect range. In your hunt, consider that for hundreds of years, the world's two powerhouse producers of elite knives have been Japan and Germany.

Japanese knives are customarily crafted from high-carbon hard steel. Distinguished by their lightness and blade thinness, they perform well in precision cutting and stay sharp for a long time, but they can be brittle and require care, so don't put a lot of pressure on them (no cutting of frozen foods, for instance).

German knives, on the other hand, are workhorses made from a softer carbon steel, which makes them more durable. Their thicker blades mean you will have to apply more force to cut—but they can handle that force well.

Whichever knives you choose, always hand-wash them (do not put them in the dishwasher), never let them air-dry (in order to avoid rusting), and get them professionally sharpened by a local cutler every few months.

Cookware

When it comes to cookware, an average home cook needs just seven quality items: a skillet, sauté pan, saucepan, roasting pan, stockpot, Dutch oven, and rondeau or braiser. Materials, again, are key: Look for high-performing heat-conductive metals like cast iron, copper, stainless steel, and aluminum. While nonstick pans can be convenient, the safety of the PFTE chemicals used in the coating has long been debated. (If you still want a nonstick alternative, choose modern ceramic-coated designs, made without these potentially harmful chemicals, instead.)

When cooking with high-grade materials, ensure that you're using the correct temperatures and preheating techniques for each (for instance, properly seasoning cast iron) and you won't miss the nonstick coating. What's more, you don't have to commit to one material for all of your cookware. In fact, by diversifying, you can broaden your culinary range and recipe repertoire, and take on any bigger fish to fry.

REGISTER THIS

Commit to reliable kitchen essentials that will last a lifetime.

Chef's knife: Better yet, get one for each of you. Trusted makers include Shun and Miyabi (Japanese), as well as Wüsthof and Zwilling (German).

Enameled cast-iron Dutch oven: Those by Le Creuset and Staub have long been considered the crème de la crème.

Copper sauté pan: The signature styles of the nearly two-hundred-year-old brand Mauviel are crafted from 90 percent polished copper and feature a stainless-steel interior.

À la Carte

Discovering your forte or fixation in the kitchen is gratifying as it is, but finding a mutual obsession with your partner is especially worth celebrating. Whatever that may look like for you, let yourselves explore and invest in this shared passion. Sometimes going down the rabbit hole together can be a fun new phase, and other times it can be the start of a lifelong household ritual. Here are some ideas for specialty equipment to add to your collection—and geek out over together.

For the Breakfast Clubbers

Rise and shine with all the essentials: a griddle (for everything from bacon to flapjacks), a grill press to keep your bacon from curling, and a batter dispenser for pancake precision (or, for a Belgian-inspired breakfast, a waffle iron). For excellent eggs, get a few sets of eggcups and egg spoons (for soft-boiled eggs on the shell) and egg rings (for those who like them fried). And don't forget the toaster and toast rack.

For the Pasta Chefs

You can opt for an electric or manual pasta machine, or, for a more old-fashioned approach, a *mattarello*-style rolling pin. Though there are hundreds of types of pasta, you will be well equipped to make myriad varieties with these handy tools: a drying rack; cutting wheels and stamps; spaghetti tongs; a wooden board and dowel for gnocchi and cavatelli; piping bags; and a ravioli tray.

For the Baristas

Keep your beans fresh with a coffee grinder. A drip coffeemaker is great for a classic cup of joe in the style of your favorite American diner; for a more nuanced brew, you'll want a French press and/or a pour-over coffeemaker. Use a kitchen scale and gooseneck kettle for the full experience. Lastly, invest in an espresso machine with a built-in (or separate) milk frother to master everything from *ristrettos* to cappuccinos.

For the Wellness Enthusiasts

A powerful blender is indispensable, as is a cold press for extracting fresh fruit and vegetable juices. Use ice-cube trays to freeze liquid smoothie bases or batch-made blends to defrost and drink later. For homemade ingredients, consider a yogurt maker, which will ferment milk in just hours, and/or a nut-milk maker, which will transform nuts, grains, and seeds into plant-based drinks.

DATE NIGHT

TOP CHEFS

In many marriages, one person will take the lead as the home cook, perhaps because the other is not as comfortable in the kitchen, or simply because the practical realities of daily life might make cooking together feel more like a luxury than a must.

One way to put a fresh spin on things and make collaborating in the kitchen more of a feasible, festive occasion is to prepare a three-course meal together. You can each choose one course to take on solo, and cook the third as a pair. For instance, maybe the more seasoned cook will take on the main course while the other whips up a simple dessert, and together you'll tackle an appetizer that's more effortful (see page 84 for a recipe for one such starter). Choose a theme for the menu, be it a type of cuisine, a star ingredient to be highlighted in every course, or a more conceptual inspiration like beloved family recipes—a beautiful way to share a piece of your heritage with your partner. Discuss the dishes and finalize a menu for the evening, then make a shopping list of what you'll need and head to your grocer to gather the ingredients together.

As you work side by side and cook up a storm, allow for the possibility that you have different cooking styles and be open to learning new techniques from each other. If your partner is less experienced, be courteous and supportive of their efforts—never high-handed. Regardless of the outcome, savor the moment and appreciate the time you're able to commit to one another. Make the most of the endeavor by sitting down to properly enjoy the meal together without interruptions, which can be rewarding in and of itself. And a quick tip: If you both clean up as you go, there will be less to do after the repast is done. At worst, the whole experience will be an epic day to remember, and at best, you'll enjoy the meal so much that you'll find yourselves adding it into your regular dinner rotation.

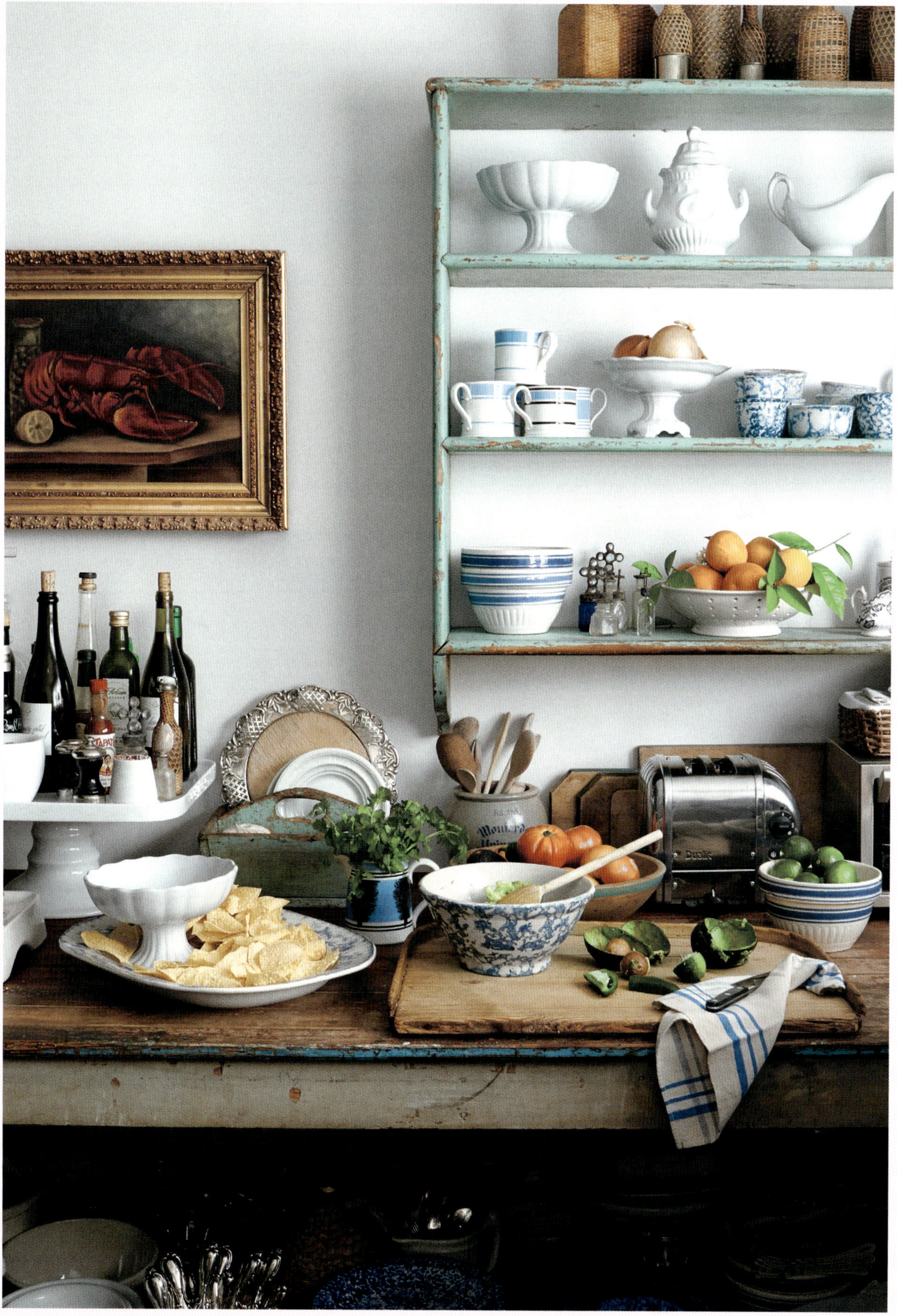

Mediterranean-Style Dolmades

This recipe for traditional, vegan rice-stuffed grape leaves is courtesy of my Greek-born Armenian grandmother. A great option for a date night starter that you can make together (see page 82 for more on playful ways to join forces in the kitchen), the dish invites conversation. While it is not overly complicated to make, it *can* demand meticulousness—so much so that even the most territorial home chef would welcome a helping hand. The process of wrapping each dolma requires patience, and it will take an hour or two to wrap them all, but by joining forces you can speed things up and use the occasion for some invaluable one-on-one time. Put on some background music, pour some refreshments, and have a cozy chat as you work alongside each other.

The dolmades can be served either chilled or at room temperature as a mezze or appetizer, side dish, or snack, and will keep in the fridge for up to five days, so you can make them when you both have the time to slow down. The resulting dish—an herby, lemony, brightly flavored Mediterranean classic—will be a testament to your teamwork and give new meaning to the phrase "made with love."

Makes 45 dolmades

2 cups (418 g) uncooked medium-grain white rice

½ cup (118 ml) extra-virgin olive oil

2 large onions, finely chopped

4¾ cups (1.1 L) water

2 teaspoons salt

2 teaspoons black pepper

1 teaspoon paprika

½ cup (25 g) finely chopped cilantro

½ cup (25 g) finely chopped Italian parsley

½ cup (25 g) finely chopped dill

½ cup (25 g) finely chopped mint leaves

One 16-ounce (454 g) jar of grape leaves in brine

Juice of ½ lemon

Lemon wedges for serving (optional)

Rinse the rice thoroughly, then set aside.

In a large, lidded saucepan or deep pan, heat the olive oil over medium heat. Add the onions and cook until lightly browned, about 15 minutes. Add the rice to the pan and mix well. Cook the rice and onion mixture for about 8 minutes, stirring constantly. Add 2¾ cups (651 ml) of the water, plus the salt, pepper, and paprika. Stir to combine.

Cover the pan and let the rice mixture simmer until the water is fully absorbed, about 5 minutes. The rice will not be fully cooked at this stage. Turn off the heat and stir in the cilantro, parsley, dill, and mint. Place the lid back on the pan and remove from the heat. Let the rice sit, covered, until it reaches room temperature, 30 to 45 minutes.

Remove the grape leaves from the jar and rinse them thoroughly to wash off the brine. Wring them dry, and pluck off any stems.

To make each dolma, lay 1 leaf on a flat plate or cutting board with the shiny side facing down and the stem side facing you. Scoop about 1 heaping tablespoon of the cooled rice filling into the center. (You may need to adjust the amount of filling used depending on leaf size.) Fold the bottom of the leaf up over the mixture, then fold in the two sides and roll the dolma upward tightly as if you were rolling a cigar. Repeat the process until you have used all the filling.

Line the bottom of a large rondeau or braiser with a layer of grape leaves. Set your dolmades seam side down on top of the grape leaves, packing and layering the dolmades in closely. Add the remaining 2 cups (473 ml) water and the lemon juice. Lay a heatproof plate facedown on top of the dolmades to secure them, and place the lid on the pot. Bring to a boil, then reduce the heat to low and cook until no water remains, the rice is thoroughly cooked, and the grape leaves have softened, about 30 minutes.

Turn off the heat. Let sit, covered, until the dolmades reach room temperature. Serve the dolmades as is or with a squeeze of fresh lemon juice.

Table for Two

"Party of two" is a phrase you've no doubt repeated countless times when dining together at restaurants. And at your most beloved haunts, you might even have a favorite booth or table that you hope to snag. It's a phenomenon that many of us experience: feeling comforted by being in the same little spot where we've sat time and again.

 Well, what if you were to create a cozy spot at home for those sweet one-on-one moments? An everyday dining nook, breakfast table, bistro set, or even a kitchen counter with a couple of stools can be a dedicated meeting place for you and your partner. You might use it every morning for a quick breakfast together before you head off to work, or to savor some afternoon tea on the weekends. Where you have your home-cooked evening suppers or those midnight bowls of cereal you indulge in before bed. Maybe it's where you read together, plan out your schedules, or simply check in with each other (see opposite for one such conversation to have here). By creating the space, you will organically open the door to ordinary yet precious moments.

 Make this special spot extra inviting through your décor and accessories, such as a vintage tablecloth, a vase of flowers, novelty salt and pepper shakers, or a lazy Susan with beckoning bits and bobs like a deck of artist-designed playing cards and a fanciful bottle opener. You can also use lighting to enhance the intimacy of the space: Think a single hanging pendant light, a dainty table lamp, or a votive candle à la your favorite romantic restaurant. And don't be so precious about it. This corner is *yours* and meant to be used daily. Embrace the inevitable imperfections (like wine stains on a wooden table from an impromptu post-dinner toast) as evidence of the love you've nourished here.

CHECK IN

BALANCING ACT

When we think of daily kitchen tasks, we may consider only the basics of cooking and washing dishes. In actuality, keeping a home kitchen running smoothly requires far more: stocking the fridge and pantry; planning and prepping meals; reorganizing, tidying, disinfecting surfaces; sweeping and mopping; wiping appliances; taking out the trash—the list goes on.

Often, when one person in a relationship takes on the brunt of household duties, many of the chores being done go unnoticed while still being expected by the other partner—a phenomenon called "invisible work" (a term first coined in 1987 by sociologist Arlene Kaplan Daniels). And for the person carrying the project-managing load, it can be physically, mentally, and emotionally taxing. It's no wonder, then, that division of labor is such a prevalent obstacle for many couples. But through mutual respect, good communication, and thoughtful planning, you can not only steer clear of such issues but also create harmony and true comfort in your home and relationship.

Start by breaking down the workload, either by room or by day, then divvy up the tasks you will each be responsible for and talk through each point until you are in agreement about what's fair. Keep weekly agendas and/or to-do lists until you both feel fluent in your share of obligations, and try to actively recognize—and express gratitude for—each other's contributions over the days, weeks, months, and years.

Naturally, everyone's routines and habits are bound to change at some point, be it suddenly or over longer periods of time. Schedules and priorities can shift, and with them, the dynamic you've worked so hard to create at home. Be mindful of each other's well-being and circumstances and make an effort to actively check in with each other about the domestic workload.

If you notice that your partner is struggling with their share of tasks, offer to lend a hand to meet them in the middle. Or if you realize that you are both feeling overwhelmed, look into options that will allow you to take a breather together, like ordering ready-made meals or booking a housekeeping service, budget permitting. Having open discussions on the matter—and staying patient and compassionate through it all—can help nip any tension in the bud, and ultimately bring the distribution of household duties back into balance.

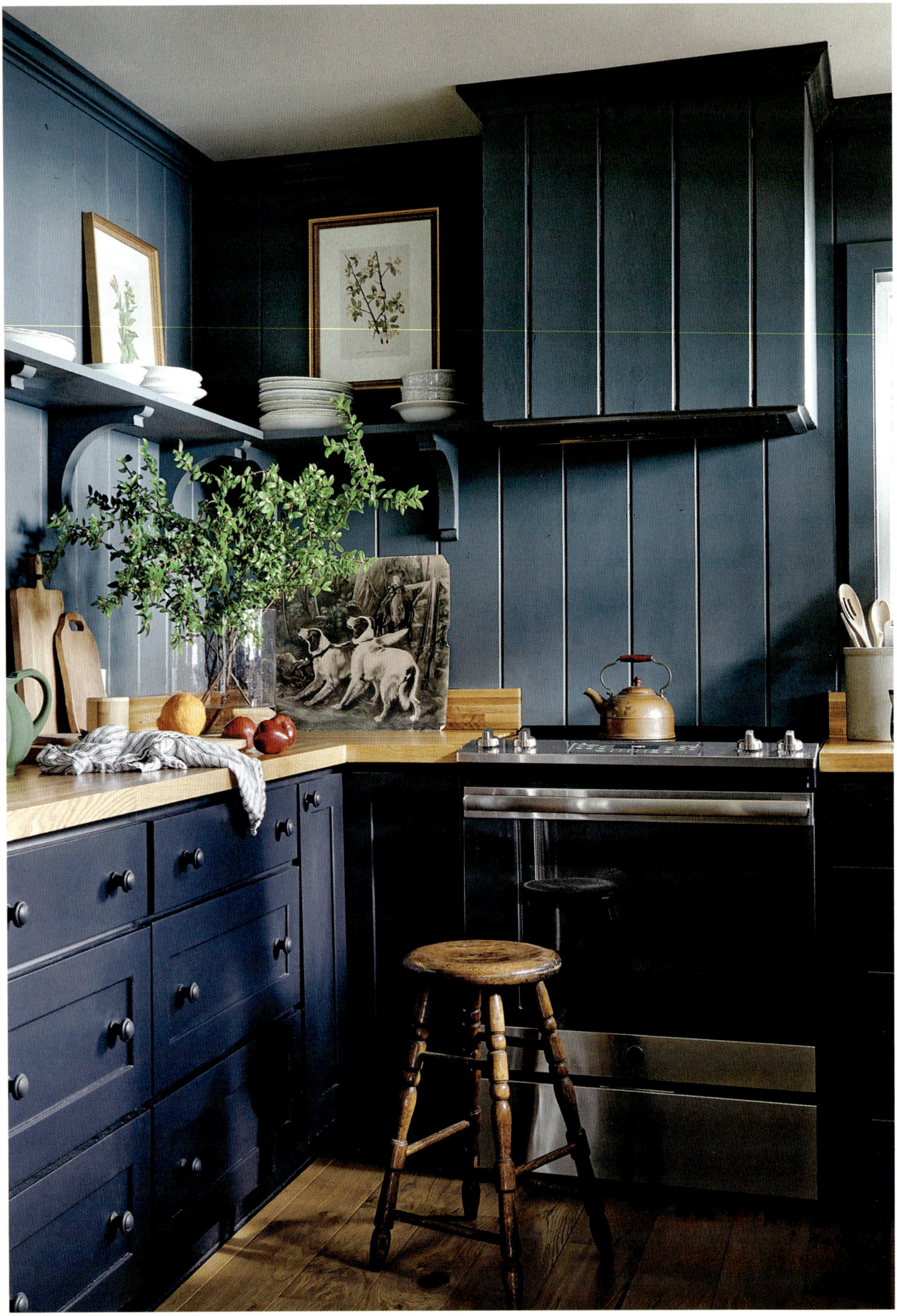

Finishing Touch

While there are few furnishings in the kitchen, there are still plenty of details you can introduce to personalize your space. If you don't know where to start, focus on incorporating details that are tied to your stories to bring your kitchen to life: Your most-loved cookbooks can live on an open shelf or on the countertop between bookends for easy access. A letter board can hang by the window, welcoming grocery lists, weekly menu items, or just notes between soulmates. Treasured heirlooms like hand-painted tole trays and porcelain plates can be upgraded to wall art via spring-style hangers. If you have a beloved family recipe, commission an artist to illustrate it for a one-of-a-kind artwork, or if you have the original handwritten copy, make a duplicate and frame it to create a print of your own. Similarly, you can frame memorable menus from dinner dates past, or the menu from your wedding reception.

Small potted herbs—the ones you regularly use for your homecooked meals—can freshen up the space, as can floral bouquets in vases, jugs, or pitchers. Use a large pedestal bowl to hold citrus, bananas, or apples—whichever fruits you reach for most. And choose kitchen linens (like tea towels and pot holders) and practical countertop items (like a butter keeper and spoon rest) that reinforce your kitchen's special spirit. Finally, consider tying everything together—and visually defining the room—with a kitchen floor mat, indoor/outdoor runner, or vinyl rug in a colorway that complements your décor and accessories.

Special details, like a salvaged wooden counter stool, antique copper teakettle, framed botanical prints, and decorative branches foraged from the yard and bunched in a vase, can be instrumental in cultivating a warm, inviting spirit in the kitchen.

Get Together

THE DINING ROOM

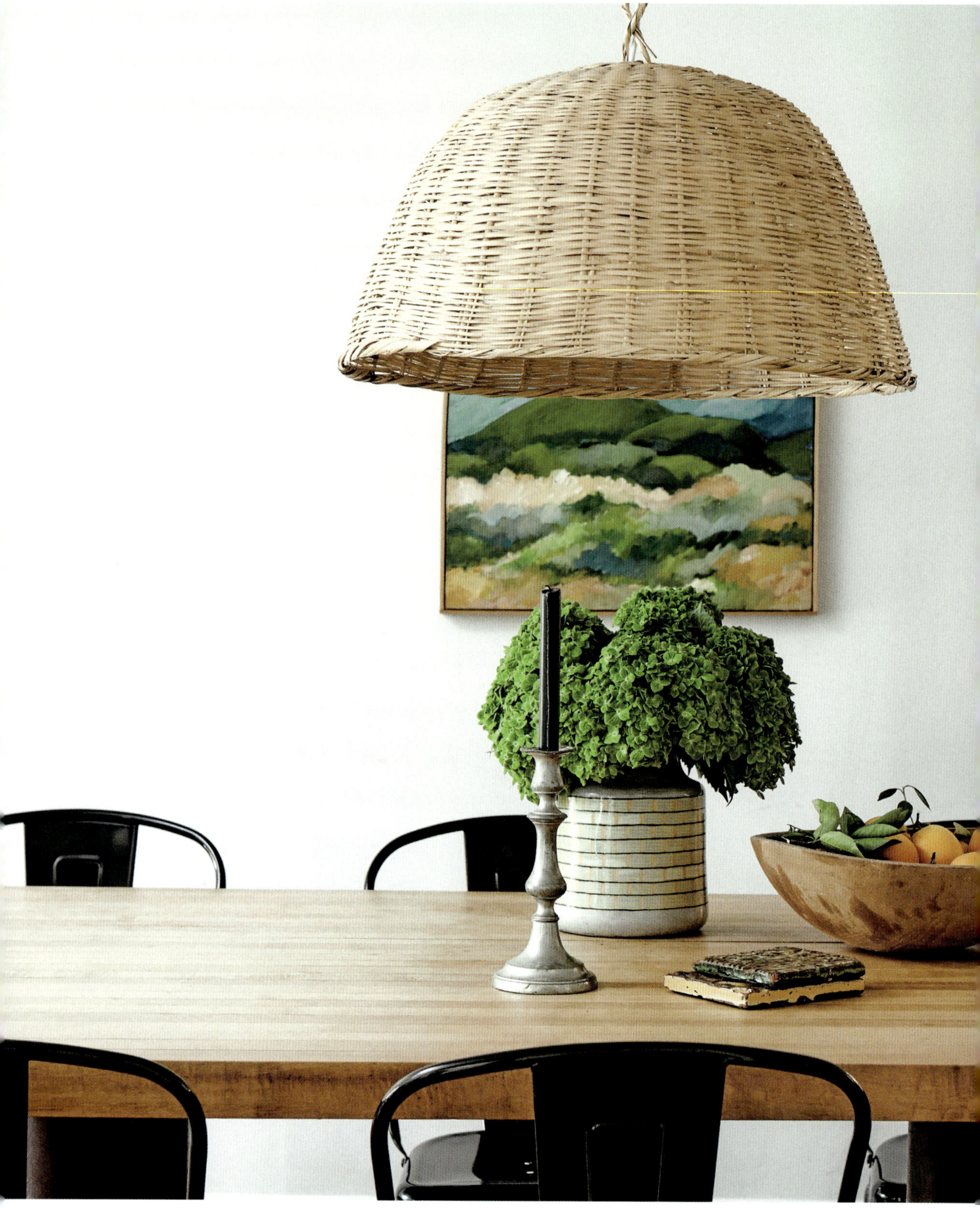

Whether you're planning a candlelit anniversary dinner or hosting the holidays together for the first time, the dining room will certainly play a key role in your household events and, more important, your relationship. It will be the site of countless shared meals, dinner parties, and celebrations, and since it will be regularly used when company's over, blending your personalities in this space will help make your occasions more memorable.

Nowadays, it might be tempting to forgo a formal dining room altogether, especially if you have a dining area in the kitchen, but if you have the space for it, there are many perks to having one, particularly for couples starting a new chapter together. And really, it doesn't have to be so "formal" if that's not your style. See, the dining room isn't so much a place to dine as it is a place to connect—with your partner and with your guests. Whether it's over a decadent multicourse family meal or takeaway coffee with friends, it's the enriching conversations that naturally unfold here that really define this space. It's where you will not only bond with company and get to know each other's circles but also have the opportunity to see your partner through their loved ones' eyes, which can be a very profound and powerful thing. The beauty often comes after dinner, when bellies and hearts are full, walls are down, candles are burned, and you find that you've lost track of time. Long, languid meals with your love or your visitors will give your home a deeper identity—one that will linger in your memory even if you one day move.

    That said, don't give in to using the dining room only on special occasions, which will lead to its gathering dust. Dining rooms can be extremely adaptable, morphing on an as-needed basis to accommodate household tasks, projects, office work, game nights, and so much more. The idea is to integrate the room into your lifestyle and not be too precious about it. In the end, the many memories made here, during festive fêtes or cherished one-on-one time, will be those you look back on for many years to come.

SWEET TALK

HOSTING AS A COUPLE

What does entertaining at home look like for you? You and your partner might be natural "hosts with the most" who find joy in the art of setting a table and cooking a special-occasion meal. Or perhaps you're potluck enthusiasts who love nothing more than a full house of family and friends. And then, of course, there are those couples that get flustered at the mere thought of organizing a dinner party and prefer to lie low on a Friday night with just a few pals.

For many newlyweds, throwing formal dinner parties might feel like something that's expected of you in this new era, but there's no one right way of hosting company. So long as you and your partner are on the same page, you will find your own style of entertaining friends and family. Before you splurge on fancy china, make your way through this lighthearted pop quiz together to get a better understanding of where you land on the hosting spectrum as a couple, talking through each point in the chart until you come to a consensus. That way, you can better understand how to stock your sideboard or buffet and cater your dining room to you.

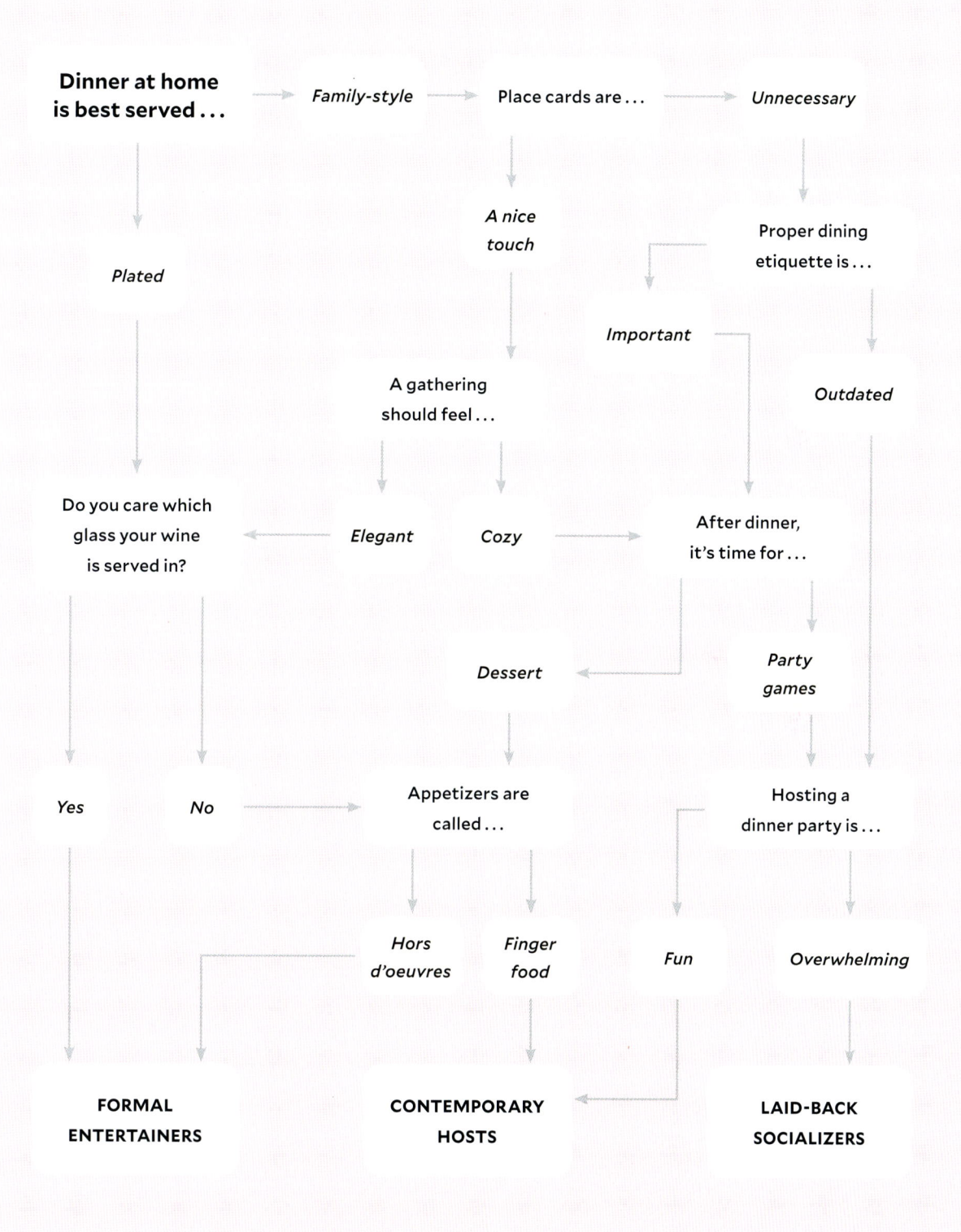

Dinner at home is best served... → *Family-style* → *Place cards are...* → *Unnecessary*

Place cards are... → *A nice touch*

Unnecessary → *Proper dining etiquette is...*

Proper dining etiquette is... → *Important*
Proper dining etiquette is... → *Outdated*

Dinner at home is best served... → *Plated*

A nice touch → *A gathering should feel...*

A gathering should feel... → *Elegant*
A gathering should feel... → *Cozy*

Important → *After dinner, it's time for...*
Cozy → *After dinner, it's time for...*

Plated → **Do you care which glass your wine is served in?**

Elegant → **Do you care which glass your wine is served in?**

After dinner, it's time for... → *Dessert*
After dinner, it's time for... → *Party games*

Do you care which glass your wine is served in? → *Yes*
Do you care which glass your wine is served in? → *No*

No → *Appetizers are called...*
Dessert → *Appetizers are called...*

Party games → *Hosting a dinner party is...*

Appetizers are called... → *Hors d'oeuvres*
Appetizers are called... → *Finger food*

Hosting a dinner party is... → *Fun*
Hosting a dinner party is... → *Overwhelming*

Yes → **FORMAL ENTERTAINERS**

Hors d'oeuvres → **FORMAL ENTERTAINERS**

Finger food → **CONTEMPORARY HOSTS**

Fun → **CONTEMPORARY HOSTS**

Overwhelming → **LAID-BACK SOCIALIZERS**

Get Together

Formal Entertainers

If you are both up for keeping the tradition of formal sit-down dinner parties alive, it's well worth investing in the time-honored practice and going for the whole shebang. The star of your dining room will be your table settings, so find eight or twelve five-piece dinnerware sets in fine china (made of ceramic) or bone china (a more durable porcelain made of a mix of ceramic and bone ash and considered to be of the highest quality) that you both feel represent your household well. Beware of vintage ceramicware, whose glazes may have traces of lead, and instead consider heritage brands with timeless styles like Wedgwood and Royal Copenhagen, both of which date back to the eighteenth century. Stay within the same china pattern for your chargers and serveware (like bowls and platters), and use plain tablecloths and napkins to let the dinnerware shine. You will also need eight or twelve special-occasion red wine glasses, white wine glasses, champagne flutes, and water glasses (be they fine crystal or glass) and five-piece silverware sets (in fine silver or even stainless steel). Get a second collection of dinnerware, flatware, and glassware in more relaxed, dishwasher-safe materials for everyday use.

Evergreen and sophisticated, a classically set table will always be in style. Monochromatic bouquets are a good choice for formal centerpieces, as are matching taper candles.

REGISTER THIS

Set things right with these classic tablescape essentials.

Tablecloths: Two or three linen, cotton, or silk varieties in neutral colors for a refined base layer.

Chargers: Weighty brass or nickel decorative plates to help your formal table shine.

Vases: A set of three low-profile vases for floral arrangements. Stick to glass or a finish that matches your chargers.

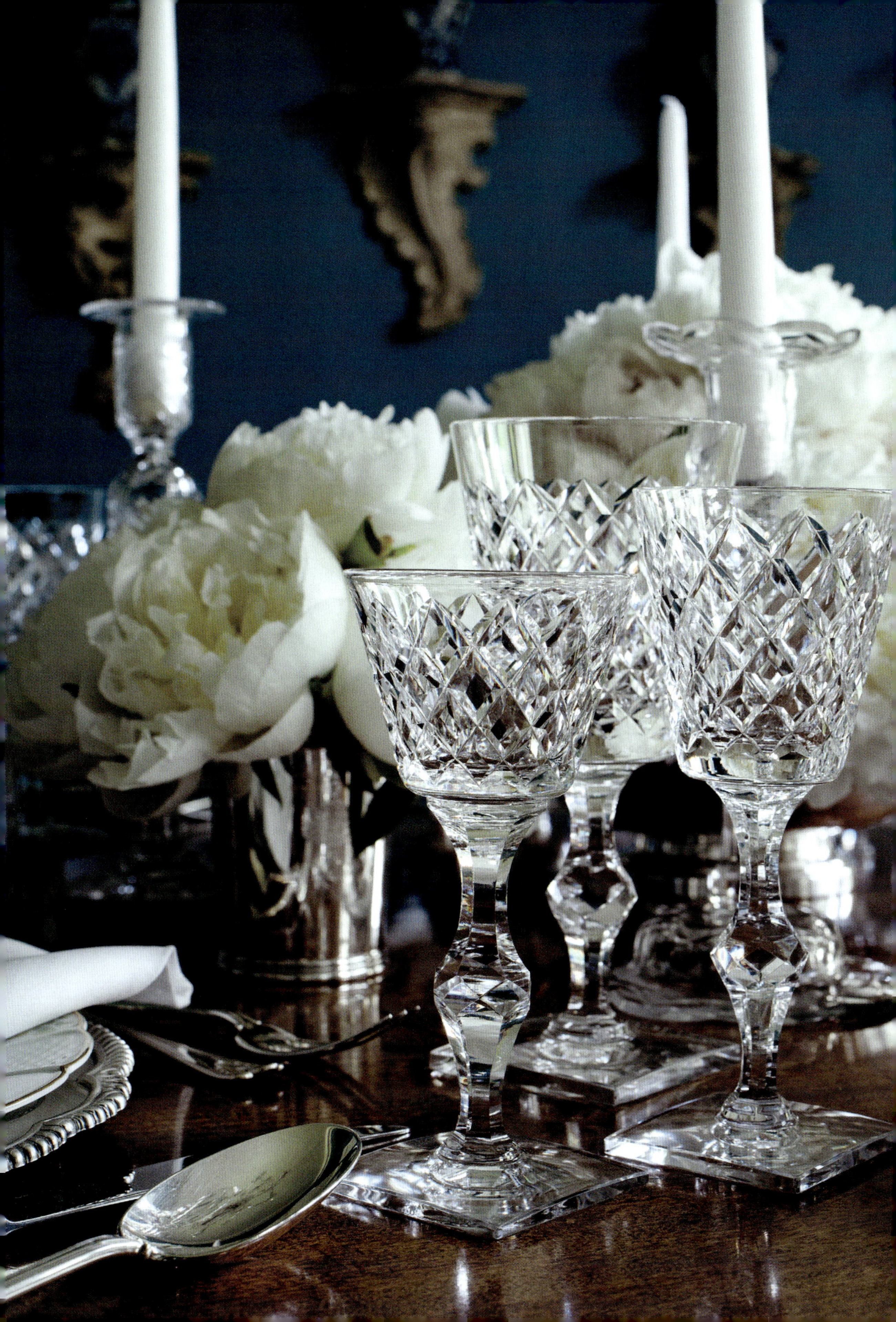

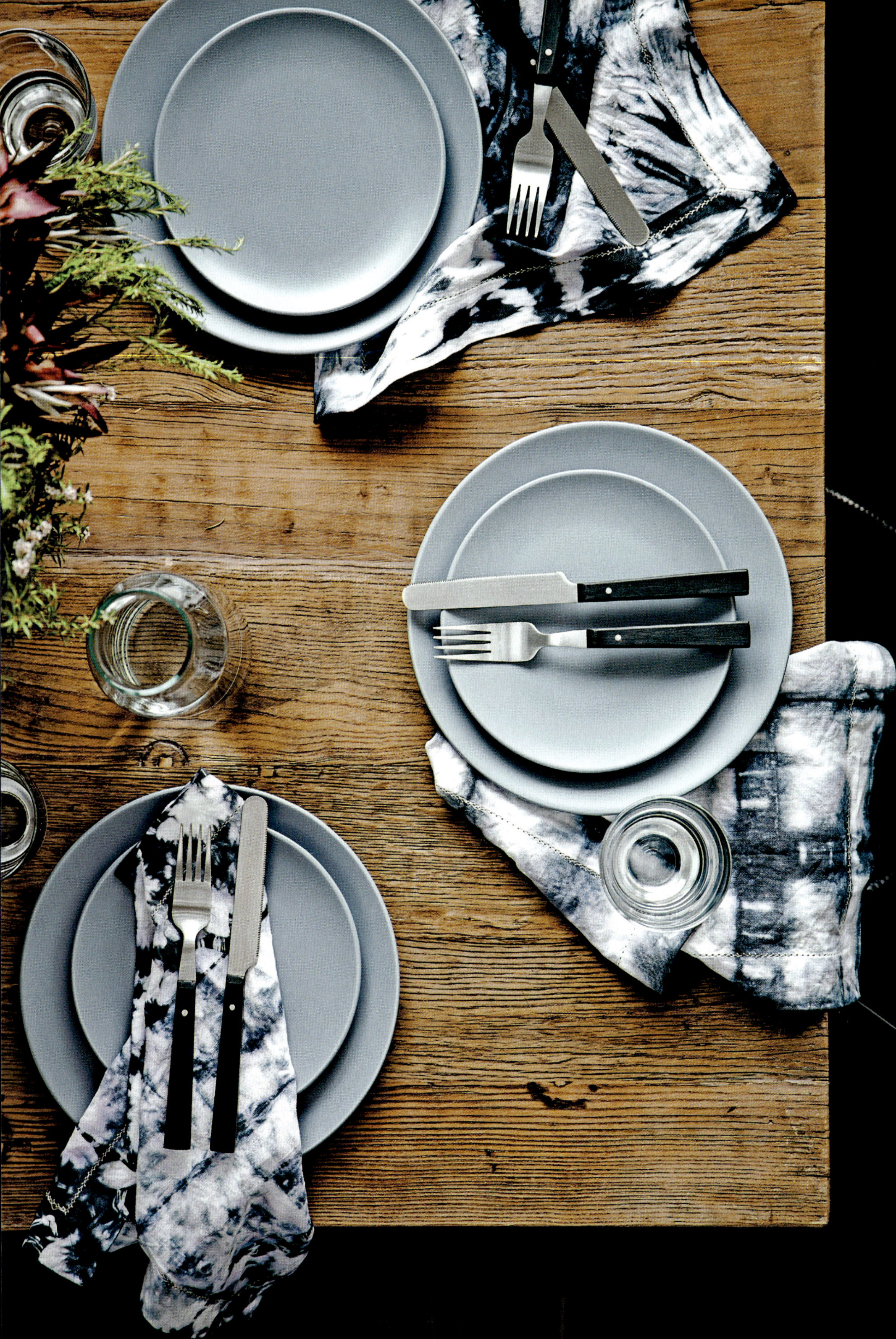

Contemporary Hosts

If you fall into this category, then dinner parties are a beloved pastime for you. You appreciate a well-set table—you're just not so precious about it. Choose twelve sets of slightly elevated everyday dinnerware (instead of fine china) for your family-style or buffet meals, plus twelve universal wineglasses, water glasses, and sets of flatware. If you're unsure of which designs to select, hark back to your favorite date-night spots and travels and aim to re-create those milieus through your tableware. Acquire a range of serveware as well, including a couple of oversize salad bowls, salad servers, platters, pitchers, charcuterie boards, and cheese knives. Pick a color scheme or material that you both love and choose items that incorporate it—that way you can build your collection over the years.

Even with only one pattern each of dishware, glassware, and silverware, you can still achieve a multitude of tablescape designs by adjusting the details, so invest in different table linens (tablecloths, napkins, runners, and place mats) and accessories (chargers and napkin rings) to change things up from one fête to the next.

A modern-day approach to entertaining means you get to pick and choose which traditions you observe—and which ones you don't. Cloth napkins, for instance, can feature bold colors and patterns for a more relaxed vibe.

REGISTER THIS

Noticeable details for you and your guests to feast your eyes on.

Place card holders: Fanciful holders to display hand-lettered guests' names or food labels on the buffet table.

Place mats: Rectangular and/or circular place mats that will add flair and showcase your dining table.

Cloth dinner napkins: Two or more sets of linen and/or cotton napkins in different patterns and colorways that riff off your place mats.

Laid-Back Socializers

If neither of you is the dinner party type, you likely still entertain at home from time to time, but in a more low-key fashion. Your dining room will still be your party zone, but your gatherings will tend toward casual hangouts with your nearest and dearest. You should have (at least) eight sets each of presentable everyday dinnerware and flatware—both for you to use and in case you have company—as well as eight universal wineglasses and water glasses. For your relaxed get-togethers, have absorbent coasters and a few chip-and-dip bowls on hand. You'll also get a lot of use out of eight (or more) dessert plates, for sweet and savory bites alike. Wooden or ceramic nesting bowls can be used for both mixing and serving batches of quick snacks like cinnamon-sugar popcorn, while small nut bowls can hold everything from almonds to olives to berries. Consider a set of cappuccino cups and saucers for coffee dates, and specialty barware (like martini glasses or whiskey tumblers) for cocktail hours. And instead of having formal china sitting unused in your sideboard, use the available storage for your board games or records.

Hosting doesn't have to be a grand ordeal. For the most casual gatherings, nothing more than some elegant glassware and a few small serving bowls for grazing snacks will do the trick.

REGISTER THIS

Keep it fun and breezy with a few reliable party staples.

Cloth cocktail napkins: A set or two of playfully embroidered linen or cotton napkins for beverages.

Deluxe board games: Heirloom-quality editions of your favorite classics in premium materials like leather and wood.

Centerpiece: An oblong bowl or circular tray for a perpetual and adaptable dining table attraction.

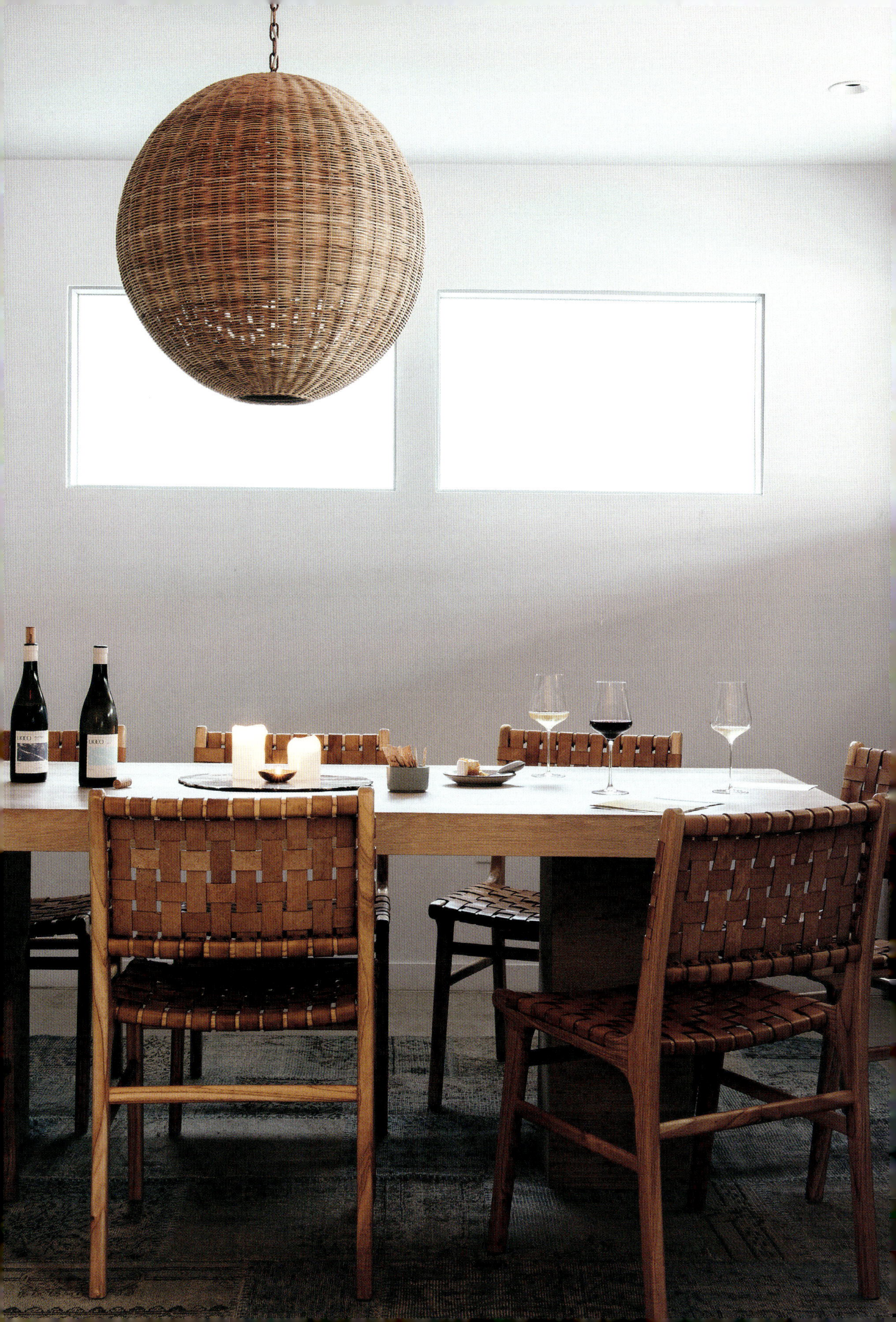

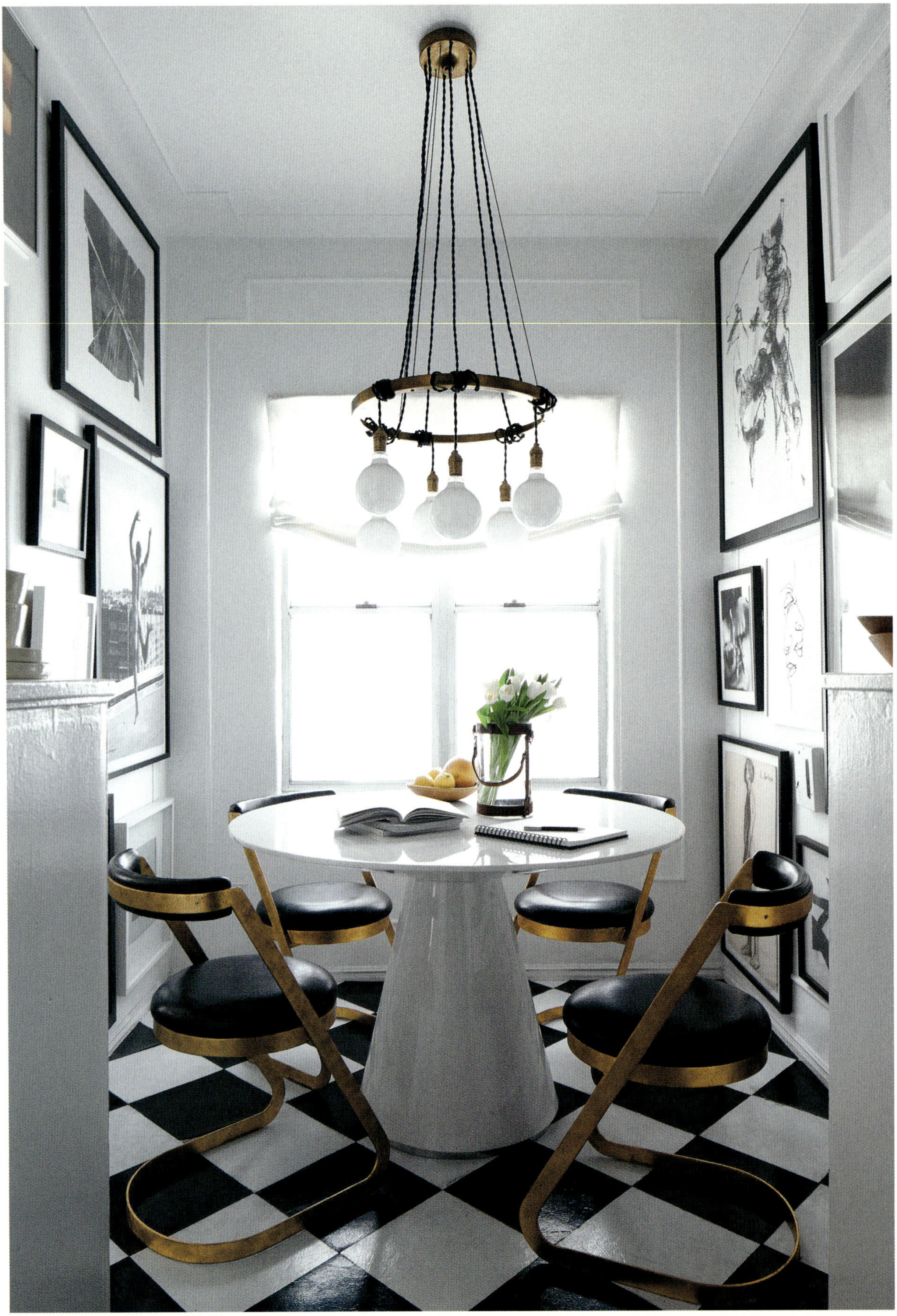

MAIN SQUEEZE

THE DINING TABLE

The dining table is a major showpiece—one that has the potential to anchor the entire home in a particular style. In fact, if a dining table is not in harmony with the rest of your décor or has the wrong dimensions for your space, it can really throw off the atmosphere of your home and ultimately become an eyesore. Plus, it's arguably the one element of your home that friends and family will be most acquainted with as they congregate around it over the years, thus leaving a lasting impression of your home (and the time spent with you as a couple).

Considering the impact this single piece can have—and the fact that it is one of the pricier furniture expenditures—take the time to weigh the pros and cons of different styles and calculate what size and shape are best for your dining room before committing to the purchase. As you narrow down your search, deliberate together on the longevity of the design and materials, the area the table will take up, and how it will accommodate both everyday life and special occasions. Reflect on the following factors as you set off on your quest.

Size

Dimensions are key when determining the right table for your dining room. If a table is too small, it will feel awkward and isolated, perhaps even uninviting. If a table is too large, it will appear unbalanced and be inconvenient to use. The rule of thumb is foolproof and simple: Allow for at least 3 feet and no more than 6 feet (about 1 to 2 m) of space between the table and any wall or other furnishings. With this guideline, you can determine the range of table sizes that your dining room can accommodate. If you love the idea of a grand dining table that can fit more guests but your space cannot permanently accommodate it, consider an extendable table, which includes a leaf or two for expanding the tabletop, giving you the flexibility to host larger parties if and when you need to.

Silhouette

A pivotal factor in deciding what shape of table you should get is actually what sort of chairs you want to employ. (See page 107 for tips on choosing dining chairs.) Small square and round tables typically work best with armless chairs all around, while rectangular or oval tables can accommodate armed chairs at both ends. Meanwhile, an extra-large table (one that seats ten or more), no matter the shape, will give you the option of surrounding it with armed chairs. In addition to the shapes of dining tables, survey the different kinds of legs and bases (a few common ones shown below) to help you identify your favorites.

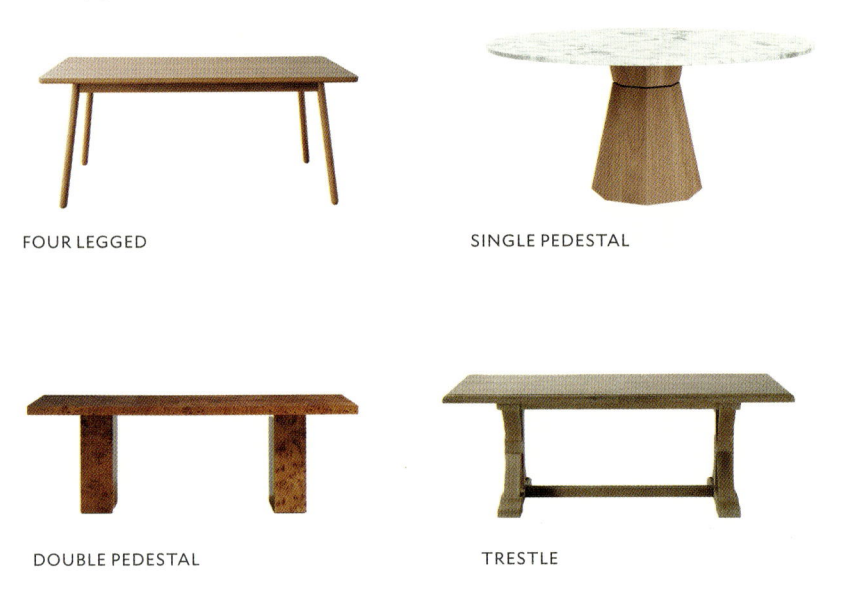

FOUR LEGGED

SINGLE PEDESTAL

DOUBLE PEDESTAL

TRESTLE

Material

The quality and durability—and by association, the required upkeep—of your table are just as important as its visual impact, so consider which materials work best for your homelife and habits as you search. Solid hardwood (like oak, cherry, and walnut) and softwood (like pine) are the most popular and versatile but can show signs of wear, from scratches to water stains. You'll want to dust a wood table weekly with a soft cloth, avoid harsh chemical cleaners, and use protective coverings like table pads (under tablecloths). Glass-topped tables, on the other hand, are nonporous and therefore easier to keep clean—and they can make your space look larger—but they will require more frequent wiping (since smudge marks are inevitable). Lacquered tables can be a happy medium between these two categories, especially for those aiming for a more contemporary look. The maintenance for stone-topped dining tables will be dependent on the type of stone used. Durable options include quartz and granite; marble, though luxurious, is more susceptible to stains and scratches.

Style

The spectrum of dining table designs is vast and varied, from Shaker and French country to art deco and modern—and everything in between. Start by browsing together, be it in-store, online, or in look books. Take notice of which features you love, hate, or are neutral about, and compare your findings with those of your partner. And look for design motifs and shapes that call back to the other furniture pieces in your home, like tapered legs and scalloped edges, to ensure visual flow. This will help you narrow down your search in what is a seemingly endless sea of options until you find "the one." The goal is to trust your taste and that of your spouse and find the design elements that speak to you both.

Opening Up

If you don't have a designated dining room but have a large living room or an open floor plan, you can use furniture to divide the space and create the illusion of a dining area. For instance, arranging your sitting room with a sofa or an L-shaped sectional facing away from the dining table will organically distinguish the two areas. Alternatively (or additionally), simply adding an area rug beneath your dining set can effectively separate the space and make it feel self-contained. (Tip: When choosing a rug for any dining area, make sure it is low-pile or flat-weave for easy maintenance, that its shape mirrors that of your dining table, and that it is 2 to 3 feet / about 60 to 90 cm larger than the table on all sides so that the chairs do not snag on it.) For exceptionally tight spaces or in homes where there is simply no room for a permanent, full-size dining table, consider the convenience of a drop-leaf table, which can convert to a dining table when needed but otherwise serve as a console or intimate bistro table.

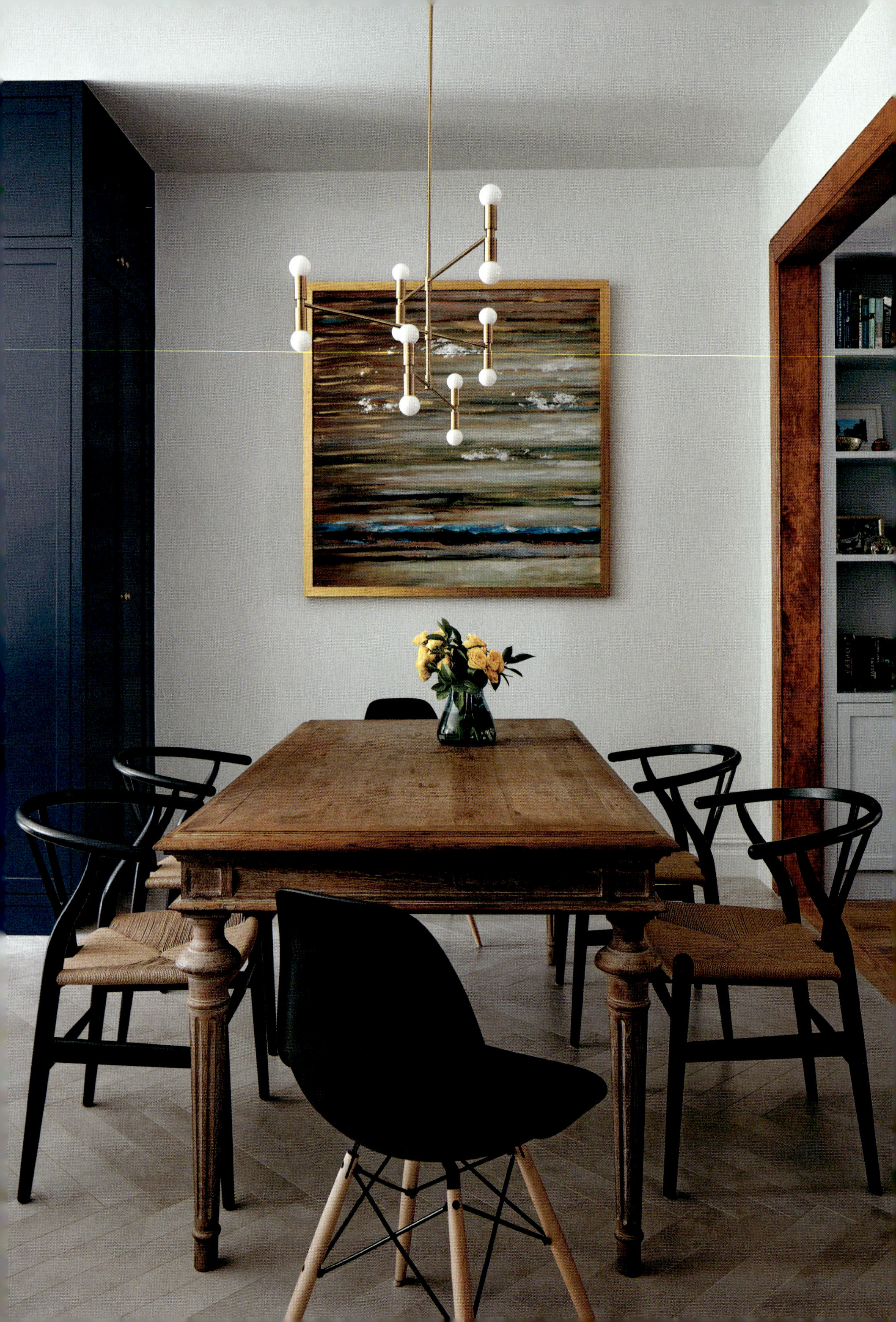

Have a Seat

The right dining room chairs will not only ensure that you and your guests are comfortable but will also have a major influence on the design of the space. In some cases, dining tables will be sold as a set with seats, but this can leave your dining room looking dated or generic. You're more likely to get a dynamic, unique aesthetic—one that speaks to your personalities—if you purchase seating separately from your table. With this approach, simply make sure you can draw some unifying lines between the table and chairs, be it in material, color, and/or design style (like Parisian-inspired or brutalist). How similar they are to each other is entirely up to you and the level of contrast you want to achieve. Here are a few other things to mull over with your spouse as you shop around.

Consider the materials used: Upholstered seats tend to be luxurious and formal, and are certainly comfortable, but can be costly and require upkeep like regular vacuuming and stain removal. If opting for fabric-covered seats, look for durable textiles like real or faux leather or performance fabrics like polyester or other synthetic blends. Meanwhile, wood chairs are generally more affordable, pragmatic, and lower maintenance, and complement a more contemporary look, but sitting on them for long stretches can lead to discomfort. When choosing wooden chairs, look for solid, quality construction and sturdy materials like oak and mahogany. If you're looking for rattan seats, find coated varieties for easy wiping, and for woven rush seats, note that natural fibers will require more maintenance. For more cushion, you might like to add seat pads with washable covers and ties—a great way to infuse more texture and color into the area. Metal chairs are another option, if you like a more industrial, casual look.

You may also consider a bench in lieu of some or all of your chairs, which can help open up the space, making it look bigger than it is, and offer more flexible seating. It's also a sweet addition for couples who like to sit side by side. Drape a knitted or faux fur throw over it for added comfort.

Once you have a better idea of what you're looking for, it's time to visit purveyors in person to test chairs out together, because ultimately, you won't really know which ones work best for you both without actually *sitting* in them. Factors like the height of the chairback or the size of the seat can go unnoticed by one of you but be deal-breakers for the other. Keep the dialogue going as you explore what feels most comfortable for you both—aka the Goldilocks principle—and soon enough, your picks of which chairs are "just right" will align.

If you and your partner are having trouble agreeing on a specific style and aren't opposed to a more eclectic look, mismatched chairs can be a creative compromise. Just make sure to stay within the same range of formality, and look for other commonalities like color palette or height.

Glow Up

If your dining room design is feeling flat, you likely need to remedy the lighting. By incorporating multiple sources of light throughout the room, you will give yourselves the freedom to adjust the ambience of the space for various events, be it an intimate dinner for two, a festive occasion with your nearest and dearest, or a joint work-from-home session.

    The centerpiece of your dining room lightscape will be your chandelier. Choose a dimmable style—equipped with warm white LED bulbs—to deliver just the right amount of light for functionality and romance. With chandeliers available in a great array of designs and materials, you can find one that either blends into the room, commingling with your dining table, chairs, and room accents, or shines bright on its own as a bold statement. Whichever style you choose, make sure the chandelier hangs 30 to 40 inches (about 76 to 102 cm) above the center of the table. If it is too high, you'll lose the intimacy. Install a backplate or chandelier canopy (the decorative piece that sits flush to the ceiling and hides the wiring) to make the fixture's presence even more impactful.

    Then, layer in other sources of light, like a pair of sconces or floor lamps. If you have a sideboard, you can add a buffet lamp (taller and slimmer than a table lamp) or two, which can be especially helpful when guests are serving themselves. To spotlight specific pieces in the room, use accent lights. For instance, indoor uplights can be used on the floor behind large houseplants, and picture lights can be used above works of art on the walls. And for that extra touch of romance, use taper candles in holders to add a shining element to the dining table—be it a pair for a special date or a sea of them across the length of your table for an unforgettable holiday feast.

CHECK IN

A HELPING HAND

Entertaining at home can be a big, intimidating undertaking, even for the most proficient of hosts. There are the pre-party tasks, from grocery shopping and cleaning the home to cooking and setting the table. Then there are the host responsibilities during the event, which can include serving food, topping off drinks, and staying attuned to everyone's needs or requests. Of course, once you've seen your guests out comes the most daunting phase of all: cleanup.

With the physical and mental demands each of these stages can bring, it's important to be in constant communication with your partner before and throughout it all, particularly about how you can fairly divvy up the responsibilities at hand. In the case that you find yourself buried in the work, don't be too shy to ask for help and delegate tasks to your partner—and conversely, if you finish something early, check in with your spouse to see how they can use a hand. It's vital that both partners be willing to help each other and take on more or less as the event progresses. If you actively work together and embrace the collaboration, you might not only get more done in less time, allowing both of you to be present when the company has arrived, but also find that you can actually enjoy the whole process of successfully hosting as a team.

Dinner Is Served

At face value, setting the table can seem like a dull, redundant chore. Take a step back, though, and you'll see how this modest task actually represents so much more. Rooted in rich histories, the practice of preparing a dinner table—methodically arranging plates, glasses, utensils, and other tableware—is actually a precious act of human ritual, whose iterations span many generations across the globe. Reframing it through this lens can, hopefully, reenergize your approach and get you eager to create table setting traditions of your own.

No matter your style, it's beneficial to learn the customary American (by way of Europe) table settings of today. (Note, soup bowls and spoons are not pictured here. If serving, in both settings the bowl would go on top of the napkin, and spoon farthest to the right.)

INFORMAL PLACE SETTING

1. Salad fork
2. Dinner fork
3. Cloth napkin
4. Salad plate
5. Dinner plate
6. Dinner knife
7. Water glass
8. Universal wineglass

The Newlywed Home

FORMAL PLACE SETTING

1. Bread plate and butter knife
2. Salad fork
3. Dinner fork
4. Dessert spoon and fork
5. Cloth napkin
6. Salad plate
7. Dinner plate
8. Charger
9. Dinner knife
10. Salad knife
11. Water glass
12. Red wine glass
13. White wine glass

DATE NIGHT

CHECKMATE

Carving out time to dine together at home is essential, but after a while, shared meals will feel less and less like dates and more like, well, life. Planning special dinners for each other here and there is always a great idea, of course, but for those idle evenings when you want to do something casual but different, consider an intimate game night.

Pour some drinks, prepare an assortment of snacks, put on a record, and park yourselves at the dining table for a one-on-one chess tournament—or play checkers, cards, a board game, or whatever floats your boat. The idea is to linger with your love and embrace a little bit of respectful competition, which, in small doses, can help couples hone their communication skills, set healthy boundaries, and strengthen their bond through play. Plus, on the occasion that you're feeling frisky, you can put a racy twist on the game by wagering items of clothing, perhaps—wink-wink.

If you find that one or both of you tend to get *too* competitive and that things become a little heated, opt for a more collaborative activity, like a cooperative board game, crossword, or jigsaw puzzle. The point is to have fun, spend quality time together, and take pride in each other. And if you don't use your dining table regularly, consider keeping out an ongoing game of chess or a jigsaw puzzle that will beckon you to sit at the table and take a pause together when you otherwise wouldn't have.

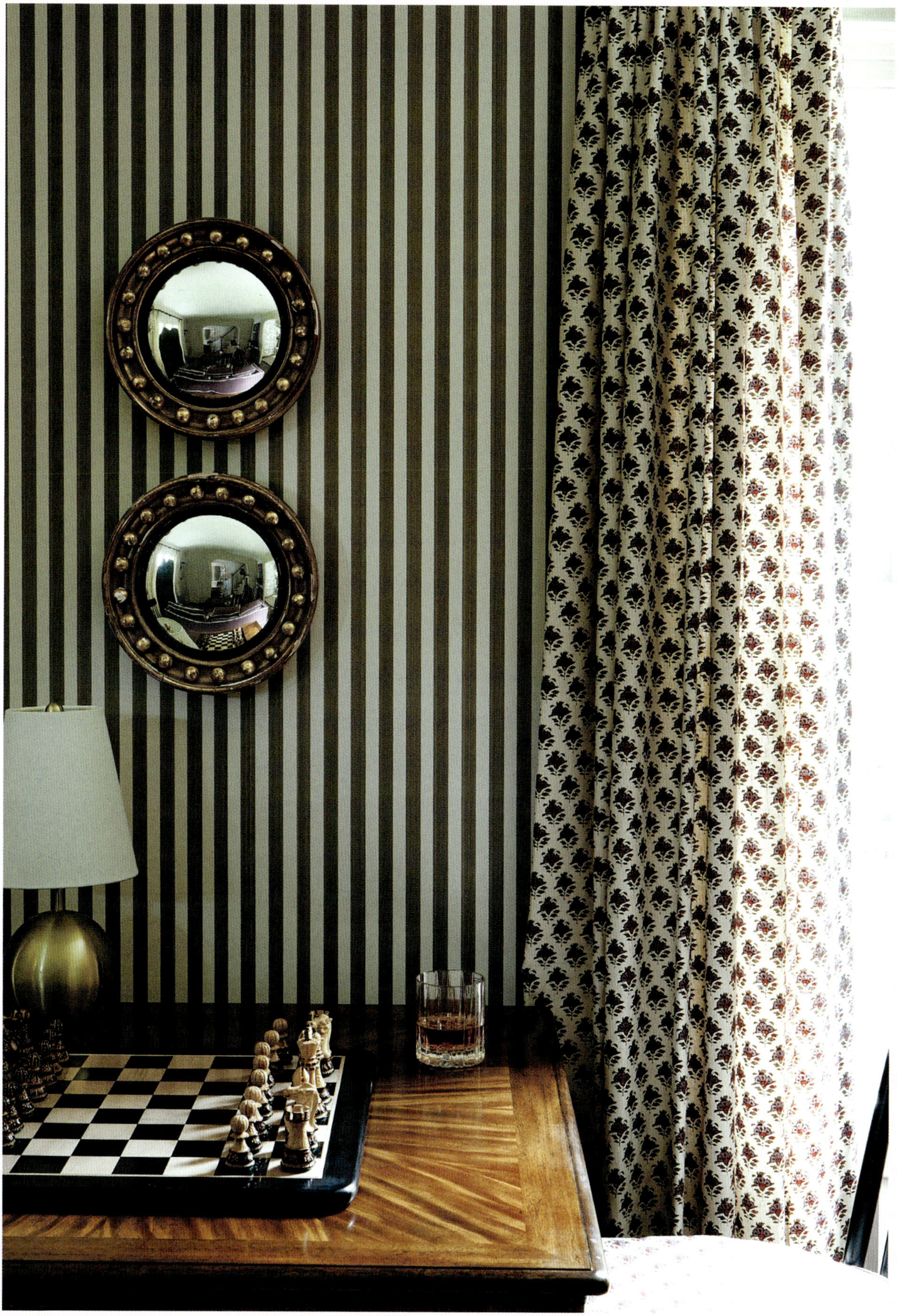

Raising the Bar

For couples who like to imbibe, a bar cart or cabinet is a fabulous addition to a dining room. Not only can it bring an interactive element to dinner parties—shaken cocktails to order, anyone?—but it can serve as a sultry spot to meet your companion at home for a nightcap (or two). And when curated and decorated with care, it can also be a nice conversation starter.

Before you go shopping for a new piece of furniture, check your combined inventory of unspoken-for furnishings to see if there's, say, a small desk or old cubby that can be refurbished and repurposed as a dedicated bar. By doing so, you can give new life to an otherwise unused item while adding an extra sprinkle of charm and history to your dining room. If you like that idea but don't have such a piece, don't be afraid to hunt one down at a local flea market or vintage shop. It might be more work, but it will be a delightful activity and result in yet another talking point for visiting guests. If a classic bar area is more your style, go ahead and find a bar cabinet that matches the rest of your dining room. In the case that you don't have space for a permanent bar station or prefer a more affordable unit, bar carts are an excellent option for their compactness and mobility. You can park it next to the dining table, move it to the living room when you want to have drinks there instead, and tuck it away as you wish. Whatever you decide to go with, just make certain it is sturdy and can hold weight without wobbling, as glassware and full bottles can get quite heavy.

Personalize your at-home bar experience by mastering a signature cocktail or two that you can whip up for cocktail hour—perhaps the same drink(s) served at your wedding, for nostalgia's sake. Better yet, work with your spouse to come up with your own unique recipe (or put a distinctive twist on a classic) to create a one-of-a-kind drink that guests can look forward to having only at your place. For bartending pros, a custom printed or hand-written menu of house cocktails in a tabletop picture frame can be a charming inclusion, too.

If you don't partake of alcohol, there are plenty of ways to still have a fun bar feature in the dining room. A stationary bar cabinet can, instead, be a coffee bar with an espresso machine, a milk frother, flavored syrups, an assortment of demitasses, and a (regularly refreshed) jar of biscotti, for example. A movable bar cart, meanwhile, can have myriad uses when company is over, like as a retro-inspired rolling dessert cart with a selection of sweets, a hot cocoa bar for when it's nippy out, or a mobile sundae station for hot summer days.

When styling a bar cart, keep your most-used bottles, as well as any decanters, décor, barware, and glasses, up top. Use the bottom shelf for your special-occasion wines and spirits and for any bottles you wouldn't want your guests helping themselves to.

LILLET
LUXARDO
BULLEIT
FRONTIER WHISKEY
APEROL
EL DORADO
12
RUM

ANATOMY OF A WELL-STOCKED BAR

A selection of hard liquors:

Vodka

Gin

Brandy

Tequila
(one blanco and one reposado or añejo)

Rum
(one aged and one light)

Whiskey
(choose from bourbon, Scotch, single-malt, Japanese, and Canadian varieties)

A few liqueurs and fortified wines:

Triple sec
(for margaritas)

Cointreau
(for cosmos)

Vermouth, dry or sweet
(for martinis)

Campari
(for negronis)

Coffee liqueur
(for espresso martinis)

A digestif or two:

Limoncello

Sherry

Amaro

Port

Anise spirit

> Plus wine and beer, of course. Always have a couple of bottles of red, white, and sparkling wine on hand, and keep your fridge stocked with crisp cold ales and/or lagers. If you find a bottle of wine or beer you both love and regularly enjoy, buying it by the case will be more cost-effective.

116   The Newlywed Home

Learn to build your cocktail station like a pro and you'll be well-prepared to whip up practically any drink of choice, whether that's a rum and Coke or an extra-dry martini with a twist. The chart opposite covers the necessary bases—aka the booze—but feel free to make tweaks to the list if you'd like a specialized bar catered to your and your partner's libation preferences. If you're both Cognac fans, for example, you may want to have a brandy-forward selection. And don't worry about stockpiling everything all at once. Amass your collection at whatever pace suits you, and then see below for the ingredients and accoutrements you'll need to channel your inner mixologist.

With your bases covered, it's time to get mixing.

- **Shake things up** with classic mixers including bitters, grenadine, simple syrup, Worcestershire sauce, and Tabasco.

- **Get fizzy with it** and stockpile your favorite carbonated drinks, from club soda and tonic water to ginger ale and ginger beer to cola and lemon-lime soda.

- **Sweeten the deal** with your favorite fruit juices, including orange, cranberry, pineapple, grapefruit, tomato, and various blends.

- **Add a twist** with fresh garnishes like limes, lemons, mint leaves, and berries, and jarred garnishes like olives and maraschino cherries.

- **Get your tools in order.** The basics: a bottle opener, corkscrew, ice bucket with tongs, and bottle stoppers. The enhancers: a jigger, muddler, citrus squeezer, cocktail spoon, shaker, and strainer. And the conveniences: a cutting board, paring knife, peeler, zester, and swizzle sticks. Bottoms up!

Cherry Stem Cordial

Here's a lovely summer project you can take on as a pair: making cherry stem cordial. It's important to do this in summer because not only is that when cherries are in season but you'll also need the generous sun and its warmth to brew this beautiful, unique liqueur. Not to be confused with cherry liqueur, which is made with the sweet flesh of the fruit, this cordial uses just the stems, resulting in a combination of fruity, earthy, spiced, and slightly bitter notes on the palate. Enjoy it on its own as a digestif or mix it with sparkling water over ice for a cool, refreshing fizzy cocktail. Or better still, experiment with the cordial to make your own signature drink.

Makes 3 cups (830 ml)

2 pounds (908 g) organic cherries

1¼ cups (250 g) sugar

1¼ cups (300 ml) water

1 cinnamon stick

4 to 6 whole cloves

1 cup (230 ml) vodka or moonshine

Wash the cherries, pluck the stems from the fruit, and dab the stems dry with a clean towel. Place the stems in a 16-ounce (500 ml) sealable glass jar. Add the sugar, fully covering the stems. Seal the jar tightly and leave outside in the sun until the sugar has melted and a syrup has formed, at least 1 month and up to 2 months.

Strain the syrup through a fine-mesh sieve and into a jar. You should have about 1 cup (230 ml) of syrup. Reserve the stems.

In a small saucepan over medium heat, combine the water, strained cherry stems, cinnamon stick, and cloves to taste. Bring to a boil, then immediately turn off the heat. Let the water cool for a few minutes. Measure out 1 cup (230 ml) of the spiced water and pour it through a fine-mesh sieve into the jar of syrup. Discard the strained cinnamon, cloves, cherry stems, and any leftover spiced water. Cover the mixture and let rest until it reaches room temperature.

Funnel the syrup and spiced water mixture into a 34-ounce (1 L) sealable glass bottle to use as a nonalcoholic base for mocktails or cocktails. To make the cordial, add the vodka (or moonshine for a stronger drink) to the glass bottle and gently shake to mix. Store the cordial (or syrup) in the refrigerator for up to 1 month.

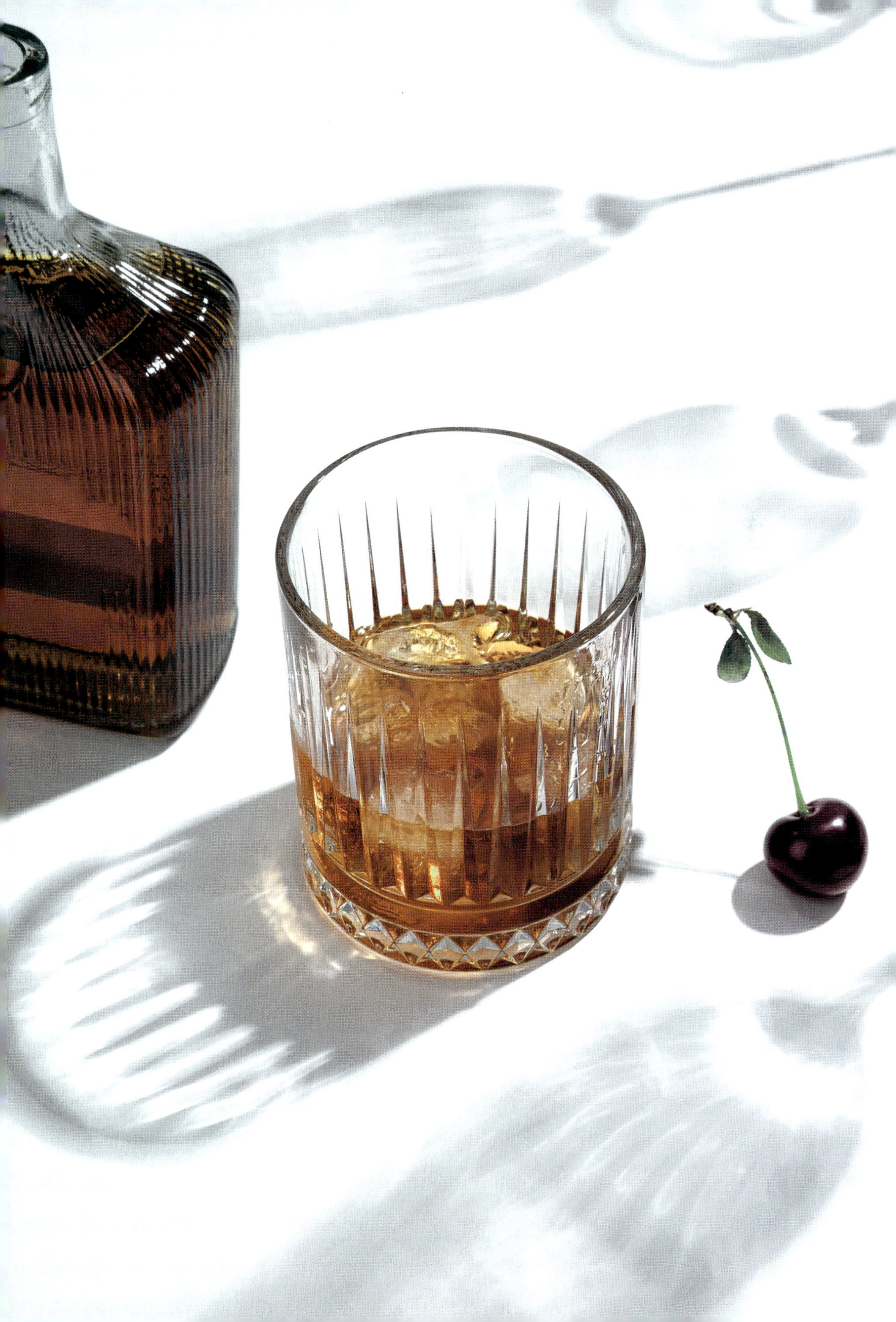

Pillow Talk

THE BEDROOM

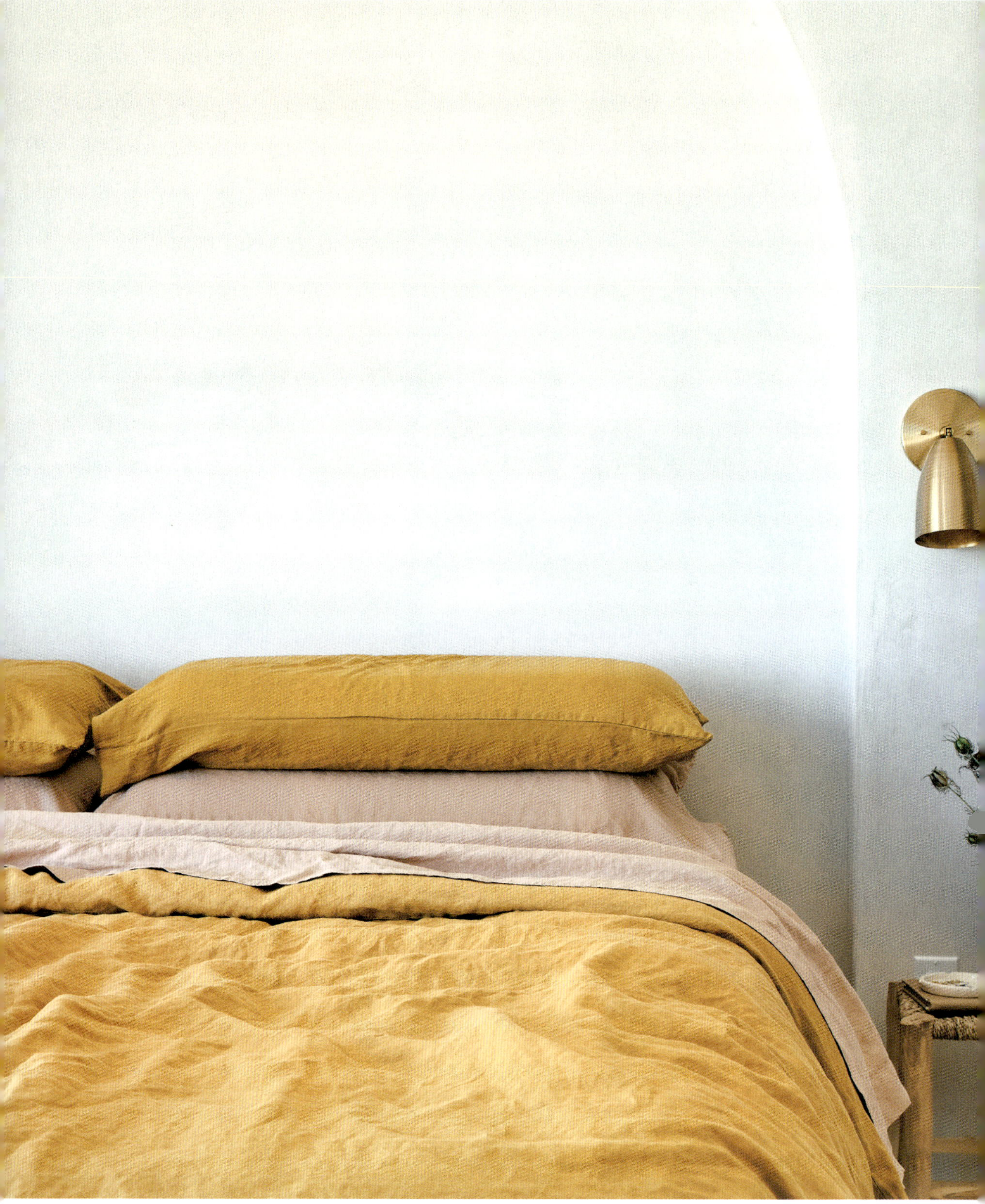

There is a time-honored toast often recited at Armenian weddings that translates to "May you grow old on one pillow." The romantic expression—a loving blessing bestowed upon newlyweds to wish them a lifetime of shared dreams and intimacy, in body, mind, and soul—is a testament to the belief that the bedroom is the most sacred and private space for a couple. It's where vulnerability, sensuality, and one-on-one attention are honored, and respite and relaxation are prioritized. A peaceful buffer between your private selves and the rest of the world, if you will.

Keep these pillars in mind as you turn your hand to planning and realizing your primary bedroom. The strategy should be to craft a space that is serene and conducive to restful sleep for you both, and cozy enough for you to want to linger in that precious alone time with your partner. You want to feel a sense of calm when you walk in, slip into something comfortable, and settle in for the night. Thankfully, you can rest assured: Tranquility is something you can cultivate.

    The very personal nature of the primary bedroom also has a major upside in that your private chambers will rarely be seen by others, which can take a lot of the pressure off as you dream up this space. That's not to say, though, that you shouldn't strive to make its design stand apart. On the contrary, your bedroom has the potential to be your matrimonial sanctuary, tailor-made to suit your wishes and preferences as a pair. And while it may seem like a challenge to evoke a distinct sense of style when the bedroom typically only needs a few standard furnishings, the thoughtful choices you make for this room—from bedding and pillows to window treatments and nightstand displays—will come together like a patchwork quilt that brings you comfort.

    As you take the time to transform your bedroom into an alluring, cozy retreat that serves you both, concentrate on honoring each other's comfort above all. Being considerate and mindful of your own needs and those of your partner will help create a safe space where you can both let your hair down and show up as your most authentic selves, and in turn pave the way for intimacy in all its forms.

SWEET TALK

SLEEPING TOGETHER (LITERALLY)

Even the most laid-back of folks have certain bedroom hallmarks and practices that, to them, are mandatory. Familiarity and habituality can bring about comfort, and comfort is the underpinning of the bedroom, so preferences this way or that are only natural. But when you're bedmates, these biases need to be presented as requests, not demands, as the space is just as important to your partner as it is to you. If you wait too long to address these matters or don't handle them with care, these conversations might devolve into arguments or resentment, or cause one or both of you to lose sleep for more reasons than one.

The following issues are the bases of some common bedroom tiffs that you can nip in the bud. Remember, health and wellness should always take precedence, so when faced with a stalemate, lean toward the solution that promotes better-quality sleep. Make your way through the list to see which conversations need to be had, and in those instances, join forces to problem-solve and set your bedroom's ground rules. Get to the bottom of *why* you want things a certain way and try to differentiate between preferences and necessities. Ask yourselves what you are willing to compromise on. And as you negotiate, work to balance the scales so that everything doesn't end up in one person's favor.

ISSUE: Whether your pet should be allowed on the bed

SOLUTION: If one of you is not having a restful sleep with a furry bedfellow, consider resolutions that can still keep your beloved dog or cat close to you as you slumber. One option is to add sleeping accommodations for your pet at the foot of your bed, like a platform dog/cat sofa in the style of your bedroom. Another route is to upgrade your dog bed or cat bed to one that mimics the feel of your mattress and keep it close by your bedside. In fact, some mattress brands offer pet beds designed with layers of memory foam and/or spring coils, so you can rest easy knowing that your pet is still comfortable.

ISSUE: Different sleep schedules

SOLUTION: If one of you is a night owl going to bed at two a.m. and the other is waking up at five a.m. for a workout, the best-case scenario is that you are two ships passing in the night. The worst-case scenario? You disturb each other every time you come to or get out of bed. In these cases, both partners' sleep can greatly benefit from interventions like a white noise machine, sleep masks, and earplugs. You may also consider a memory foam mattress for its motion-isolating properties (for more on mattresses, see page 127). Most important, be mindful of each other and careful to not make extra noise.

ISSUE: One of you runs cold, and the other runs hot

SOLUTION: To remedy this incompatibility, you can swap one large, shared duvet for two separate twin-size duvets in different densities. This will allow you to accommodate your dissimilar preferences and still sneak in cuddles under one blanket if you're feeling cozy. Alternatively, there are some innovative split-bed heating/cooling climate systems that you can look into.

ISSUE: Whether there should be a TV in the room

SOLUTION: If one of you loves watching their favorite shows from bed but the other can't fall asleep to the sound of the television, perhaps the viewer can use Bluetooth headphones and/or the sleeping partner can wear a blackout sleep mask (some designs also help dampen noise). If neither of these compromises sits well with you, you may need to negotiate specific no-media hours for the bedroom, or have the viewer use a small personal device like a tablet with earbuds instead of a TV.

ISSUE: Different mattress preferences

SOLUTION: There are a few options for couples who like different mattress firmness levels: Add half-bed toppers and/or pads on one or both sides until you are both comfortable and satisfied, or consider a split mattress with an adjustable base (for more on mattresses, see page 127).

ISSUE: Whether food should be allowed

SOLUTION: A hotly debated topic, regularly eating in bed can be a pleasure for some and an ick for others. Those who are for it might find it to be a nostalgic, comforting part of bedroom life, while opposing parties might take issue with the discomfort of sleeping among crumbs or spills, or worse, the risk of attracting ants, roaches, or mice. Some compromises to consider are that the diner use a bed tray to keep things neat and take responsibility for a biweekly laundering of the bedding.

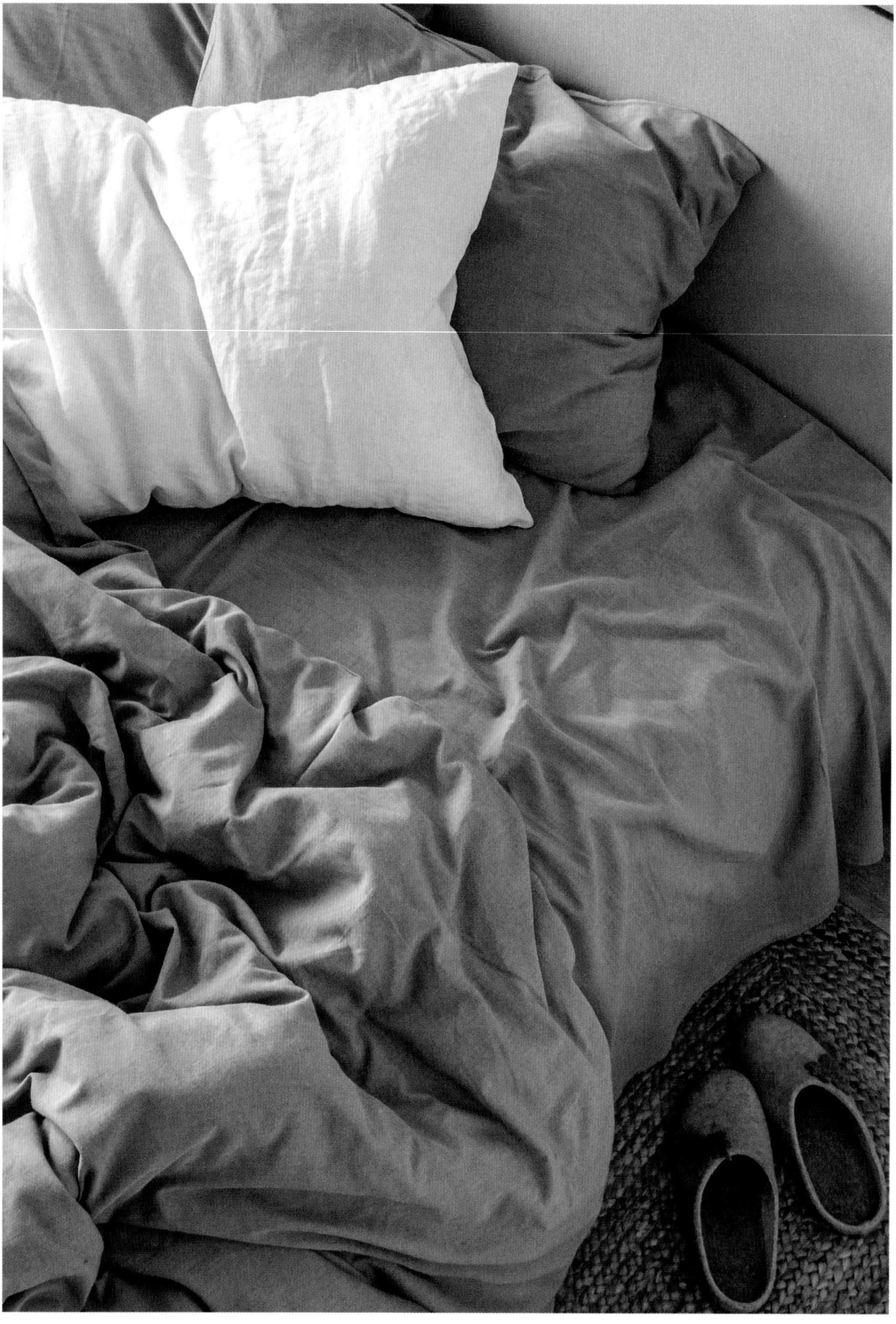

MAIN SQUEEZE

THE MATTRESS

If rest and relaxation reign supreme in the bedroom, then the mattress is the crown jewel. Unfortunately, a bad or worn-out mattress will almost certainly disrupt your slumber, and poor sleep can lead to a multitude of negative effects on your health. (Plus, if you're tossing and turning at night, your partner likely is, too.) Spending on a quality mattress means investing in your wellness and relationship, so save up and hunt down the perfect one for you both. That said, a good mattress can cost a pretty penny (with queen sizes going for anywhere between $1,000 and $3,500—even $10,000 and up for luxury offerings), so first things first: Decide on a budget. You should buy the best mattress you can afford, but financial stresses alone can turn you into an insomniac, so be clear about what you can set aside. With that established, you can get down to brass tacks and start shopping around. Use these guidelines to narrow your search.

Size

The dimensions of your room will determine what size mattress (and bed) you can accommodate. Aim for at least 2 feet (61 cm) of space on both sides of the bed for clearance and convenience. There are four standard North American bed sizes that are suitable for couples, and reviewing their dimensions in terms of both your interiors and your lifestyles is an important first step.

Full: 54 inches (135 cm) wide by 75 inches (191 cm) long. Also known as a double bed, this is the smallest available option for two people, but if you're not the cuddling type or are 6 feet (180 cm) or taller, you may feel cramped.

Queen: 60 inches (150 cm) wide by 80 inches (203 cm) long. This is the most popular size, and understandably so, as it can accommodate most couples and fit well into a standard bedroom.

King: 76 inches (193 cm) wide by 80 inches (203 cm) long. Though it features the same length as a queen, the king size offers a more spacious width, making it ideal for partners who each prefer their personal space in bed.

California king: 72 inches (183 cm) wide by 84 inches (213 cm) long. Perfect for very tall individuals, this is the lengthiest mattress size available. While it is longer than a standard king by 4 inches (10 cm), it is important to note that it is also 4 inches (10 cm) narrower.

Material

The main players in the mattress composition game are innerspring (imagine a classic, cushy hotel bed that is springy to the touch); memory foam (the popular body-conforming synthetic material invented by NASA—yes, NASA); gel foam (memory foam infused with temperature-regulating polymer gel); and latex (a natural, supportive material that is considered more premium and eco-friendly). If you are a light sleeper, you may prefer memory foam for its motion-isolation properties. If you run hot in your sleep, you might like the airflow that comes with an innerspring mattress or the cooling effects of gel foam. If you have respiratory issues, you may want an organic latex mattress for its hypoallergenic quality. And if you are struggling to see eye to eye or have several, more nuanced needs, look into hybrid designs—coil-foam, coil-latex, or foam-latex—that could serve you both.

Comfort

Everyone has unique sleep needs, so try to find the right balance between firmness (how soft or hard a mattress feels, and how much it contours to your body) and support (how well a mattress supports your body and spine and relieves pressure). Note: Mattresses tend to get softer over time, especially with two users, so it's better to lean on the firmer side if you're on the fence. Make a date out of browsing (and bouncing on) different models in person—test out your favorite sleeping positions, talk to the experts on-site if you need some guidance, and take advantage of any sleep trials until you start homing in on what you like and where your preferences align. If you find that your preferences aren't quite the same, consider fine-tuning the two sides of the mattress with toppers and/or pads. And a word to the wise: While there's a glut of direct-to-consumer brands out there that offer a quick, easy shopping experience, when it comes to comfort, trying out a mattress in person is unmatched. Mattresses-in-a-box typically do not stand the test of time, and by buying one online, you aren't able to assess if it will meet your needs until it's already in your home. That said, this type of mattress is often more affordable than one you'll purchase in-store.

Base

Some mattresses require a box spring or a proprietary base from the seller, so be sure to look into the warranties of models you're interested in. This is especially important for those who hope to use an existing bed frame. For folks with more specific needs, smart beds with adjustable bases can offer customized sleep solutions, allowing you, for instance, to tweak the mattress's temperature, raise and lower the head or feet, modify the height, or even get a massage. Naturally, you will need to find a mattress (or mattresses, for split beds) that are compatible with the smart base in question.

Upkeep

The lifespan of a good-quality mattress is typically around eight years, so once you find yours, take good care of it. Different mattress types have different maintenance requirements that you'll want to take into consideration during your search. Most hybrid, latex, innerspring, and memory foam mattresses should be rotated about every six months, while some models are dual-sided or reversible, requiring that they be flipped as well. Extend the life of your mattress by vacuuming it a few times a year and using a fitted mattress pad for protection.

Sleep on It

The centerpiece of the bedroom, your bed is where you will start your days, check in with yourself and each other, look forward to meeting at night, and perfect the art of pillow talk. Beyond its role in your relationship, though, your bed frame will set the design tone of your private quarters. Whether it be an ornamental showpiece that announces a glamorous style, a simple silhouette that evokes a quiet coolness, or something in between, the choice is yours. Here is some info—along with some dos and don'ts—to help guide you in your search for the bed of your (sweet) dreams.

Platform Beds

With low profiles and sleek, compact shapes, platform beds with slats or solid bases are a great choice for a contemporary aesthetic and/or smaller spaces. (Many designs include built-in storage, too.) However, because they do not require a box spring, they can limit your mattress options depending on the bed's structure and weight capacities. (See page 127 for more on choosing a mattress.)

Box Spring Beds

From four-poster to upholstered panel styles, bed frames that feature box spring foundations are available in more design varieties, spanning contemporary and traditional aesthetics. However, these options are generally bulkier, which can affect your room's configuration.

Headboards

A headboard can serve as a pleasing focal point for the bedroom but will take up space, and in the case of an upholstered headboard, can require maintenance. Note that your room's architectural features may dictate where you can place a bed with a headboard (for example, do not obstruct the view by covering the window with the headboard).

Footboards

Offering a classic, more formal look, a footboard can add structure to the bed and help keep bedding in place, but if one or both of you are taller than average, you might run the risk of banging your toes on it in your sleep—ouch!

Dream Room

More than any other part of the home, your primary bedroom has the potential to impact your psyche and quality of life. Getting a full night's sleep can significantly improve your physical and mental health and can positively impact your relationship by balancing your moods and reducing stress. So when you are ready to shift your attention to outfitting your primary bedroom, focus on optimizing it for serious rest and relaxation. Everyone's routines and needs are different, but here are a few best practices to maximize tranquility and make your private quarters your shared little piece of heaven.

Embrace minimalism. Clutter is overstimulating and is the ultimate nemesis of a good night's slumber. A quiet room equals a quiet mind. Therefore, prioritize storage solutions to keep the bedroom as mess-free as possible and think "less is more" when it comes to décor—you don't want there to be too much for the eye to take in. Get savvy with double-duty pieces like upholstered storage ottomans, and utilize out-of-sight areas like the space underneath the bed by employing sliding drawers or flat bins and boxes. A well-designed laundry hamper that is easy to access is a great way to discourage dirty clothes from being strewn about. If space allows, you can also have an oversize basket into which you can toss clothes that are not quite dirty but might pile up after one wear.

Keep the palette neutral. If you want to optimize relaxation, avoid washing the primary bedroom in loud colors. Choosing an overall palette of light or neutral hues—everywhere from your walls to your bedding—will make for a more restful atmosphere. To add some flair to the muted tones, you can incorporate accent pieces like vibrant lampshades for a pop of color and/or get creative with textures throughout. Limewash on the walls and ceiling can add rich depth and character to the room, as can textural wallpapers. For bedding, layer different fabrics within one or two complementary tonal families to add dimension and create a cocoon of comfort. Subtle patterns and design motifs are nice, too. From percale sheets and muslin duvet covers to cashmere throw blankets and velvet pillows, you can get adventurous by overlapping textiles that beckon you to bed.

Soften the light. Soft, diffuse lighting in layers is a must in the bedroom to help you achieve the perfect ambience. Utilize bedside table lamps, or choose wall-mounted sconces or hanging pendant lights above the nightstands. Whichever you choose, go with dimmable options and use warm LED bulbs so as to not disturb your partner if you are up later than they are. When choosing window treatments, be sure to find those that will allow you to filter and block the light. Explore combinations of sheer and blackout curtains and shades—as well as insulating and noise-reducing varieties—until you find what will suit you both. (See below for tips on hanging curtains.)

Improve the air quality. Bring in a HEPA-filtered air purifier to help eliminate allergens, pathogens, odors, and other contaminants from your environment and make your space healthier overall. And don't worry: With so many good-looking and subtle designs available nowadays, finding one that fits into your bedroom aesthetic won't be a challenge. You can also introduce pollutant-reducing indoor plants like a weeping fig or golden pothos to further freshen the air—and look—of your bedroom.

Window Shopping

If you're using drapes or curtains for your window coverings, dimensions and materials are of the utmost importance. Here are some tricks of the trade to consider before you place your order.

- When selecting curtains, consider which fabrics will best suit your style and needs. Linen, for instance, can infuse the space with an airy, romantic quality, but it will let in more light. Velvet, on the other hand, has a richer, more glamorous look and provides great insulation and noise cancellation, but it is generally pricier and can be tricky to clean. Note that the color of the curtains will also influence how much light they absorb (the darker the curtain, the more its blackout abilities).

- Decide if you want to use curtain tracks (mounted to the wall or ceiling for a discreet, modern look) or rods (the more common and decorative option). If the latter, be sure to choose the correct rods for your curtain weight. A heavier fabric like damask will need a much sturdier rod (in brass or cast iron, for instance) than cotton or polyester designs. Consider, too, the additional hardware that you will need, such as hooks, rings, and tiebacks.

- To hang drapes correctly—in a way that flatters your space and gives the illusion of taller ceilings—you want to hang them at least 4 to 6 inches (10 to 15 cm) above the window trim. For ceilings higher than 9 feet (2.7 m), aim for about halfway between the window trim and the ceiling.

- Use a hanging rod that extends 8 to 12 inches (20 to 30 cm) on either side of the window. This will make your windows look larger and ensure the curtains won't block the view even when they're pulled back.

- Once you've determined the placement and length of your rod, choose curtains with the correlating length—they should just kiss the floor. For a more dramatic look, you can have extra-long drapes that puddle on the floor, but this approach requires more upkeep and obstructs the floor space, making it less practical in the bedroom, where real estate is at a premium.

Blanket Statement

Making the bed in the morning is a habit that can have a positive ripple effect in other areas of your lives, so when it comes to choosing your bedding, be honest with each other about your tendencies and levels of energy for the chore. Truth be told, nothing can drag down your bedroom—and the rest of your day—like an unmade bed. If both of you are fully on board with a multistep, traditional bedding setup, then go for it and embrace the layers: flat and top sheets, a comforter or duvet and duvet cover, a quilt or coverlet, two to four sleeping pillows, up to six accent pillows, and a throw blanket. If that amount of bedding feels overwhelming

A bed can have anywhere from two to ten pillows, depending on its size and your preferences. For a king mattress, a popular combination is four sleeping pillows stacked in twos, three Euro pillows, and a lumbar or bolster pillow.

The Newlywed Home

to one or both of you, don't commit yourselves to a complicated setup, because soon enough, at least one of you will grow tired of making the bed every morning. Instead, simplify your bedscape and make it easy to maintain by sticking to the basics: A bed with a fitted sheet, a duvet with a machine-washable cover, a pair of sleeping pillows, and a long lumbar throw pillow can be hastily made and still look polished and inviting.

As for upkeep, plan to wash everything that comes in contact with your bodies (sheets, pillowcases, and duvet covers) once a week, and everything else (duvet and pillow inserts, blankets, and mattress toppers) about once every three months. Use a natural linen spray between washes to freshen up your space and add an extra layer of comfort to your bedroom. (Consider incorporating this step into your bed-making routine to reinvigorate the space daily.) And think twice about high-maintenance materials like linen, which, while luxurious and hypoallergenic, wrinkle easily and therefore require ironing or dry cleaning. If you prefer machine-washable / -dryable materials, steer toward cotton, which is breathable and has moisture-wicking properties—great for all types of sleepers. Generally, Egyptian cotton is considered the best in this category for its softness and longevity, whereas percale-weave cotton, though not as soft to the touch, is more affordable and available in a range of thread counts.

REGISTER THIS

Sleep tight with luxurious bedding fit for a king or queen.

Sheet sets: Three sets (with a fitted sheet, flat sheet, and pillowcases) in single-ply Egyptian cotton with a thread count of at least 300.

Duvet: An all-season down (or down-alternative) baffle box-stitched duvet insert—the ultimate indulgence.

Duvet covers and pillow shams: Two covers and four shams in your style of choice, monogramming optional.

The Right Headspace

The wall space above the bed is often a glaring blank canvas waiting to be filled. Here a curation of art—or a single large-scale piece—can shine bright and spruce up the bedroom. A grand painting or photography print, diptych, or triptych is a classic approach. Alternative ideas include a pair of framed scarves, a floating shelf with an assemblage of lightweight artworks and objects, an oversize tapestry or map, a woven wall hanging, or an eclectic gallery wall. Just make sure that whatever you choose is very securely mounted to the wall to avoid any accidents. The most important factor to bear in mind is balance—no matter what you choose, you'll want to get the scale right. A few pointers:

- Use kraft paper—cut into the accurate measurements and taped to the wall—to map out the piece or pieces.
- The width of your showpiece should be at least 75 percent (and not more than 90 percent) of the width of your bed frame, centered over your bed.
- The lowest point should be about 8 inches (20 cm) above your headboard (or, if you don't have a headboard, about 15 inches / 38 cm above your pillows).
- The space between your ceiling and the piece or pieces should also be at least 8 inches (20 cm). Anything less will feel top-heavy.
- The space above the artwork(s) may not be of equal distance to the space below the wall art, and that is totally okay. Remember, it is better to have extra room above than below so as to avoid its looking awkward.
- For those with four-poster and canopy beds, aim to have a smaller artwork centered within the posts against the wall. Alternatively, you can give the illusion of a framed artwork by hanging a statement pendant light in the center of the room.

A powerful work of art above the bed can transform the room into a unique, personalized space. Use accent lighting to further cement the piece as the focal point of the bedroom.

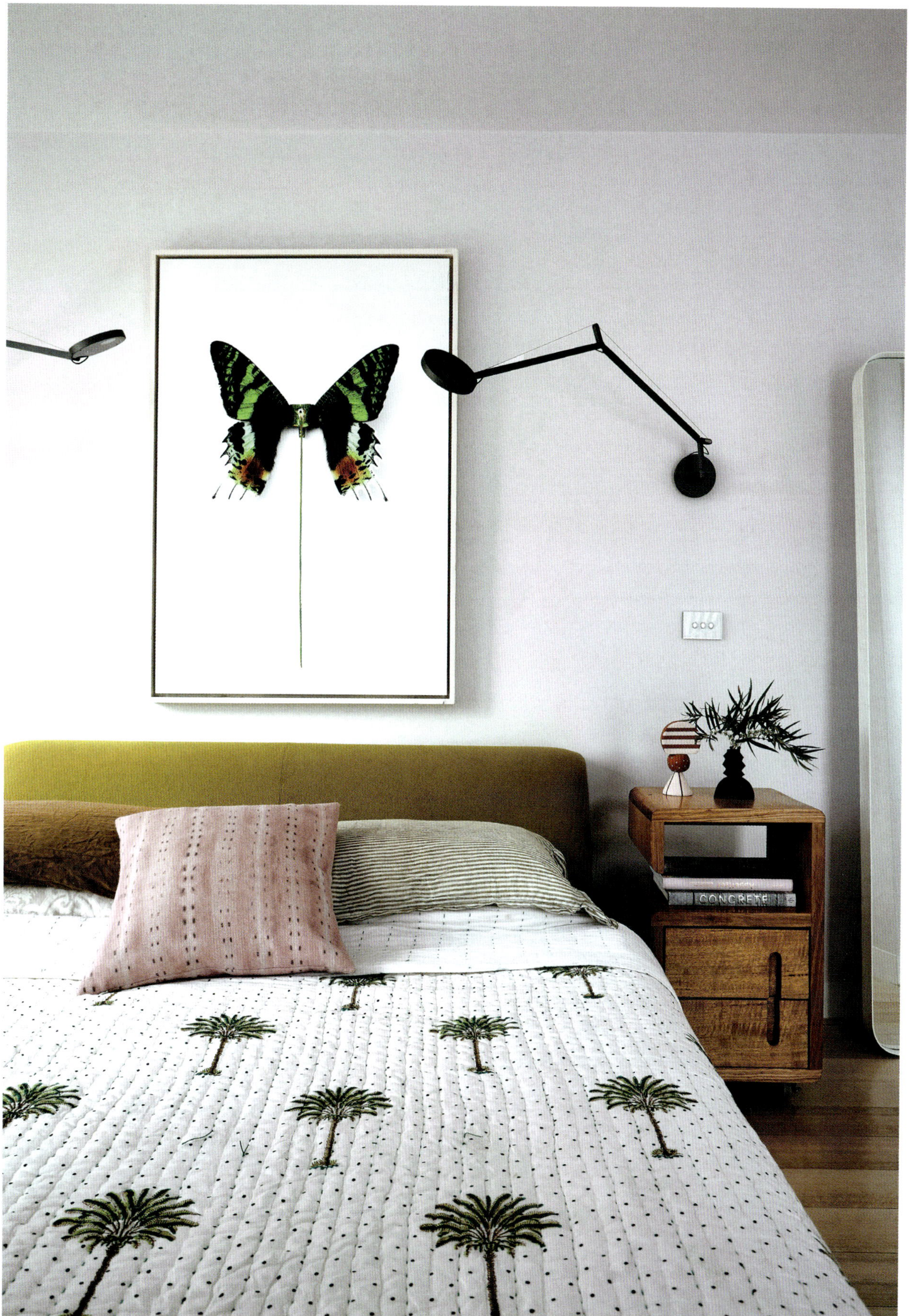
CONCRETE

Two-Night Stand

The bedrooms we've inhabited throughout our lives can tell the full story of who we have been and, as a result, who we are today. From humble nurseries outfitted by loving parents to teenage bedrooms with poster-plastered walls to the bare-bones studios of early adulthood, our private quarters have always been extensions of our identity. Perhaps that is why sharing a bedroom with a romantic partner for the first time can be such a daunting shift—despite its being such a beautiful, positive step in a new stage of life—because in a way, you are giving up your designated personal space, and doing so indefinitely. And while your shared primary bedroom will, of course, still represent who you are, that reflection will be intertwined with that of your partner and your relationship. There is, however, one small but mighty area that will belong to you and you alone: your bedside table. In addition to catering to your personal needs, nightstands can be a fantastic canvas for self-expression.

Start by choosing the furniture that works best for each of you. Not only do you not have to get matching nightstands, you don't have to use classic nightstands at all if they don't suit your needs; a writing desk, an oversize trunk, a petite bookcase, an end table, or a small chest of drawers are some alternatives you can explore. Whatever speaks to your character and requirements will work, as long as the height of the tabletop is level with or within 5 inches (13 cm)—higher or lower—of your mattress and allows for a couple of inches (5 cm) of space between it and the bed for your comfort and convenience. If you don't want to get too eccentric, look for two pieces that share a common thread, whether that is a color palette or design style.

As for the surfaces of the nightstands, that is where you can each get really creative. If you are a bookworm and love to read every night, it's only natural that you'll have a book or two or five living on your tabletop. If you have an elaborate skincare routine you like to do in bed, your surface will likely have a collection of creams and potions. If you are the techy sort, you might have a charging station for gadgets proudly on display. And in addition to accommodating nighttime habits and practices, your tabletop vignettes can also hold sentimental, artful, or miscellaneous objects like framed images or a vase of fresh flowers. Water carafes, candles, lamps, desk clocks, and tissue-box covers are also worth looking into as functional yet visually appealing pieces with a plethora of options that can suit your fancy. Of course, you do still share the bedroom with your partner, so there may need to be dialogue about what is exhibited on the tabletops, but try to approach the topic with grace and give each other the space for individual expression.

Meanwhile, some (more minimalism-inclined) couples might instead agree to have perfect symmetry on either side of the bed—with matching tables and lamps and not much else on display. In these cases, bedside tables with a drawer or two are essential to contain all of your personal knickknacks and necessities. Alternatives include floating drawers attached to the wall and beds with built-in nightstands. You might also consider identical catchalls in which you could keep your small personal belongings tidy while staying cohesive, or personal photographs in matching tabletop frames.

As time passes, your nightstand vignettes might evolve along with you, so don't expect that they will be static, unchanging features in your bedroom. Much like your past bedrooms and the previous versions of you they represent, your bedside table will be a still life for only a moment in time and will take its next form before you know it.

In lieu of a traditional nightstand, a quaint bentwood chair is apt for small spaces and can be on standby when you need an extra seat in the house.

DATE NIGHT

DO NOT DISTURB

Sometimes you're due for a vacation with your partner, but between travel expenses, scheduling conflicts, and other logistics, a lavish, relaxing getaway might seem out of reach. To hold you over during these travel dry spells, consider bringing the five-star hotel experience to you by re-creating the luxuries of a swanky resort suite in the comfort of your bedroom.

To start, clear your agendas for a Saturday or Sunday—or take a weekday off together—and mark your calendars. (If you take the day off, set up your out-of-office auto responses as you would for a real trip.) The night before your staycation, prep, prep, prep. The idea is for you to wake up and feel as you would in a five-star hotel, so the more you can prepare, the less you will have to think about the day of. Dress your bed in crisp, clean sheets and get any necessary housework out of the way. Set up a tray with new, quality toiletries and essentials for the day and place it on your dresser or nightstand. Stock a mini fridge or cooler with your favorite bottled refreshments and packaged or premade snacks. (Chocolate-covered strawberries are always a good idea.) And put a bottle of Champagne in your refrigerator in case you feel like celebrating.

When morning comes, sleep in to your hearts' desires and be sure to tuck away your devices to make way for a day of unplugged bliss. Upon waking, instead of getting properly dressed, opt for slippers and plush robes as your comfy vacation uniforms. Enjoy a leisurely morning and afternoon in bed together, and when you want to hop out to, say, grab a pot of coffee from the kitchen, you can riff on the hotel theme by using a rolling bar cart as a "room service" trolley. If you want to level up the experience, make use of local food delivery offerings or treat yourselves to professional in-home services like a mobile massage therapist—or housekeeping for the following day. For those with a TV in the bedroom, embrace the "whatever is on" vibe of a hotel room and put on a classic movie or sitcom reruns, or binge-watch an entire season of a new-to-you reality show. Read side by side, embrace the art of conversation, and just bask in the beauty of having nothing to do. After all, when was the last time you let yourselves be bored?

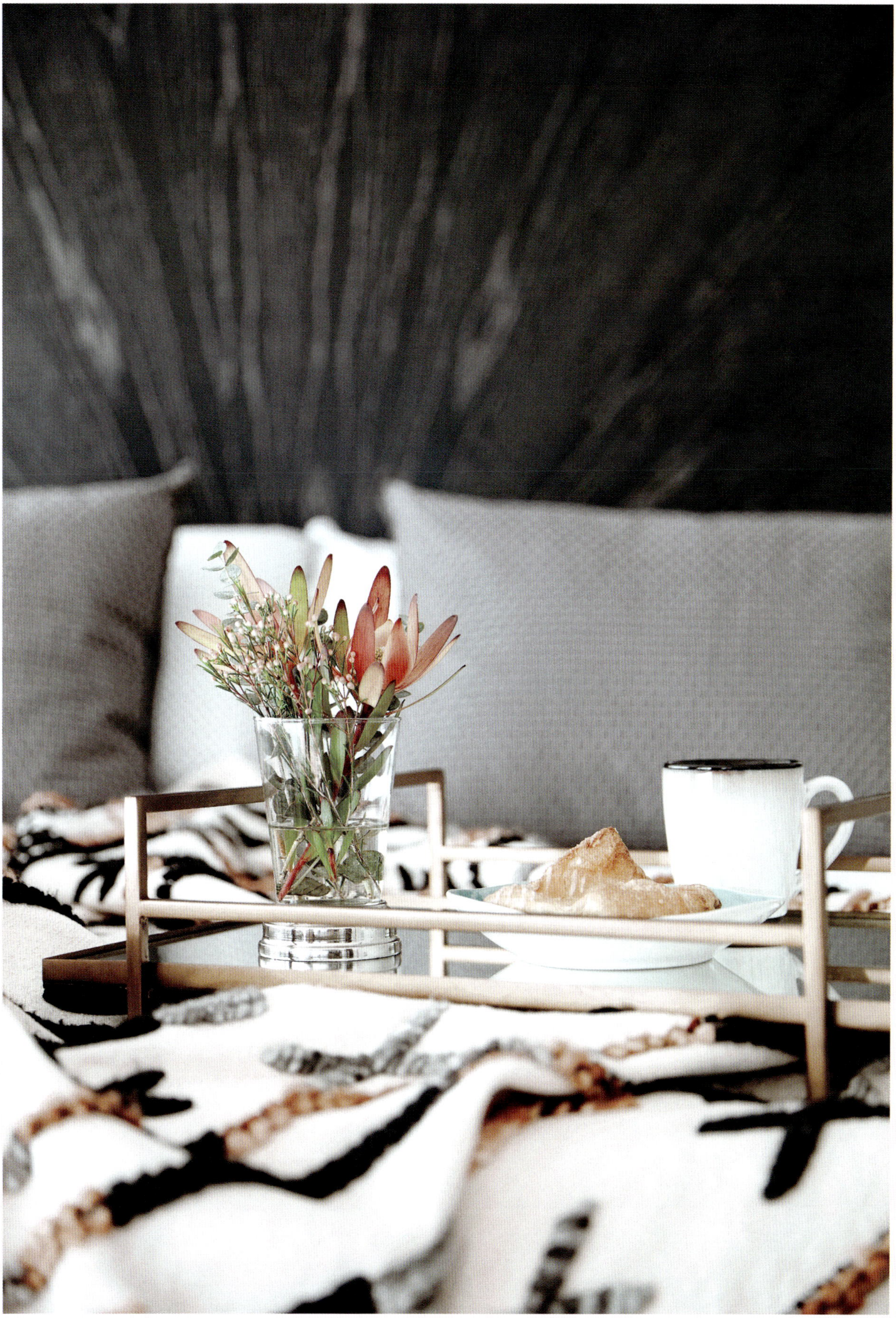

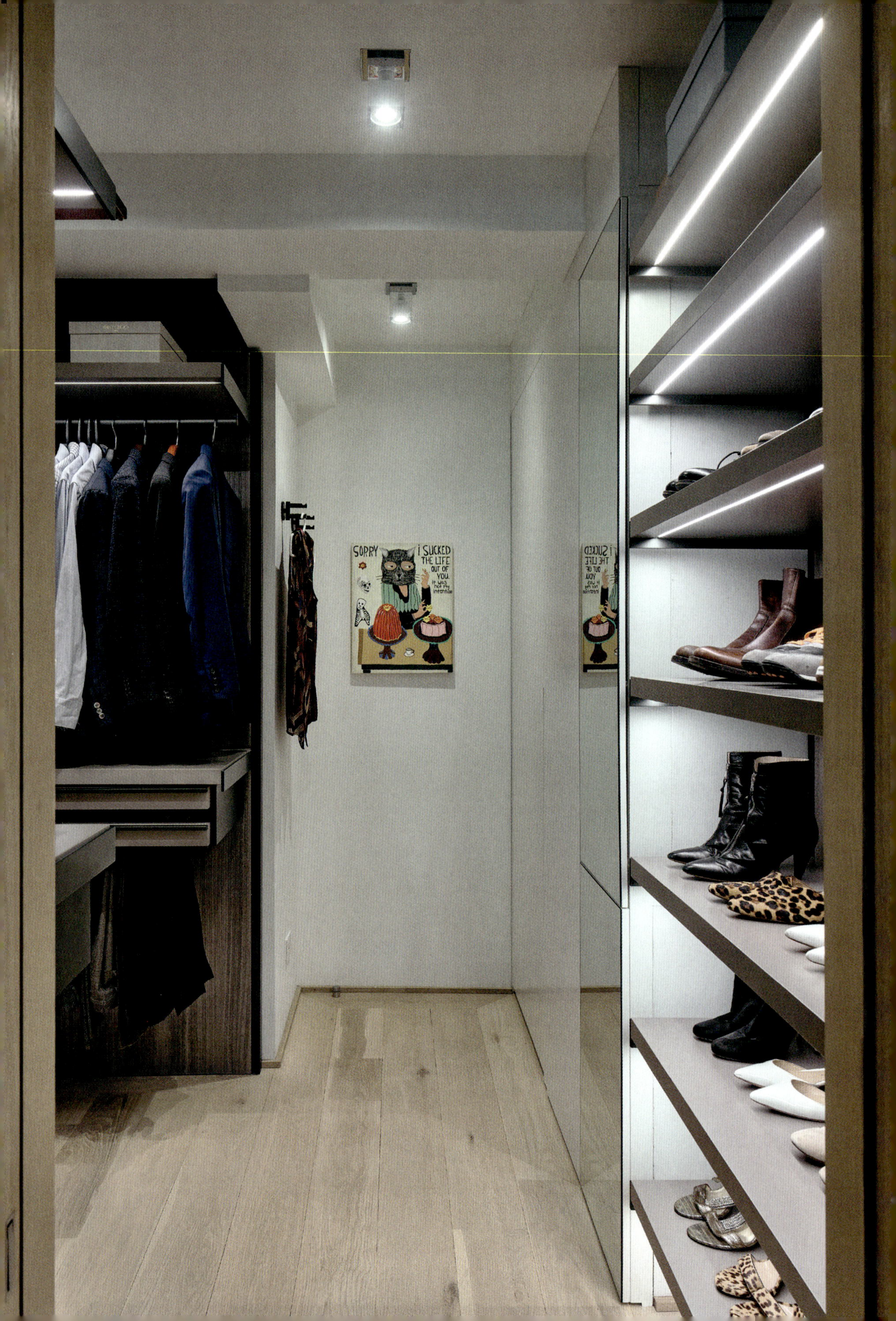
SORRY
I SUCKED
THE LIFE
OUT OF
YOU.
it was
not my
intention

Clothes-Minded

In an ideal world, each partner would have their own walk-in closet. If that is the case for you, then consider yourselves among the lucky few. Those who have to share a closet—often a small one—know that it can quickly become a battlefield if left unkempt, overstuffed, or unreasonably divided. To keep yours from causing quarrels, come up with a strategy from the outset and be prepared to compromise, make sacrifices, and keep your ends of the bargain. Otherwise, your plan may fall apart at the seams. Here are some reliable tips and tricks to help you maximize closet space, stay efficient, and organize like a pro.

Weed your wardrobes. Seriously. Methodically evaluate your clothing and accessories item by item and purge your collections of things you don't and won't wear. (See page 206 for a cheat sheet on how to decide what to keep.) If closet space is extremely tight, commit to rotating your clothes seasonally, or consider whittling your pieces down to capsule wardrobes, each with a select few clothing items and accessories you love that can be mixed and matched for a variety of outfits.

Divvy up the real estate. Review your edited wardrobes side by side and decide together if you will split the closet fifty-fifty or, say, seventy-five–twenty-five. Based on your agreed-upon ratio, calculate how many (and which) drawers, shelves, and hooks you each get, as well as how much hanging and floor space you're allowed. Incorporate visual dividers, like a hanging closet organizer, to create a clear buffer between your sections.

Go high and low. Use the shelves that are hardest to reach and/or the space beneath your bed to house storage boxes of out-of-season clothes. Use multi-hangers to stack articles of clothing, as well as hooks—mounted on the inner closet walls or hanging behind the door—to forge more usable space.

Color coordinate. Use hangers in two different colors—one assigned to each of you—to distinguish your hanging clothing items. Use this same method for storage boxes, bins, and other containers. Organizing your wardrobe by color will also make your pieces more easily accessible and leave your closet looking tidier and more put together.

Keep yourselves in check. Consent to a rule for new purchases, like the one in, one out method wherein you get rid of one similar article of clothing every time you buy something new. Alternatively, you can agree to purging your wardrobes twice a year.

Proper illumination can take a closet (no matter its size) to the next level. Under-cabinet LED light bars and in-drawer sensor lights add a touch of luxury while making garments and accessories more easily seen.

Pillow Talk

Inn Style

There is a simple art to hosting an overnight visitor, and it begins with getting the guest room ready. The area itself should be furnished sparsely to accommodate your guests' belongings and make it easy to keep neat. Stick to the basics—a bed (or pullout couch, futon, rollaway bed, or Murphy bed), a nightstand with a table lamp (or two of each), and storage space by way of a closet and/or dresser will do just fine. If you, too, use the room for storage, ensure that at least one drawer is completely empty for visitors to use, and that there is enough free hanging space for their clothes. Uncluttered floor space and/or a luggage rack for baggage will also be greatly appreciated. As for decorating, do so with a light hand to allow for enough usable tabletop surfaces. (Tip: Avoid strong-scented candles in case your guest is not a fan of fragrances.) With your foundation in place, you can begin arranging the amenities.

 The absolute essentials you should provide are freshly washed bedding and towels, but that is the bare minimum. Whether the friend or family member staying over is an out-of-town visitor, a local who needs a place to crash, or a house sitter for the weekend, you'll want to make them feel as comfortable as you can. So, with your partner, imagine what you might hope for when you are away from home and use your wish lists to guide your decisions. Some basic conveniences to consider providing include an extra blanket in case your guest needs an added layer for warmth, a cooling fan and/or space heater to allow them to control the temperature, disposable house slippers, a newly laundered robe, a wastebasket, and an accessible outlet for their electronics. (See page 163 for tips on stocking a guest bathroom.) A welcome basket is always a nice touch; fill it with bottled water, nonperishable snacks, and instructions for accessing the Wi-Fi and using other home features. Additional optional comforts include a laundry basket for their wash, a sound machine and/or disposable earplugs, a washable eye mask, and a few books (and perhaps a local guide) to peruse during downtime.

 And some quick notes on etiquette: When your guest arrives, greet them warmly—perhaps with a refreshment—and offer a brief tour of your home, giving them a rundown of where they can find everything, be it extra towels or coffee filters. Then, especially if they have been traveling, give them some space and let them get situated and make themselves at home.

Less is more when it comes to decorating a guest room. Minimal furnishings and uncluttered floors will help visitors settle in with ease.

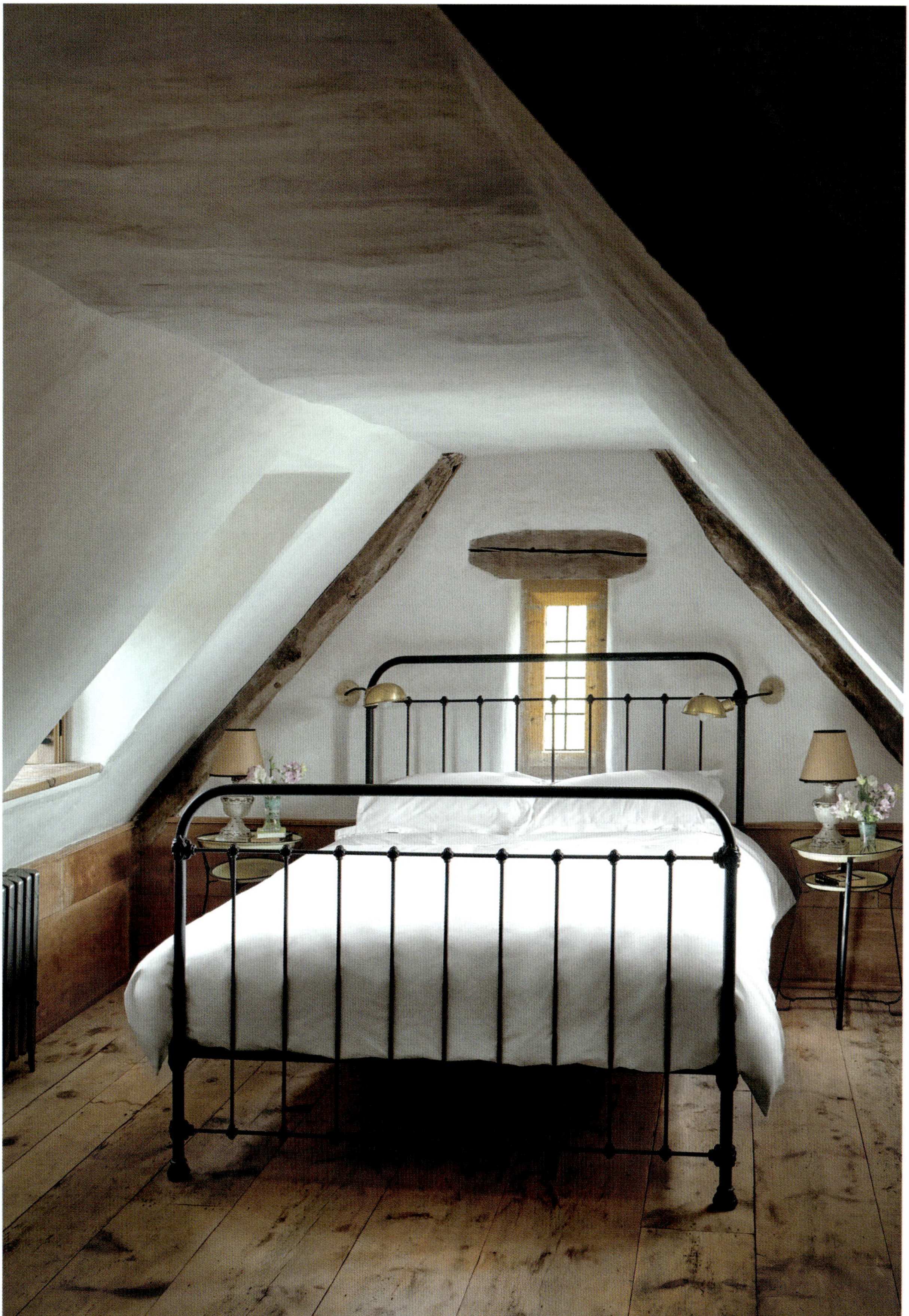

Vanity Fair

THE BATHROOM

There is a stage in most relationships, typically when you're dating exclusively and beginning to sleep over regularly, when one partner will suggest to the other that they keep some toiletries at their place. This is one of the first signs that your relationship is growing deeper—a shift toward commitment. Some couples may discuss the implications of this, but more often than not, what goes unsaid is that when you both agree to leave something of yours behind—a comb, a toothbrush, facial cleanser, or what have you—you both agree to make space for each other in your separate homes and lives.

For many of us, the bathroom is a refuge, a place to take a pause and practice self-care. It's where we check in with ourselves and get ready to present ourselves to the world. Ultimate privacy is the essence of the bathroom, and that is what makes sharing it so intimate.

In this new era, with a proper couple's bathroom, try to focus on those feelings of appreciation and excitement you had when you entered the "toiletries phase," if you can. Remember how sacred this space can be for both of you, and understand how this time, it's terrain that you will share equally. The objective should be to make room for each other and respect those boundaries, and to cultivate a bathroom style that is soothing and tranquil for you both.

In the end, your bathroom does not have to be extraordinary or conform to a rigid decorating style. It could be extremely simple, or it could be exaggeratedly luxurious. It will come down to what you each agree is maintainable and comfortable, and feels nurturing to your personal needs. What's important is that you both *feel* good when you're in your bathroom performing your daily routines, freshening up, or taking a breather. By setting the foundation for self-care in your primary bathroom for not just yourself but for your spouse as well, you are paving the way for calm coexistence and, hopefully, more simple gestures of love and undying commitment.

SWEET TALK

SHARING A BATHROOM

"Separate bathrooms." That is the half-serious advice for a successful marriage that you may have heard. Sure, having your own private restrooms could allow for more mystery in a relationship and perhaps result in fewer squabbles, but if it's not in the cards, all hope is not lost. With the proper preparation and maintenance, you can achieve a satisfactory level of discretion and harmony within a joint bathroom.

Find time to have this precursory conversation—the questions below will get you started—to gauge each other's comfort levels, forecast possible disputes, and establish rules of organization and etiquette. By doing so and committing to upholding these boundaries together, you will both find that you can peacefully share and cohabitate in the space and still keep the flame alive. Naturally, you will each have to compromise here and there, and likely still tolerate certain inconveniences like a fogged-up mirror, but in the end, you just might find yourselves cherishing the charmingly ordinary rendezvous you will have in your bathroom day after day. And if your home *does* have two or more bathrooms, and you find yourselves butting heads throughout this conversation—anticipating that sharing one bathroom will cause a lot of friction in your relationship—you can take the plunge and establish separate primary bathrooms after all.

Have you ever shared a bathroom?
Sharing a bathroom could be more challenging for those long accustomed to having their own. Did one or both of you grow up in a household where there was one bathroom? Did you have to share it with siblings or parents? How about sharing one with former roommates or partners? Compare and contrast your individual past circumstances and take note of any challenges (such as the other's products overtaking the storage space) and successes (like effective tidying practices) that you came away with. It's also likely that the two of you have already shared a bathroom with each other, in which case this could be an opportune time to gently—but honestly—analyze that experience as well. This line of conversation will help you get the ball rolling on some ideas for preliminary ground rules. Just remember to be tender and

understanding—never antagonistic or defensive—as you talk, because after all, the endgame of this entire exercise is more peace, not less.

How many products do you use?

Take stock of the self-care items and products you use—seriously, count them. How many of them do you reach for daily? How about weekly? Which ones are rarely in use? Bathroom routines are highly personal, so do not try to sway each other from your practices or toward downsizing your collections. Compromise will instead come in the form of how you will divvy up the available storage space and how much (or how little) you will have on display. You may also consider finding products that you both love—think toothpaste, facial cleanser, and shampoo—to avoid duplicates. (See page 156 for more on bathroom organization.)

How much privacy do you need?

Some people are fine leaving the bathroom door open while they handle their business, while others flinch at the thought of another person—even, or sometimes especially, their romantic partner—being anywhere near the closed door. The spectrum of comfort is wide here. For instance, you might absolutely loathe the idea of your spouse intruding on you while you use the loo but don't mind at all if they are in the bathroom while you shower. Get candid about your levels of comfort by going over scenarios, and if your preferences clash, establish the more conservative boundary to make sure no one ever feels awkward or exposed against their wishes. Privacy is precious, but our ideas of personal space can vary, so just make sure you come to a mutual understanding of where your individual boundaries lie.

How different are your schedules?

Getting ready at the same time in the morning can be stressful. Discuss your daily agendas—including when you need to be out the door—to find out how much overlap there is. Share your bathroom routines, noting any time-consuming steps like shaving or applying makeup, and be honest about how long it takes you to get ready. Depending on both of your privacy preferences, if your timetables are synced something may have to give. For instance, if you take twice as long in the bathroom as your partner and you both need to get ready simultaneously, you will have to get up earlier to get a head start so you're not causing them to be late, or perhaps do part of your routine (like your makeup application) elsewhere in the house. Write out a realistic schedule to abide by, and check in with each other after a few weeks to make certain your system is working well for you both. And if one or both of you are chronically late or always rushing, you might benefit from having a little table clock in the bathroom to help you keep track of time.

What are your bathroom cleaning habits?

Because this is your shared bathroom, you will need to team up to tackle its maintenance and agree upon your household's cleanliness standards. Generally, a deep cleaning every two weeks is necessary to keep mold and mildew away, while daily wipe-downs are highly recommended to rid surfaces of nasty germs and keep your space in tip-top shape. Come up with a housekeeping plan and schedule that you are both content with, like taking turns or designating zones for deep cleanings, and establish house rules, like squeegeeing shower doors after every use, as needed. And as a general rule, promise each other to always clean up after yourself and leave the bathroom looking as tidy as (if not tidier than) when you entered it. Now if only you could agree on which direction your toilet paper roll should hang…

A Strong Foundation

Bathrooms can begin to feel outdated fairly quickly, typically needing a refresh every five to ten years. If your bathroom is move-in ready and perfectly suits your fancies, you can jump right in to organizing and decorating. But if the space is leaving you uninspired or feels noticeably passé, you might need to roll up your sleeves before you can focus on the details. The bright side is that you don't have to fully renovate your bathroom to revamp it and make it feel more like *you*. If it's within your budget, a few key replacements can go a long way and give the illusion of a major makeover without the heavy lifting.

    Read on for a list of possible updates, ordered from quick and easy fixes to more involved overhauls. Make your way through it to sort out which swaps are crucial, which would be nice, and which are low priority, unneeded, or just too costly. Come up with a game plan for which tasks you will take on yourselves and which ones you'll need professional help with (though the majority of these suggestions are DIY-friendly). If you have the capacity for only a couple of updates, assess the bathroom's condition and make note of the main features that are eyesores, bothersome, or absolutely impractical, and concentrate on fixing those for now. A leaky old toilet, for instance, should be remedied tout de suite, but a retro vanity could be something you embrace by incorporating vintage-inspired elements. Find the common thread between the existing elements you're working with and the new items you're looking to introduce, and lean into what will be most comforting to not only look at but also interact with on a daily basis.

Functional swaps: In minutes, you can install a new toilet seat in a more suitable design and material (like mahogany) or a bidet attachment to your existing toilet for a super-swift but noticeable upgrade. You can also level up your daily routines by swapping your showerhead with one that satisfies both partners' water-pressure wishes.

Lighting and mirror(s): Subtle yet seriously powerful, the right vanity lighting and mirror(s) can cue a desired aesthetic for the bathroom. Trade generic sconces for those in line with your taste and preferred ambience, and opt for white bulbs for more flattering, task-friendly lighting. When choosing mirrors, reflect on the frame style and shape for the right artistic accent, and be careful about sizing. A large mirror can make a small bathroom appear bigger but can also overtake the room if it's not a good fit, so stick to one that is a couple of inches (5 cm) narrower than your vanity. For double-basin vanities, consider if you want two small mirrors—one above each sink—or a single, wider one that spans both.

Vanity Fair

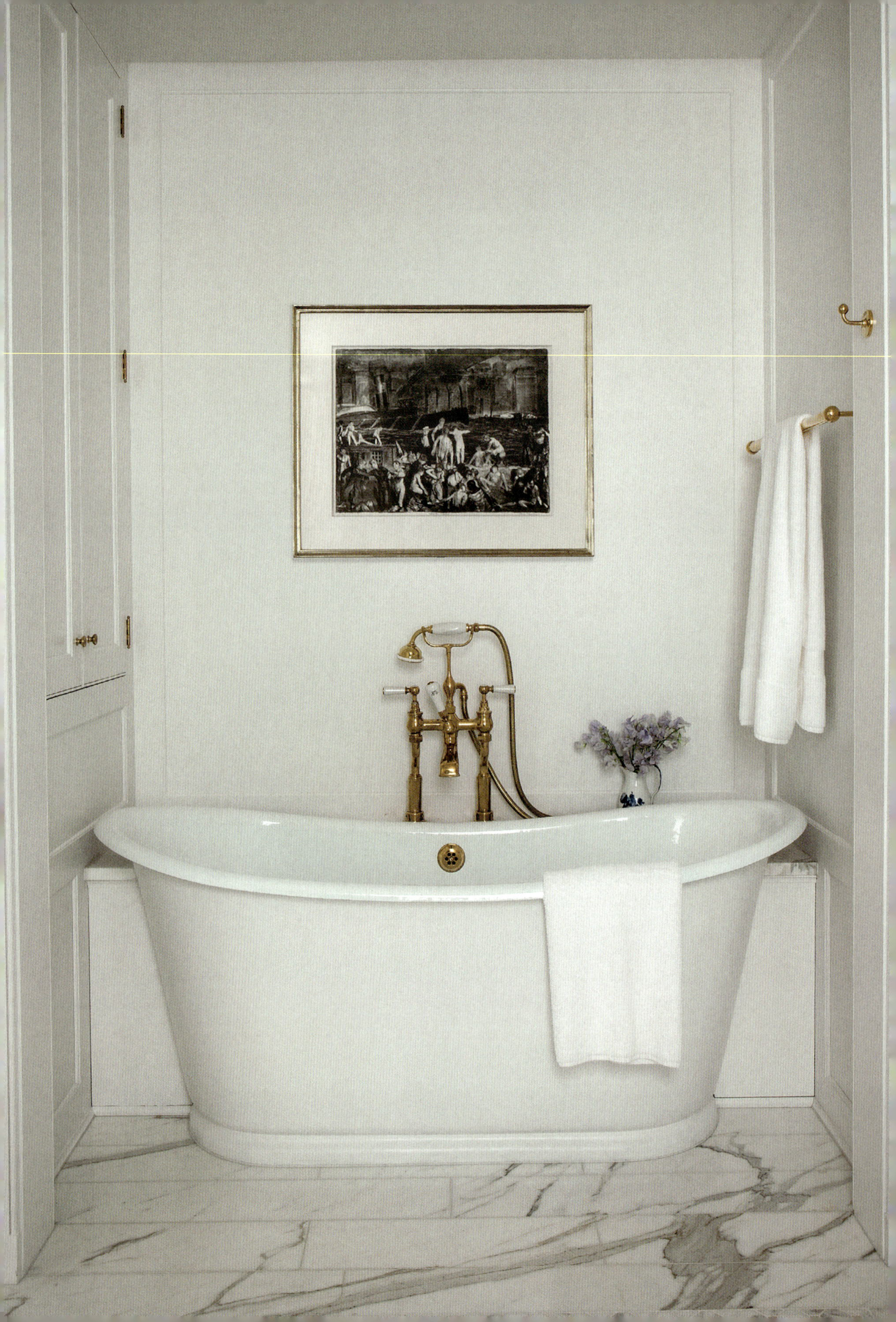

Window treatments: Privacy is essential in the bathroom, but so is natural light, so the proper window coverings are key. Light-filtering blinds and roller and roman shades are great options that can introduce a clear design style. Other options include peel-and-stick window films, available in sundry styles, as well as linen, cotton, or polyester curtains—just make sure they are sheer enough to let sunlight through but not so translucent that you are exposed to your neighbors.

Fixtures and hardware: Replacing your fixtures and hardware can help usher the bathroom into a new era. Think faucets and hoses, knobs and handles, towel bars and rings, switch plates and hooks, and even toilet paper holders and flush levers. Pieces in brass, nickel, bronze, and steel are all on offer in nuanced finishes including aged, brushed, polished, stainless, and matte black. Just be sure to stay consistent with the metal and finish you choose.

Walls: A fresh coat of paint or some design-forward wallpaper is a fantastic way to refresh the bathroom. While it can be tempting to go bold, you may want to stick to more organic, soothing hues and patterns for your primary bathroom, as this is a place of daily refuge. (Guest bathrooms, on the other hand, are a great canvas for eclecticism. See page 163 for more about this.) Add texture via plaster finishes or panels—though these may require more delicate maintenance than water-resistant semigloss paint—and consider two-tone walls or one accent wall for more dimension.

Vanities: Updating the vanity is one of the most significant ways to overhaul your bathroom. A fresh coat of paint on your cabinets, a new stone countertop, or a statement-making new vessel basin will immediately transform the room. If you decide to update it all, explore some color and material combinations until you find what best anchors the bathroom in your desired aesthetic.

Flooring: Redoing the floors is a very serious to-do, but if what you're working with is unacceptable and you want a quick fix, tile-mimicking vinyl floor mats can cover a lot of ground and offer a striking temporary solution. Chalk paint is another shortcut you can use to update tile flooring. Just use a couple of coats and seal it with a water-resistant lacquer.

Toilets and tubs: Swapping out a used, faulty, or unattractive toilet can not only make you feel more comfortable but, with a variety of styles available—from ultramodern to vintage-inspired—can also give your bathroom a facelift. You can get it done within a day. Replacing a bathtub, on the other hand, can be a very convoluted and pricey undertaking; if you have an old enamel- or porcelain-coated cast-iron or steel tub in fairly good condition, you can instead opt to refinish it to give it a second life.

Coordinating bathtub fixtures and hardware with your art and accessories is a lovely way to create continuity in a small space.

Mine and Thine

The secret to an attractive bathroom is organization, organization, organization. Every single item, no matter how big or small, should have an assigned place, and as a couple, you should agree upon a system that feels intuitive for you both so that maintenance is a breeze. Without the clutter, you can achieve a tranquil tone in the bathroom and set the stage for your design details to shine. Of course, not everyone is a neat freak, so be sure you're creating organizational solutions that are practical enough for you to both commit to for the long haul. Here's how to get started.

Step 1: *Assess your inventory.* Before all else, you should get a good understanding of how much stuff you each have—and more important, how much of it you actually need. There is a tendency to accumulate a surplus of toiletries, so purging every few months is a good practice, and when better to start than now? To begin, check the expiration dates on all personal hygiene and skincare products and dispose of anything that is past its prime. If you can't remember how long you've had something, it's likely too long. (Going forward, you can note the dates of purchase on the products with a permanent marker to help you keep better track.) Other criteria for decluttering your toiletries and beauty appliances: Do you use it? Like it? Have only one of it? If yes to all three, keep it. (For more tips on editing down your belongings, see page 206.) As for towels, how many you each have is ultimately up to you, but aim to own two to four sets per person, and keep only one or two spare sets in the bathroom, as dormant towels in a damp room can harbor bacteria.

Step 2: *Get the lay of the land.* Gauge how much built-in storage is available. If there isn't enough space to stow all of your combined goods, you will need to bring in some additional, stylish storage. Ideas include stand-alone cabinets, over-the-toilet towers, shower caddies, medicine cabinets, towel ladders, and freestanding or floating shelves. More unconventional options include coatracks, bedside tables, or even hanging wine racks (for rolled-up towels). On open shelves or those behind glass, you can use small baskets or containers to corral loose bottles and bric-a-brac for a more sightly display. For extra-tight bathrooms, wheeled trolleys, slim pull-out cabinets, and wall- or door-mounted hooks are great space savers.

Step 3: *Chart the territories.* With a better understanding of how much stuff and space you have, confer about how you want to divvy up the areas. It's important to come up with a plan you both approve of so that you can both comfortably navigate and maintain the space. One option is to appoint sections—specific drawers, cubbies, or vessels—to each of you for your personal belongings, and others for general, shared goods like washcloths and TP. Alternatively, you can zone off sections by classification (like skincare and haircare) and utilize small bins, zippered pouches, drawer separators, or even flatware organizers to allocate separate areas for each of you within that category. When arranging your things in their designated slots, keep products more frequently used in the foreground of cupboards and drawers and rarely used items toward the back. The drawers or shelves nearest the sink are prime real estate, so use them for day-to-day essentials like hairbrushes and sunscreen. Keep towels and washcloths tidily folded and stacked or rolled in a basket or on a rack.

Step 4: *Tackle the tabletops.* If you have any counter space, limit the number of items displayed to a minimum to avoid unattractive crowdedness and make for easier cleaning. Plus, you'll need the free surfaces to use bulky items like hairstyling tools or grooming kits. Prioritize things you both use daily, like cotton swabs, hand soap, tissues, and toothpaste and toothbrushes, and use a coordinated set of bathroom accessories (holders and dispensers) to house them all. With double-sink vanities, a duet of matching trays can also live on the counter to hold your respective must-haves.

Hot and Steamy

Because of the bathroom's high humidity levels, fluctuating temperatures, and (in many cases) direct sunlight, there are some things that you'll want to avoid keeping here, contrary to common practice. These include perfume, medicine, and nail polish, all of which can quickly lose efficacy amid these conditions. That said, if you still want to house these items—as well as expensive cosmetics, creams, and serums—in the bathroom, a miniature skincare refrigerator and insulated cosmetics pouches can save the day.

Paradise Found

Personalization in the primary bathroom is not just about what you behold but about what you experience. You want to create a serene space where you can both feel grounded and at ease, and the pieces you introduce to this private space can help you reach your wished-for level of quietude. By centering your decoration strategy around relaxation, you will be well on your way to crafting a bathroom oasis tailor-made for your relationship.

One brainstorming activity to get you going is to picture yourselves where you feel most relaxed and composed, whether that is a specific spa, barbershop, bed-and-breakfast, pool cabana, or resort. Discuss what you see when you mentally replant yourself there, and make note of any elements that you think could work well in your space. Are there specific materials, design accents, or textures that contribute to your Zen state of mind? If any of the features on your list mesh well with those on your partner's, zero in on those ideas and think of ways in which you can put your own spin on them and translate them for your bathroom.

> Save the loud patterns or other experimental designs for your guest bathroom (see page 163 for some playful ideas) and focus instead on neutralizing elements in your primary bathroom. Look to boutique hotel bathrooms for inspiration in creating a serene space.

REGISTER THIS

Get the five-star treatment at home with premium bath linens—monograms optional.

Towel sets: Six sets (with a bath towel, hand towel, and washcloth) with a density of at least 600 grams per square meter (GSM).

Washcloths: Eight extra washcloths for daily use. If using them for skincare, opt for darker hues so as to not stain them with cosmetics residue.

Bathrobes: Two matching cotton terry cloth or lightweight waffle weave robes.

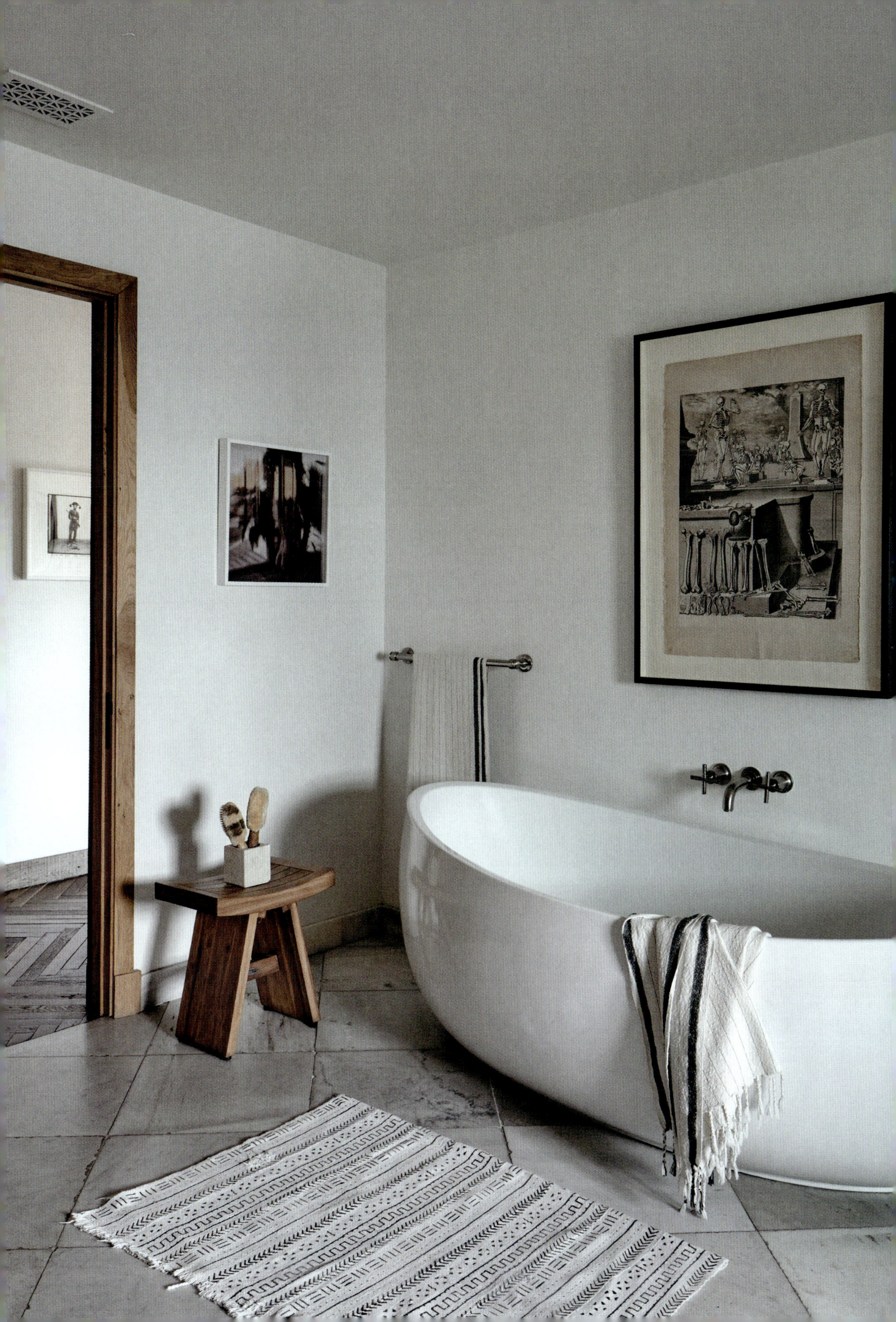

DATE NIGHT

SOAK IT UP

Some date ideas have been mainstreamed for so long that we knock them before we try them for fear of being cliché. Case in point: the romantic bath for two. But there is something to be said for soaking in the tub with your love—relieving stress, bonding one-on-one, and indulging in true TLC. It's a wonderful chance to unplug, shut out the rest of the world, and refocus on each other while resting your bodies and reconnecting physically.

For an indulgent self-care night, transform your primary bathroom into an at-home luxury spa with a menu of while-you-bathe treatment offerings to choose from. Take turns giving each other scalp, foot, or hand massages, or enjoy face masks concurrently—cucumber slices on the eyes and all. Set the mood with aromatherapy and candles, which can provide the ideal low lighting for a dreamy vibe to quiet the mind. Get creative with the bath composition by way of essential oils, bath salts, milks, bubbles, and more to address your moods and ailments.

Tailor the date experience to yourself and your partner by incorporating special features that are unique to you as a pair. Bring in a projector and have your favorite film playing on the wall opposite you, use a waterproof speaker to listen to an album from start to finish, or turn your bath into a couple's meditation enhanced with incense. Use a bathtub tray or caddy to serve up some traditional small bites like gourmet bonbons or unconventional treats like cool, refreshing tropical fruits.

And if your tub is not big enough to accommodate both of you (or you simply don't like the idea of soaking together), consider pampering your partner with a special solo bath instead. If they want to be alone to totally relax, give them that space, but if they welcome your company, pull up a chair next to them to chat and perhaps clink glasses.

Mix-and-Match Bath Soak

Channel your inner alchemists and personalize your downtime with a fragrant homemade bath soak. Use the table below to guide you as you try different combinations of bath salts, essential oils, and other enhancements to create a one-of-a-kind therapeutic blend sure to soothe your senses, detoxify your bodies, and melt your stresses away. The essential oils suggested here will provide soothing aromatherapy, while the carrier oils—which help evenly distribute the essential oils—will moisturize the skin, and the dried herbs will promote relaxation. As for the bases and powders, they can offer various benefits, including exfoliation (French green clay, bentonite clay), soothing of the skin (colloidal oatmeal, powdered milk), detoxification (rhassoul clay, cocoa powder), and pain relief (Epsom salts, magnesium flakes).

Experiment together with different combinations until you find the perfect chemistry, then jar up your concoction. When you're ready to draw a bath, simply scoop out ¼ cup (57 g) of your bath soak mix and add it to your warm bathwater—and be sure to use a tub drain strainer to catch any undissolved debris and protect your pipes.

CARRIER OIL	ESSENTIAL OIL	BASE	POWDER	DRIED HERBS
1 tablespoon (15 ml)	15 drops	2 cups (454 g)	1 tablespoon (14 g)	1 tablespoon (14 g)
Argan oil	Eucalyptus	Dead sea salt	Bentonite clay	Chamomile
Calendula oil	Frankincense	Epsom salts	Cocoa powder	Elderflower
Jojoba oil	Geranium	Magnesium flakes	Colloidal oatmeal	Lavender
Almond oil	Lavender	Pink Himalayan salt	French green clay	Rose
Avocado oil	Sandalwood		Powdered milk	Rosemary
	Ylang-ylang		Rhassoul clay	Sage

In a small cup, combine your carrier oil(s) and essential oil(s). Set aside. In a large bowl, mix your base(s), powder(s), and dried herbs with a spoon. (If using clay, avoid using a metal bowl or spoon, as metal can alter a clay's properties.) Add your oil mixture to your dry mixture. Mix well until evenly distributed. Transfer to an airtight glass jar (avoid a metal lid if using clays) and store in a cool, dry place for up to 3 months.

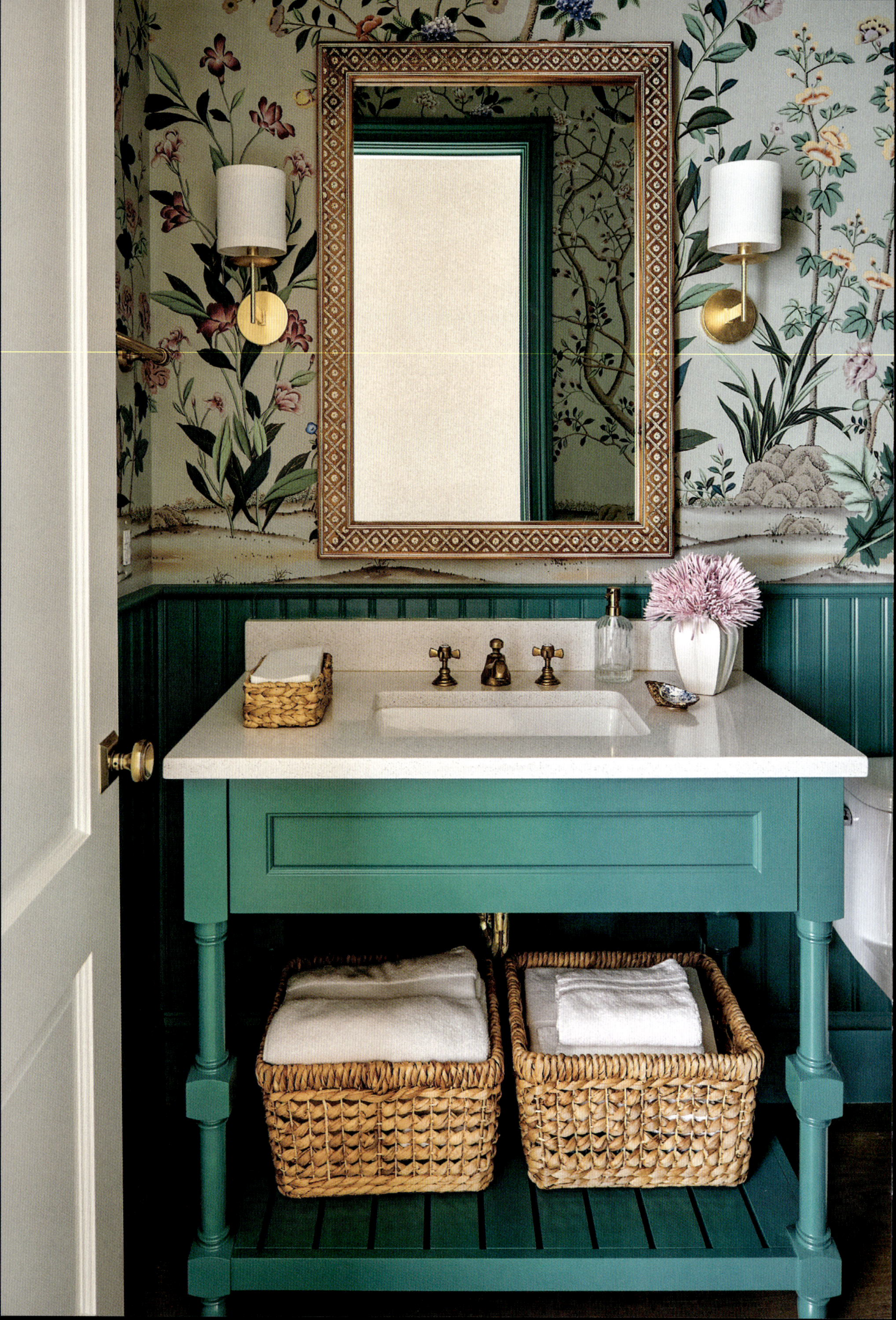

Powder Trip

The guest bathroom is one of the only areas of the home that visitors will engage with on their own. As such, the space itself—typically a powder room or half bath, classified as having a toilet and a sink—needs to be appointed in a manner that is welcoming, intuitive, and approachable. To ensure that your guest bath is comfortable and easy to navigate, integrate basic conveniences and courtesies, including a visible lidded trash bin, backup rolls of toilet paper, air fresheners and sprays, and a plunger—as well as everyday necessities like menstrual hygiene products, dental floss, and bandages for guests to privately help themselves to. Keep items in congruent, attractive vessels, like canisters for cotton swabs and tissue-box covers for facial tissue. In the case of overnight visitors, make them feel right at home with a prepared basket or tray of additional toiletries—like travel-size shower essentials, cleansing wipes, and a toothbrush and toothpaste—and, of course, a stack of freshly laundered fluffy towels.

    The guest bathroom doesn't have to be all business, though. While you may want to focus on neutralizing elements in your primary bathroom (see page 158 for tips on creating a spa-inspired bathroom), your powder room can be more playful and experimental in design. Have fun with your décor choices here. Removable wallpaper—easily applied as adhesive panels—can be used to make a bold impression, with themes ranging from tropical to nautical to whimsical. Feature attention-grabbing details like a few books propped up by elaborate bookends on a shelf, a vase of fresh flowers, and framed artworks on the walls. And consider unique accents inspired by your and your partner's collections, like jewelry dishes holding seashells or glass cloches housing antique trinkets. Dress the room up so that every corner of the space feels intentional, and try to switch things up every few months to speak to the seasons—with thematic scents and blooms, for instance—and keep returning guests impressed with the evolving display.

When opting for busy wallpaper in a powder room, consider limiting it to the top half of the walls, so as to not overwhelm the eye, and choose a classic wainscoting for the bottom half to break up the graphic print.

Love Interests

THE "BONUS" ROOM

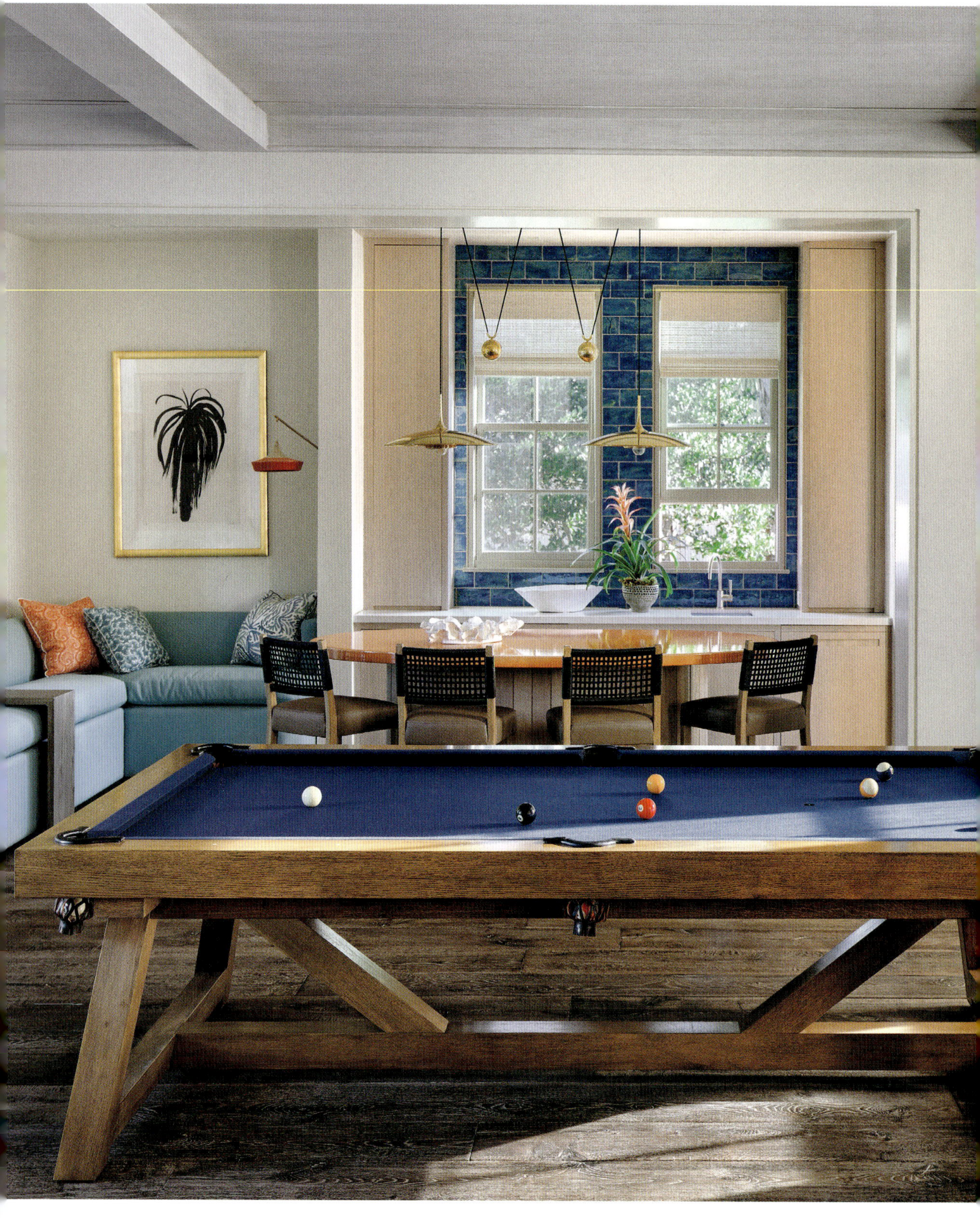

When you live solo, your work life and extracurricular activities may manifest themselves all throughout your dwelling. A pile of paperwork here, a makeshift crafting station there … But when it is time to build a family residence with your better half, these other aspects of your lives can disrupt the flow of domesticity if they are out of place. That's not to say you cannot thoughtfully and charmingly integrate them into your living areas, but it may be more considerate and appealing to have them removed from the core parts of your home, especially for couples who do not share the same pastimes.

Enter the bonus room. If you have a space that can be designated to cater to both of your additional needs and unique lifestyles (or have empty square footage that you're not sure how to utilize), then you have a very exciting—but potentially puzzling—project ahead. Of course, your multipurpose room does not have to be a literal room. It can be a spare bedroom, naturally, but it can also be a loft, a den, an attic, a sunroom, or simply an underused corner of the home. (In some cases, as with a forsaken basement or garage, you may need to finish the space and address essential concerns like insulation and climate control before you get going.) Whatever the framework may be, the intention is the same: You're creating a multipurpose space where you and your partner can both work and/or play.

  Collaborating closely, you'll need to come up with your own blueprint to build from, deliberating and defining what functions the room will need to serve, be it a workroom, an entertainment hub, or something in between. A couple of hurdles to overcome will be bridging any separate concepts you decide on and configuring a layout that maximizes efficiency. Think of it as solving a jigsaw puzzle without a reference image: It seems intimidating at first, but once you get your borders down and start to fit the pieces together, a masterpiece will soon take form. By taking on the project as a team and allowing yourselves to think outside the box, you will soon have an inimitable flex room that is customized to your and your partner's lives of productivity, creativity, and leisure.

SWEET TALK

UNCOVERING YOUR BONUS ROOM NEEDS

Given the extra space, what would your ideal use of it be? It could answer a practical need like for a fully equipped workspace or an area for showcasing a special collection, or act as a nonessential, niche feature, like a movie screening room or billiard parlor. The possibilities are essentially limitless, and the bonus room presents a rare opportunity to combine a few of these concepts in an idle section of the home. (If you'd like to use the spare room to accommodate overnight visitors instead, see page 144 for guidance on designing and prepping guest rooms.)

Because the two of you will be coexisting in this space—whether at different stations or jointly used ones—you'll need to carefully collaborate as you bring it to life, working together to survey the setting, explore ideas, and consider the compatibility of proposed concepts before making any final decisions. As you do so, try to prioritize essentials over wish lists—is it a *need* or a *want*? If you have too many ideas, you can narrow them down by finding common ground, and if you get really stuck, just go fifty-fifty: Split the space and allow each partner to have free rein in their half. Naturally, with more square footage, you can comfortably accommodate two or three different features. If space is limited, you can still achieve dual functionality, but you will have to be more calculating. Consider multifunctional furnishings like cabinets with fold-out tables and space-saving solutions like secretary desks and armoires to house equipment and stations. (For more on how to combine concepts, see page 170.)

The following guide can help you navigate a productive conversation as you ideate and devise a multipurpose room that you will both love to spend time in—alone or together.

How do you envision using your bonus room?

As a home office

If you both work from home, assess whether you tend to work simultaneously or if your WFH hours are staggered to determine if you need one desk setup or two. Consider which machines are essential—like desktop computers and printers—and keep them concentrated in one area. (See page 176 for more on home offices.)

As a creative studio

If one or both of you work with a lot of equipment and/or need a permanent station for your craft, a compact artist's studio, sewing station, or music room can allow you to get your creative work done at home and will add a great deal of character to your abode. If your pursuits don't require a static setup or take place outside of the home, you can still house your gear in the bonus room. Just stay organized with storage units like drawers or cubbies to contain your trappings and deter clutter.

As a rec room

If you don't need an at-home station for your professional or creative work, you might want an area dedicated to leisure instead. Determine if you would have shared or separate recreational setups—be it for video gaming, reading, or working out—or if you would instead like a space that's designed for group activities like movie nights or cocktail hours. Then plan to incorporate comfortable furniture accordingly, like snug personal chairs versus ample seating that can accommodate guests.

Character Study

After completing the guide on the previous page to get a better understanding of your multipurpose room needs, you will have to then ask yourselves how compatible your concepts are. If you are hoping for separate stations, walk through your schedules and daily habits to figure out how regularly you will both be in the space at the same time, and be realistic about disturbances like noise levels and messiness. Envision how those circumstances would pan out and be honest about how harmonious you find the two (or three) setups to be. If you find that the combination will be too cumbersome or discordant, take a step back and reassess your priorities until you both feel happy with the results.

Once you have your bonus room strategy nailed down, you will also need to figure out how much you can flesh out each concept. The simplest strategy here is to limit yourselves to the essentials. In lieu of a full-blown fitness center, for instance, you can have a compact home gym with the necessities for daily cardio and strength training. That way you can build on or adapt them as needed over time, and not overpower the rest of the room.

Keeping your unique stations streamlined, however, doesn't mean they can't be high-functioning or expressive. You just need to be extra resourceful and deliberate when choosing your fittings and decorations. (See the chart on the following spread for pragmatic yet stylish ideas for some popular bonus room uses.) And if one or both of you are on the fence about springing for a big-ticket item (like a specialty game table or a professional artist easel)—be it because of the cost or because you're not sure if it's just a phase—don't rush into any decisions. Instead, make a bonus room wish list with your partner and revisit it a few months or even a year later.

Designing a room that contains several concepts—such as a home office and painting studio—can be a challenge, but when done with care, it can be a truly worthwhile undertaking. An eye-catching large area rug can help bring harmony to the multifaceted room.

REGISTER THIS

Let friends and family invest in your shared passions.

Collectibles: A first edition of a favorite book, an original artwork, or a rare bottle of wine to treasure together.

Workout equipment: A Peloton, touchscreen fitness mirror, or sleek set of dumbbells to help you break a sweat in your home gym.

Experiences: Season tickets, playhouse memberships, or museum passes will make for months' worth of inspiring dates.

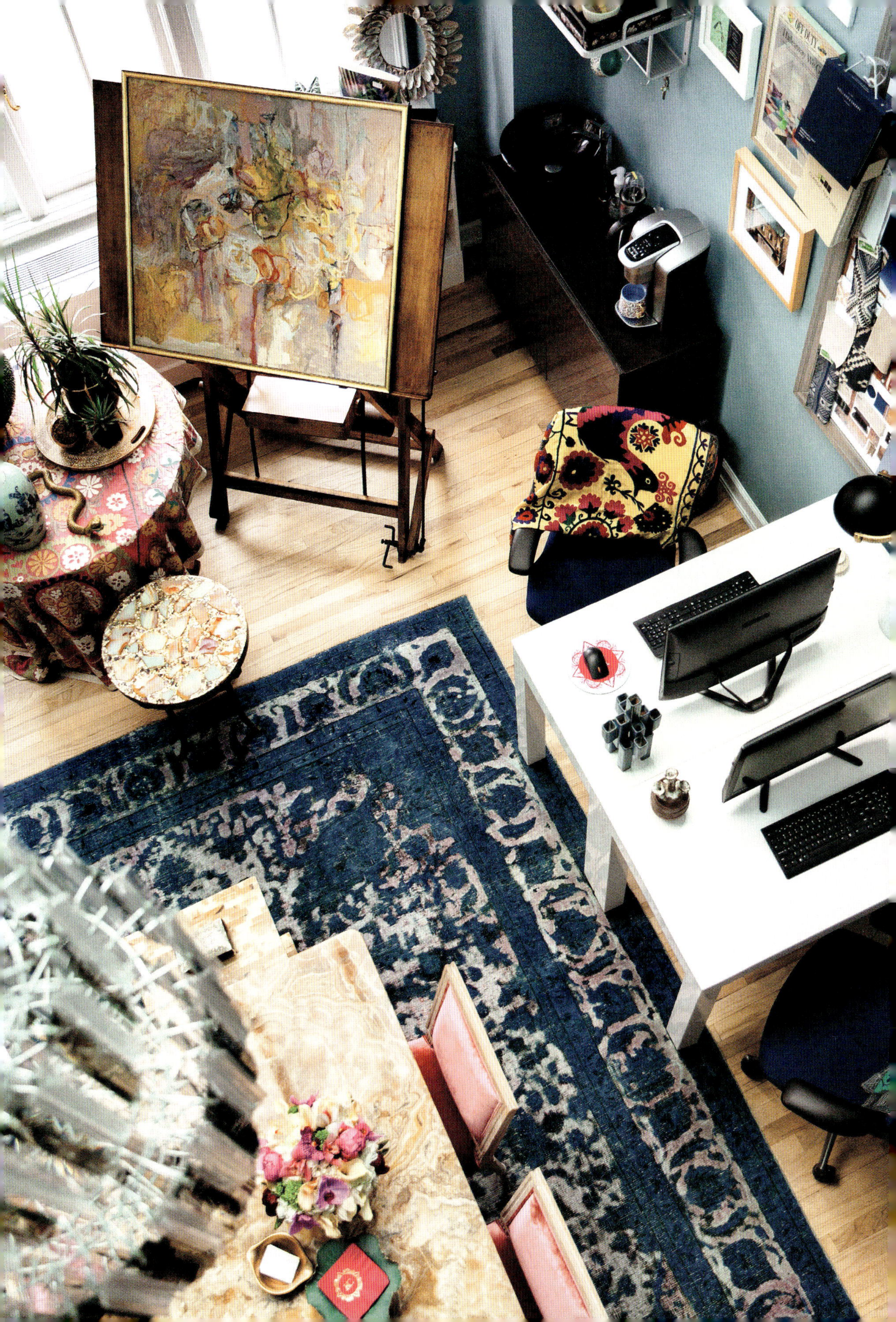

Partner Up

There might not be a readymade blueprint for your dual-purpose room needs, but uncharted territories are just an opportunity for you to pave your own path, so enjoy the process of collaborating on this unique space with your spouse. To get your creative juices flowing, here are some possible bonus room vignettes—with some fun implementable ideas for each—and examples of pairings that could be the perfect match. Once you find a partnership that works, consider boosting the harmony by incorporating mixed-use features between the stations, like a double-duty shelving system to display books and collectibles, or a TV for workout videos and movie marathons alike.

THE BOOKWORM

- A library anchored by a wall-unit bookcase to house your ever-expanding archive of books. Add a touch of whimsy with a rolling ladder.
- A reading nook with an oversize armchair, a swing-arm floor lamp, and an end table.

THE COLLECTOR

- A gallery where you can proudly display your collectibles, from vinyl to handbags to sports memorabilia.
- A designated tabletop with task lighting where you can work on hobbies like building model airplanes or repairing vintage watches.

THE FILM BUFF

A mini movie theater with plush seating, like a modular pit sofa or a pair of chic recliners. Invest in a quality sound system and boost the ambience with vintage film posters or a popcorn cart.

THE ATHLETE

- A home gym with select must-haves like a treadmill, a stationary bike, weight racks, or a punching bag.
- A yoga or dance studio with ample floor space and perhaps a ballet barre. Make sure to incorporate a large mirror.

THE GAMER

A video gaming setup with a couple of monitors and an ergonomic seat. Keep things sleek with electrical cord covers and cable management racks and opt for a proper headset for when you're sharing the room.

THE ARTIST

A creative studio fit for a budding or seasoned painter, sculptor, or mixed-media artist. Nab the area closest to the window for sufficient natural light. Use pegboard organizers or an apothecary cabinet to house your materials and tools.

THE COMPETITOR

- A puzzle-and-game room with a statement-making centerpiece like a pool table or stylish wooden Ping-Pong table.
- A board game center where you can store your arsenal and host amicable competitions with friends and family. Include a small coffee table and a few chairs or floor cushions for game nights.

THE BARTENDER

A speakeasy featuring a large corner bar cabinet with counter-height stools and art deco accents. Set the moody tone via low-light, frosted glass lamps and a dark, warm-toned color palette. Add a wine cellar with a sizable riddling rack or storage cooler.

THE MUSICIAN

- A music studio where you can exhibit and fiddle around with your instruments. Ground your layout with an upright piano or a keyboard on a stand.
- A home recording studio for your compositions. Stylishly control sound with rugs and designer acoustic wall tiles.

THE CRAFTER

An atelier for sewing, jewelry making, or knitting. Keep your station neat—and your accoutrements easy to access—with bins, tins, and other containers. Integrate task lighting along with a comfortable seat and work surface into your scheme.

Divide and Conquer

Being in close quarters with someone day in and day out can get taxing for even the most attached of couples. Thankfully, there are smart and stylish ways to separate your stations in the bonus room so you can visually define your spaces-within-a-space and always have a sense of privacy.

Room Dividers

Ranging from traditional Japanese-style shoji folding panels to ceiling-mounted privacy curtains, these partitions can add an interesting textural statement to the room.

Greenery

Incorporate a sense of the natural world with an elongated box planter or tall potted houseplants, which can provide a healthy dose of color and serenity while discretely splitting up the space.

Étagères

Backless bookcases and freestanding shelving units will not only add a geometric layer to the room but also integrate useful storage that's accessible from either side.

Seating

A pair of armchairs or a loveseat can organically divide the room and steer traffic while also providing a nice spot to take a quick break from work.

Office Romance

A home office can be a very necessary component of a modern residence, be it for your profession or simply keeping up with domestic responsibilities. If you alternate working from home or only occasionally need an office, you can elect to have one shared desk space. Since this would be a communal workstation, keep its décor pared back and neutral (a beautiful task lamp and useful desktop organizer will suffice). Use it as a center for household management and everyday business, with a small bulletin board for exchanging memos, and essentials like stationery and writing utensils. You can choose to have a household desktop computer, or if you each have your own laptop, leave the desk as a bare surface where you can perch in turns. As for your shared documents and records, decide on a filing method that you both can manage—be it a filing cabinet, accordion portfolios, or a fully digitized system—and stay vigilant about maintaining it.

If you need two separate office setups, you can take a more personalized approach to designing each one, catering them to your respective careers and styles. Think desktop accents and organizational systems that are specific to your subjective tastes and tendencies. However, if the two desks will share a room, there should be a common thread between them, whether it's matching furnishings, tabletop accessories, or a uniform color scheme. (See Strong Connection on page 179 for more ideas on creating unity in your bonus room.)

The arrangement of your joint office may be dependent on power sources, so keep outlets in mind as you draft a layout. If space is especially tight, consider a fold-out desk or escritoire. Even a spare reach-in closet can be converted to a petite office. For a more unconventional approach, you can use a large dining table in lieu of two desks, which would allow for more collaboration and creative workflows, and can function as a conference table if you ever need one—a great option for couples who are also partners in business.

Large rooms can accommodate a desk in the middle of the space, though you'll need to prioritize cable management. If you're using a desktop computer or other stationary office equipment, use floor and/or carpet cord covers to keep the area safe and neat.

The Newlywed Home

CHECK IN

WORKING TOGETHER

If you and your partner share a workspace—even if you have vastly different careers or projects—you will have to learn to be coworkers, giving new meaning to the term "work spouse." As you work closely, you may notice different sides of each other—quirky habits or alter egos that emerge when you are deep in the zone or stressed out. More commonly, you might find that you have different workday patterns or styles that may clash. There will be an adjustment period as you get accustomed to working simultaneously under one roof and learn what conditions you each need to concentrate and be productive.

To nip issues in the bud, establish some ground rules ahead of time. Much like in any workplace, a list of agreed-upon policies can help keep your arrangement peaceful and efficient. Think a phone policy (where you step out of the room to take non-work-related calls), a shared calendar with scheduled virtual meetings and visitors (so the other partner can plan accordingly), and limitations on interruptions. To lessen distractions, invest in noise-canceling headphones and use visual cues like hourglass timers to implement quiet hours. Overall, make it a point to be courteous and aware of each other, and as always, keep the communication channels clear. Check on each other here and there, kindly alert your partner when something is disturbing you, and offer extra support when they are swamped, because in the end, your partner's success is just as important as yours.

DATE NIGHT

HOT PURSUIT

Everyone has activities and topics that preoccupy them on their time off; the talents and crafts that they've honed for years. Naturally, you and your partner will get well acquainted with each other's pastimes and interests over the course of your relationship, and you will inherently expose each other to things that would otherwise never have been on your radars. You might even start to share in the enthusiasm for said subjects. But what if you were to step into an arena that is totally unfamiliar to you both? An uncharted territory in the arts, sciences, or athletics realm? Arranging an evening for you to get out of your comfort zones together and have a crack at something completely new can be a fresh opportunity for fun and letting loose—and yes, possibly making fools of yourselves, but what better place to do so than home sweet home?

Some scenarios to get you thinking and set the wheels in motion: If one of you is a cinephile and the other an avid reader but neither of you follows sports, you might learn the ins and outs of soccer and tune in to the Premier League. If one of you loves video games and the other is a seasoned yogi but neither of you knows how to play poker, you can study the rules and try your hand at the game to test your newly acquired knowledge. (Place some wagers to make things even more interesting.) If one of you is a devoted golfer and the other a skilled crafter but neither of you can sing, bring in a karaoke machine and put on a private concert that you will likely laugh about for years to come. Other ideas to consider include enrolling in an online class together, marathoning a famous movie trilogy you both somehow missed, setting up some easels and painting portraits of each other, staging a series of science experiments, or committing to a couple's fitness challenge.

Whichever novel avenue you choose to take, embrace the discomfort, be kind to each other as you both find your footing, and go all in. Dedicating yourselves to the activity will allow you to get the most out of it and possibly open up new horizons. You might walk away from the experience with the realization that it's not for you, or you might unlock a skill or interest that will surprise you. After all, it's never too late to pick up a new hobby, and if you're lucky, your partner will be equally on board.

Strong Connection

The simplest way of tying together the different elements of your multipurpose room is to ground the space in the same interior design style—for instance, American traditional, Scandinavian, coastal, or eclectic—through your furnishings and décor. Big-impact features within your chosen style, like wallpaper or a large area rug, will unify the space, as will the smaller details, like textures (staying in the same family of woods, fabrics, and other materials throughout the space) and design accents in complementary colors and motifs. Even if your respective bonus room stations are inherently different, the design choices you make for them should not clash. As for dual office spaces, use matching desktop accessories such as lamps, catchalls, and paper trays as a common thread, or, alternatively, have distinctive desktop assortments but use identical desks and chairs.

 If your bonus room will be a private escape for just you two, your design for the space can be self-contained and highly expressive. Go all in on making it your ideal couple's den and geek out over your gear, furniture, and décor. On the other hand, if you plan to welcome friends and family into your bonus room, you'll want it to blend more with the aesthetic of the rest of your home. Whether it's a recreation room, a lounge area, or a mix thereof, make sure to provide guests with ample comfortable seating.

 As for enhancing your rec room features, don't commit the number one bonus room sin: word art. Avoid anything that has a quote or obviously labels a section of the room, as it tends to be impersonal (and is sort of synonymous with faceless vacation rentals). Instead, let the furniture and configurations speak for themselves, and stay personal with your art choices. Works on display can, of course, nod to the theme at hand, but as you make your selections, stay true to who you are and steer clear of clichés. (For example, a framed movie poster is still a great idea for a media room, but instead of a widely popularized film print, choose one of a cult favorite that actually inspired your passion for cinema.)

Sun-Kissed

OUTDOOR SPACES

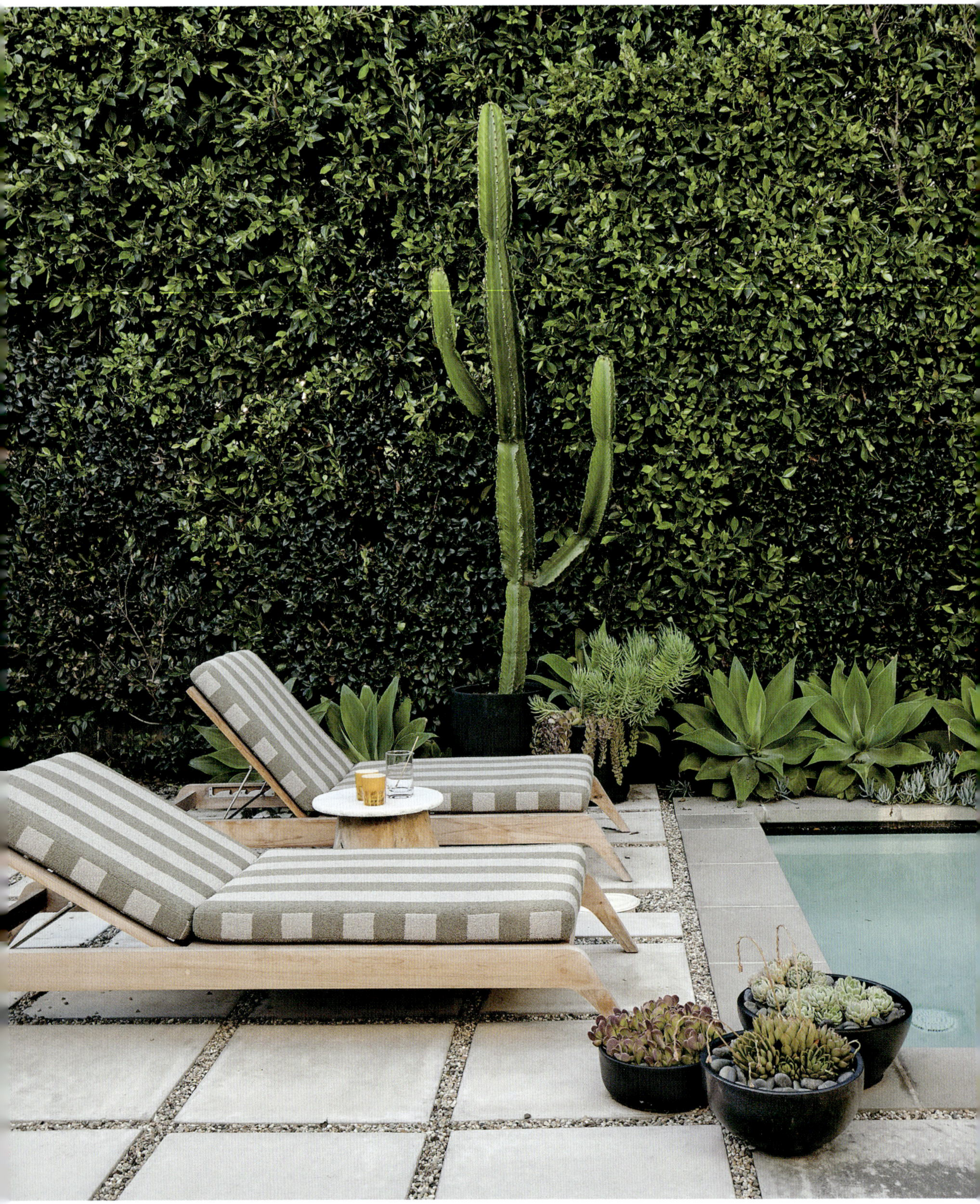

When the weather is nice, the outdoors beckon, and having an open-air retreat to call your own—even if it's tiny—is a blessing. For generations, our backyards were simply practical spaces used for hanging laundry and growing vegetables, and ornamental gardens were an uncommon luxury. It wasn't until the mid-twentieth century that the modern concept of the American backyard emerged and people began to rethink their yards as recreational features of their homes that could be customized for leisure. Since then, our private pieces of the outdoors have evolved to be more and more integrated into our lives, but we sometimes still forget just how bespoke they can be.

By categorizing your outdoor space as not separate from the home but rather an extension of it, you will gain one more hallowed place to share with your partner—one where you can bask in the sunshine and reap the mood-lifting endorphins it promotes. With that, however, comes the need to design it. We spend so much time mulling over a new home's interiors but often neglect to take that same thorough approach with our exterior living spaces. If you devote as much care and consideration to the outside as you do the inside, your slice of the outdoors—whether it's a modest balcony or a sprawling yard—can become just as enticing, significant, and personal as your living room, kitchen, and dining room.

    Luckily, this philosophy also translates to a clear-cut design tactic that will lead you to success: Approach your outdoor space as you would any other part of the home. That is to say, begin with a sincere conversation about how you imagine spending time there (individually, as a pair, and with loved ones) and tailor the pieces to your lifestyles and creature comforts. You want your oasis to lure you outside, so zero in on what your priorities are and be true to yourselves as you choose which furnishings, decorations, fixtures, and special features you both want to invest in. That way, you can ensure that your backyard will open the door to the beauty of indoor-outdoor living.

SWEET TALK

HOW YOUR GARDEN GROWS

The grounding lessons and beauty of gardening are evergreen. The age-old pastime can even be an apt metaphor for a loving long-term relationship—you know, setting down roots, nurturing them, getting excited for what the future holds, and being patient as everything grows at its natural pace. It can also be a fun, rewarding pursuit for a couple looking to spend more time together as you get your hands dirty and work in tandem toward a common goal. Plus, plants, trees, bushes, and flowers can radically transform a plain or run-of-the-mill outdoor space into a personalized oasis.

However, there is more to creating a garden than just going to a plant nursery and ambitiously filling up your cart. Factors ranging from climate and maintenance requirements to size and budget limitations can all dictate what you can actually achieve, so it's important to strategize together before embarking on this project. If your gardening interest is piqued but you're not sure where to start, talk through these six simple steps to get growing.

Step 1: *Size up your space.* Determine your available square footage, and be sure to account for any furnishings you want to include. For in-ground landscape gardening, survey how much of your ground is leveled, whether the existing soil is healthy, and whether your land features good drainage. If your viable in-ground space is limited, consider whether and where you can add raised beds or containers such as pots, urns, troughs, hanging baskets, or window boxes.

Step 2: *Identify your zone.* Reference the USDA Plant Hardiness Zone Map to learn which perennial plants can not only grow but thrive in your location. Once you know your hardiness zone, you can better assess plant tags as you shop, and this will also help you manage your expectations. (The exotic tropical garden you imagined having, for instance, may not actually be a possibility where you live.) When in doubt, look into native plants, which can thrive where you are and help preserve the local biodiversity.

Step 3: *Zero in on your style.* Chat with each other about the types of greenery you think would best suit the architecture of your home and your outdoor furnishings, and generally what you'd love to see. For instance, are you more drawn to the manicured, symmetrical gardens of France or the natural, spontaneous vibes of an English garden? Do you like the idea of an edible garden or an ornamental one? Understanding what you both like will help you further refine your vision and come up with a natural theme for your outdoor space. Together, browse local nurseries, botanical gardens, or even just your neighborhood to get acquainted with and inspired by flora.

Step 4: *Consider the cost and care of your selections.* Crunch the numbers to see how much this project will set you back. A single plant might seem cheap, for example, but when you consider how much ground you'll need to cover, the costs can add up. If the expense seems too high, you can take it slow and just start with one corner or flower bed. You'll also want to assess how much labor this project will require, both up front and ongoing, and how dedicated you both are to the necessary upkeep. If you like the idea of a classic American mowed turfgrass, for example, but aren't willing to either mow the lawn or hire a gardener to do so, you might want to look into lower-maintenance ground covers like clover lawns. Other easy-care garden ideas include low-water succulents and hardy shade-tolerant plants.

Step 5: *Build in some privacy.* Tall evergreens, from hedges to cypresses and other bushy trees, can provide privacy from neighbors while also wrapping your outdoor area in beautiful greenery year-round. Gardening accessories such as trellises and lattice fences can be used to layer foliage like climbing vines for a secret-garden effect. And don't just concentrate these features along the edges of your property: Integrating them centrally and throughout can also help you achieve privacy.

Step 6: *Welcome your (nonhuman) neighbors.* Bird feeders, birdhouses, and owl boxes will provide you with natural pest control, and monitoring them can even become a sweet new hobby for you to share. You can also attract pollinators like honeybees, ladybugs, butterflies, and hummingbirds by incorporating host plants such as milkweed and foxglove into your garden.

Sun-Kissed

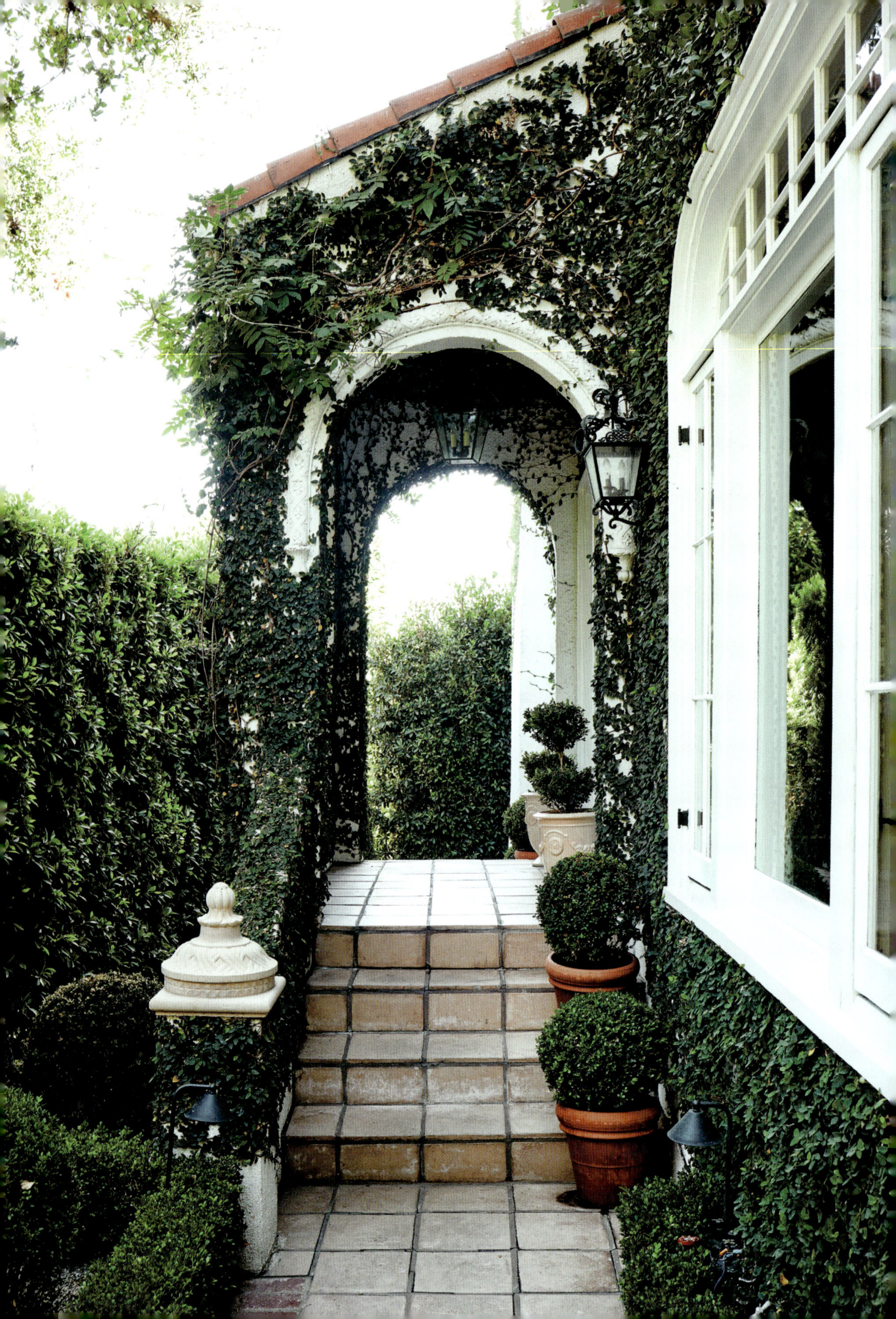

Curb Appeal

As previously discussed, your entryway holds a lot of power in giving guests a first impression of your interiors and homelife (see page 19), but visitors can actually receive a warm welcome from you even before they've stepped foot indoors. A well-kept housefront can be a thing of beauty, bringing you and anyone who encounters it a dose of joy. And who knows? It might even inspire a romantic front-porch kiss here and there, à la your first date. To curate your curb appeal, begin with big-impact updates, then work your way to the details.

While painting the exterior walls of your house is a major commitment and expenditure (costing at least—if not more than—$10,000), painting the front door will set you back only a couple hundred bucks and instantaneously give your home's façade a major facelift. Choose a quality, glossy-finish paint in a color that already appears on your home's façade for a more subtle effect, or make a statement with a bold hue like contemporary black or classic candy-apple red. Alternatively, you can sand and restain a wooden front door to give it new life.

Another high-impact change is the addition of furniture, particularly for those with a front porch. A bench, swing, or pair of chairs can be functional while also providing a preview of your interior design style.

Lighting is important to address here. A covered entry like a portico will do well with a distinct outdoor chandelier, while two matching sconces are perfect for flanking a door. Some long-lasting materials to keep an eye out for are wrought iron, brass, bronze, and resin wicker. You can also illuminate porch steps with stair lights or lanterns for both safety and style.

Now comes the fun part: personalization. With a few handpicked bits and bobs, you can quietly set your home apart from your neighbors' and allow your cultivated interior character to trickle outside. Some strategic swaps include door knockers, doorbell covers, doormats, house numbers, and mailboxes and mail slots. Aim for continuity with your picks, sticking with a color scheme, design style, and/or material for the pieces. Lastly, add your final touches via organic décor, such as potted plants (see page 58 for more on these) or wooden sculptures on either side of the door. But don't go overboard—you don't want any clutter blocking your entrance.

A vine-covered exterior can have a timeless, enchanting effect and even help insulate the home. But beware: Regular pruning and inspection are necessary to keep the vines from damaging your structure.

Sun-Kissed

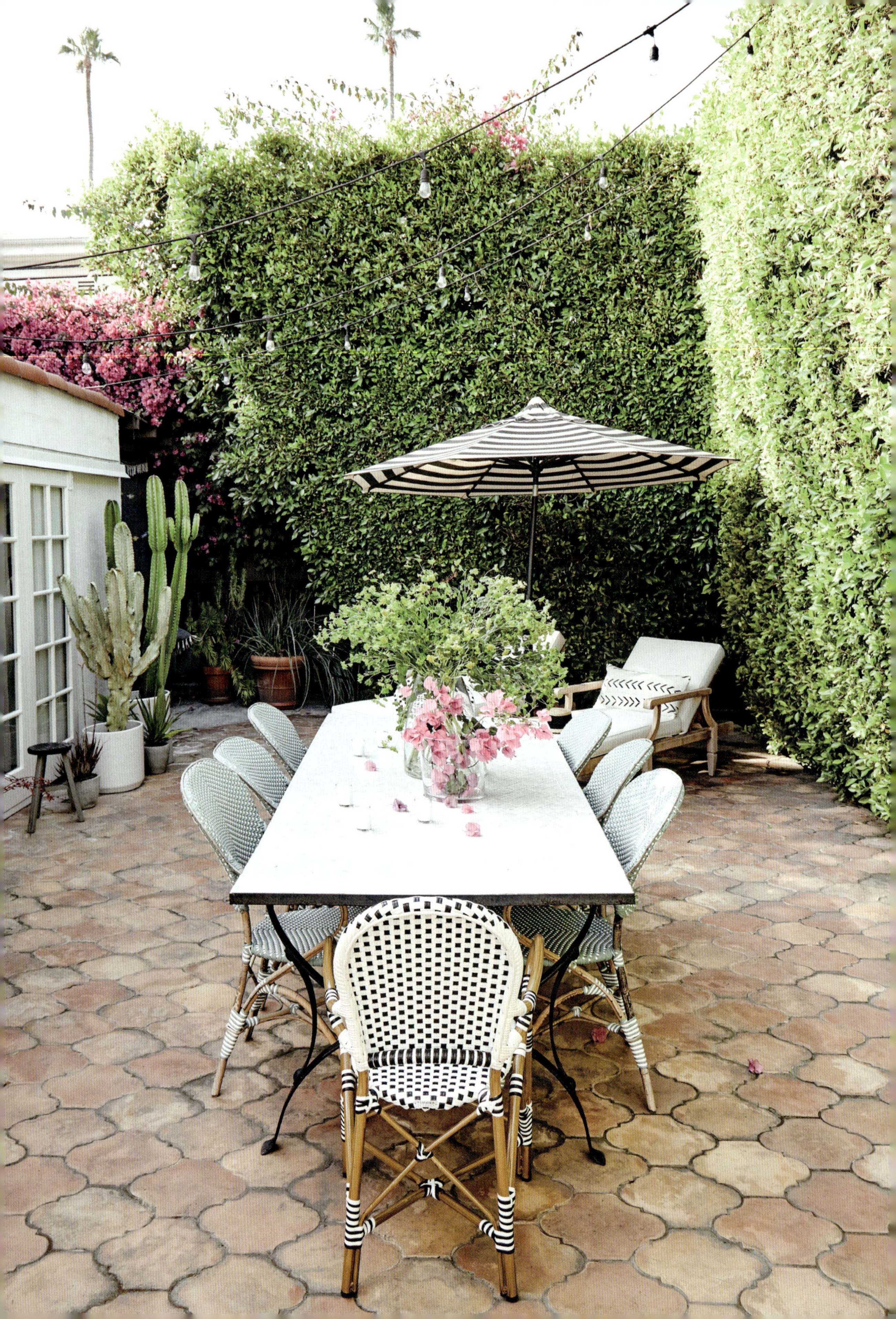

Get a Room

By approaching your backyard as an extension of your home, you can "unlock" another multipurpose living area to regularly use and enjoy—and also make the process of designing and furnishing your outdoor space way more manageable. By establishing outdoor "rooms" for different needs and moods, you can tackle the design of your backyard just as you would your interiors: one space at a time.

Figuring out how many living areas you can forge outside is the priority. Doing so early on will help you divvy up your outdoor furniture budget wisely. The most familiar approach is to feature a dining area and a lounging area—with a dining table and chairs in one zone and a more relaxed seating arrangement in another. (Petite patios and balconies will likely be able to fit just one "room." In those cases, choose one multifunctional furniture set that you can comfortably use as both an alfresco dining spot and a lounging area.) By arranging your furniture in clusters and positioning the "rooms" far enough from each other, you can make the distinctions clear, but if you'd like the separations more defined, you can incorporate additional features, from big (planter beds and cantilever umbrellas) to small (outdoor rugs and lighting).

Beyond those core "rooms," there are many options to consider: an entertaining area with an island bar, firepit, and lounge chairs, for instance; or a kitchen station with a grill, herb garden, and prep table. You might want a little nook with a bistro set where you two can have your morning coffee, or perhaps a sunbathing zone with a pair of chaises, a side table, and an umbrella in case it gets too hot. And for those who often find themselves seeking some peace and quiet, a cocoon chair or hammock tucked away in the garden can be a sweet little spot to escape to.

A chaise or two under a patio umbrella can make for a quaint outdoor "room"—a perfect little retreat for a moment of calm—whereas a large dining set will become an entertainment hot spot for company.

MAIN SQUEEZE

THE PATIO SET

The right patio set can boost the entire outdoor atmosphere. You want a lounge area that will invite you and your guests outside, and the furnishings you choose should fit your lifestyle *and* your style. Deciding what to commit to can be a challenge, particularly because many of the options on the market tend to be generic, lackluster, and flimsy, and the ones that aren't so are typically more expensive. But don't get discouraged: If you know what to look for, you can spend wisely and find an enduring, unique outdoor lounge set that will suitably ground your deck, patio, yard, or balcony—and keep you coming back out for more fresh air. Here are the key factors to consider during your search.

Scale

Figuring out the right size and number of pieces needed for an outdoor living area is tricky, especially when the parameters of an outdoor "room" are not physically clear. If your patio set is too large for the square footage, it can feel crowded, and if it's too small, it can look awkward and isolated. To help you visualize the amount of space you're actually working with, use chalk, blue painter's tape, or other indicators on the ground to sketch out your proposed borders, and use this same method to configure potential furniture layouts. Aim for about 3 feet (1 m) of space between large items of furniture, whether that's a small three-piece set (two chairs and a coffee table) or a large six-piece set (two chairs, a sofa, a coffee table, and two side tables).

Silhouette

Outdoor furniture comes in many shapes and forms, from sunbeds and daybeds to modular sofas and Adirondack chairs, plus infinite kinds of coffee tables and side tables. To help you narrow down your favorite designs, have an earnest conversation about how you both imagine using this space. If you're aiming for a conversation pit configuration, for example, you'll want a more traditional living room–style arrangement. Or if you're hoping for more of a chill-out zone, look for reclining seats or oversize pieces that you can sink into. The climate of where you live may also steer you in making this decision. For instance, if you get year-round sunshine, you may want to invest in

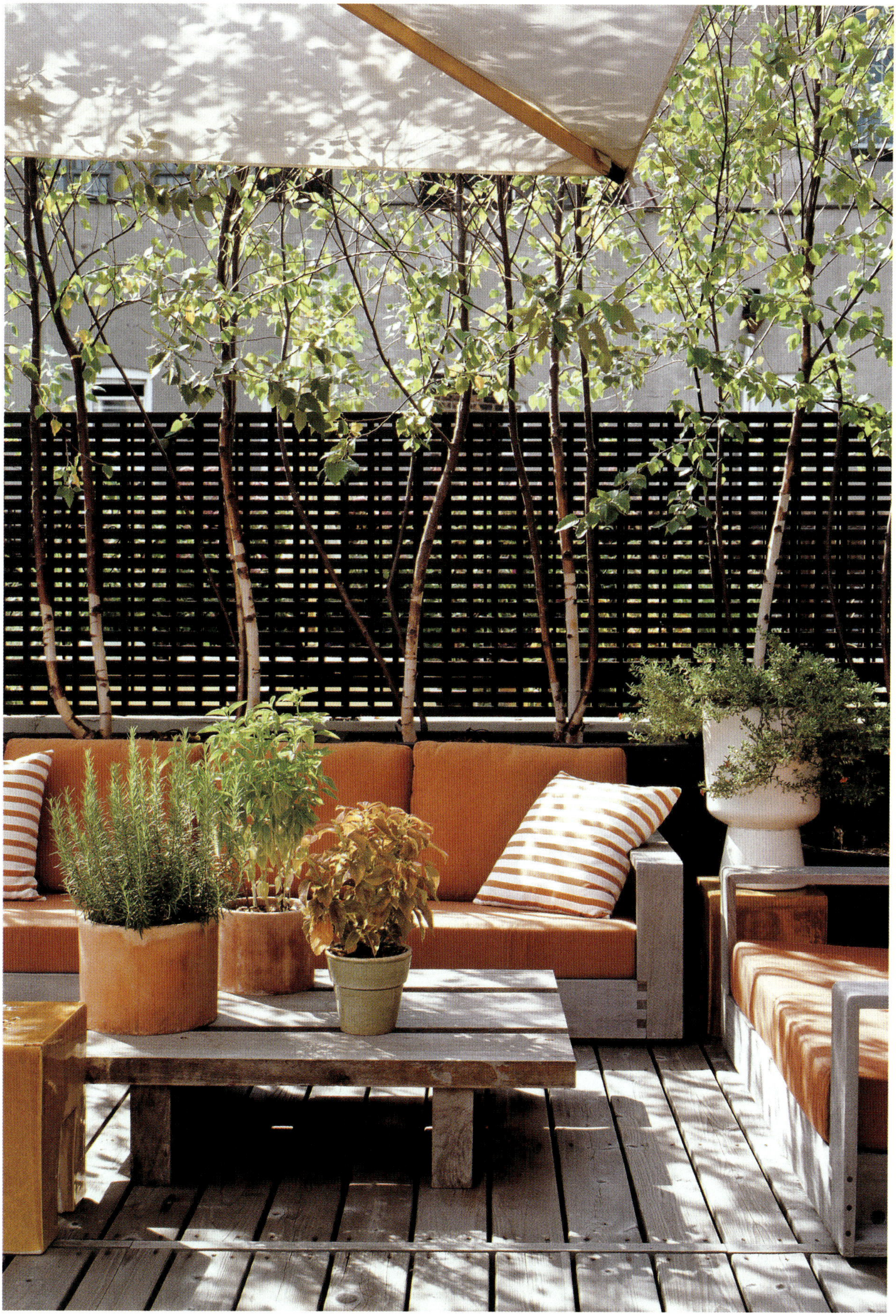

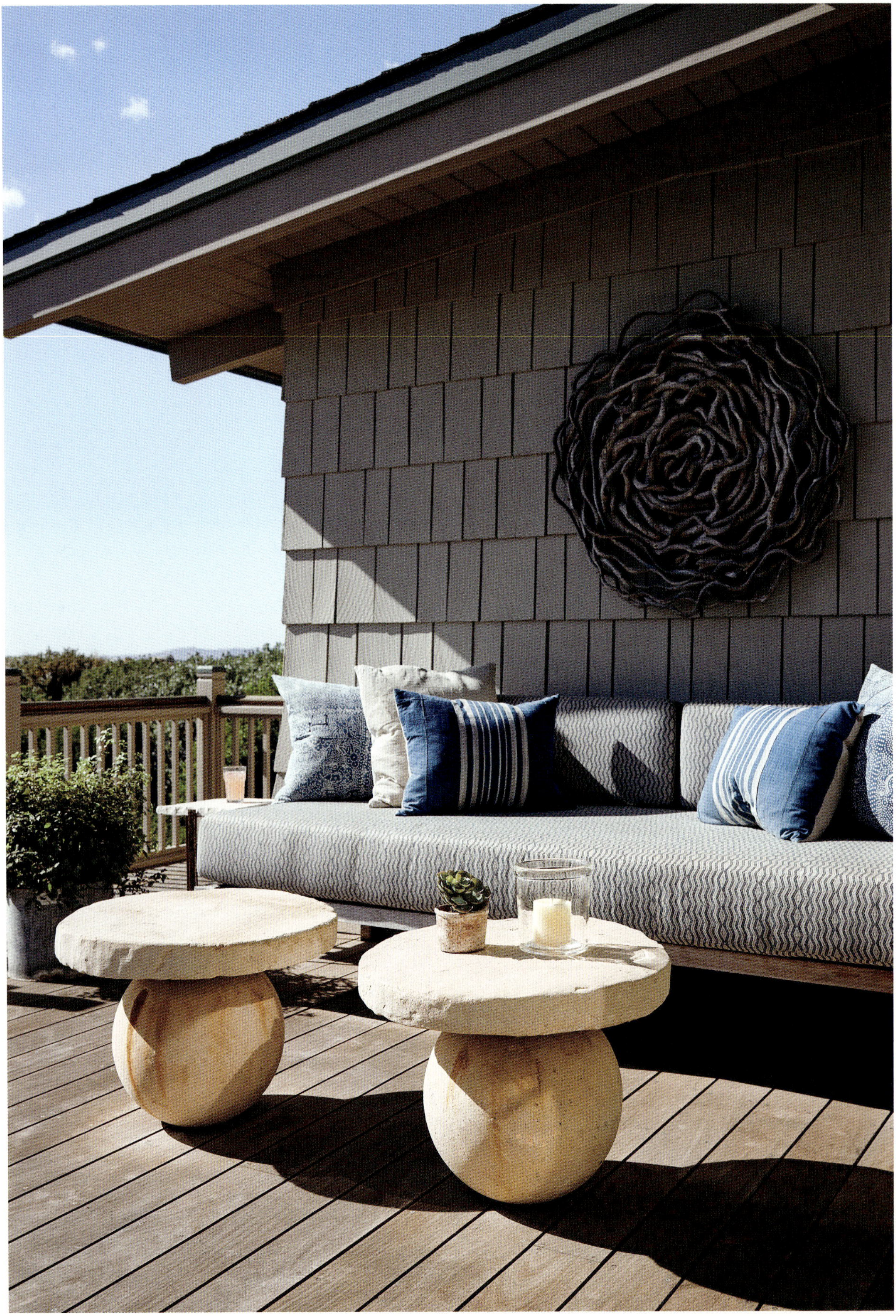

substantial upholstered seating that will remain outside at all times, whereas if you experience the four distinct seasons, you might want more lightweight pieces that can be easily transported indoors when it's cold and wet out, like folding director's chairs or sling chairs.

SECTIONAL

CHAISE LOUNGE

ADIRONDACK CHAIRS

DAYBED

Composition

You want to make sure your outdoor furniture can withstand the elements and daily use, so keep your eyes peeled for high-performance fabrics and durable frames that can extend the life of your pieces and get you more bang for your buck. For upholstery, solution-dyed acrylic textiles are preferred for their water resistance and durability, and foam fillings are the most common for cushions because they keep their shape and don't hold water. As always, testing furniture out in person is the best way to get a feel for the cushioning and support the pieces can provide. As for frames, opt for sturdy hardwood (like teak), rattan, and aluminum if you can, or HDPE plastic lumber, resin wicker, and composite if you're on a tighter budget. The latter three frame options are also easier to keep clean and looking fresh. Whatever you choose, aim to protect your furniture from wet weather conditions by covering it or storing it inside, and follow the specific care and cleaning instructions provided.

Style

Your outdoor space is an extension of your home, so aim for congruency with the rest of your living spaces. For instance, if you choose an ultrasleek, modern patio set but your interiors are retro or traditional, there will be a stark disconnect. And try to tie in the furniture to the outdoor space as a whole: think wood frames that match the siding of your exterior walls or earth-toned textiles that blend into the natural landscape that surrounds them.

Inside Out

There should be a sense of continuity between the inside and outside of your home, but that doesn't mean your outdoor spaces need to be reproductions of your living room and dining room. In other words, you can branch off but still be part of the same tree. You can unify your indoor and outdoor spaces through a design style (for example, mid-century modern) and/or foster continuity by honoring your home's architectural style through your design choices. A Spanish Revival house, for example, might feature Baroque- and Moorish-inspired furnishings and decorations throughout that speak to the structure's distinct identity. Of course, there are no hard-and-fast rules, so if you both feel confident in a bold new aesthetic—say, a Moroccan-inspired open-air retreat—that is a departure from what's inside the home, trust your shared concept and go for it.

With your furniture in place (see page 190), you can rely on layers to amplify your vision. Some ideas to explore include all-weather rugs (which are great for sectioning off outdoor "rooms"), camp throws, and patio cushions, all of which can be used to incorporate rich textures, colors, and patterns. Use the same layering tactic for lighting by adding candles in hurricane lamps and cordless outdoor table and floor lamps. You can even try hanging lanterns from a tree in place of string lights for an enchanting effect. Find décor and accessories that complement the scene, be they outdoor trays, urns, poufs, or sculptures.

And be sure to tie in your garden elements by choosing planters and pots that help you achieve the vibe you're aiming for. Think terra-cotta urns for an organic, Mediterranean look; steel troughs for a modern, industrial aesthetic; or muted ceramic and rattan containers for a cool, beachy ambience. Play around with sizing and mix extra-large planters (for trees and shrubs) with an assemblage of plants in smaller pots. (For more on choosing plants for your outdoor space, see page 184.)

> If you choose to hang paintings in your outdoor space, take precautions to protect the art. Some preventive measures include hanging the pieces in a covered area; applying waterproof, UV-resistant varnishes to the canvas; and employing weatherproof frames.

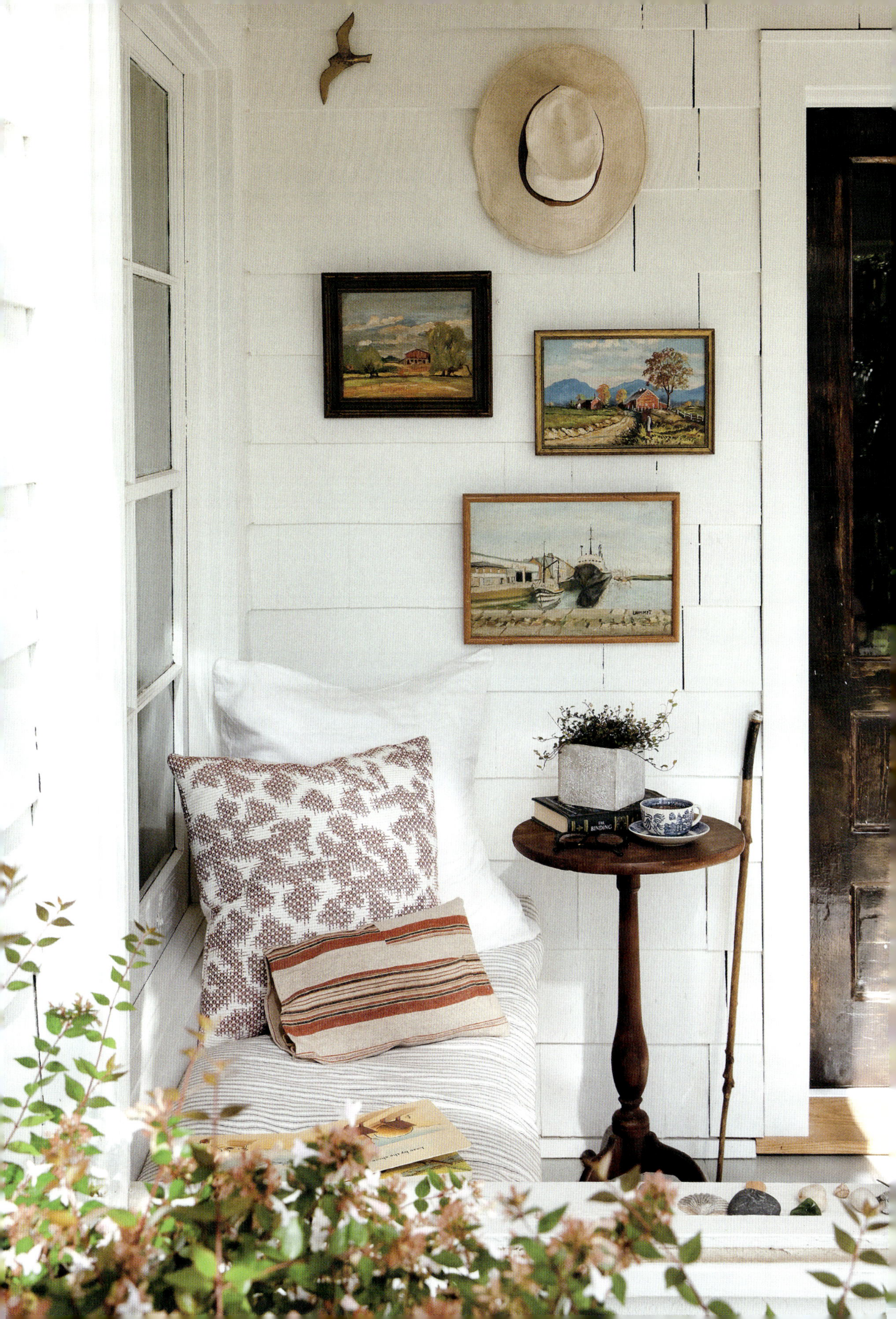

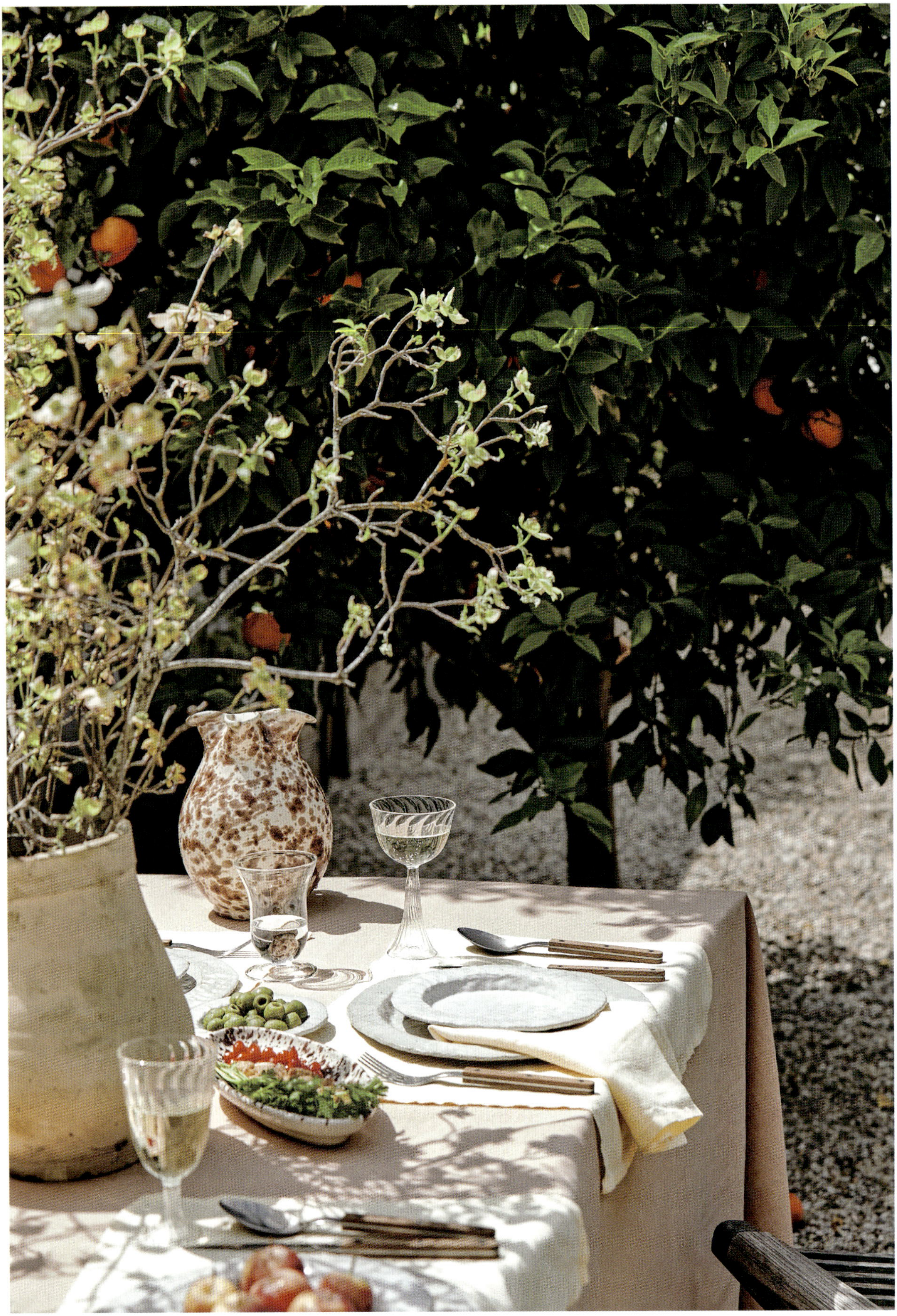

Alfresco Entertaining

From casual cookouts to chic garden soirées, hosting family and friends outdoors can be a pure delight, but if you're not well prepared, you'll find yourselves constantly running back and forth from your indoor kitchen to your backyard—and missing out on all the fun. With a bit of advance planning, though, you can get your alfresco entertaining essentials in order and be ready to put on an unforgettable, stress-free event, even at a moment's notice. Use this checklist to make sure you have all your bases covered so on the day of your next outdoor party, you can stay cool, calm, and collected.

Tableware: You don't want to run the risk of ruining your fine china or stoneware plates (and disposable plates are dreadful for the environment), so instead opt for chip-resistant ones made from melamine, bamboo, or a hardwood like acacia or walnut. For cups, look for shatterproof acrylic or BPA-free plastic, or, if you prefer glass barware, stemless varieties, which are less likely to be knocked over. Indoor cutlery is fine to use outside, but if you'd like a dedicated outdoor set, consider resin- or wood-handled flatware, which are particularly versatile and durable. As you build your collection, pick pieces that you would be just as proud to present at your indoor dining table, and those that you will be happy to use for years.

Of course, using your indoor tableware outdoors is always an option for seated meals, especially on special occasions. Mix these finer ceramics and glassware with relaxed linens and flatware to fit the bucolic setting.

Serving supplies: If you're presenting dishes family-style, you'll want to have serving utensils, platters, and bowls in varying sizes to offer you flexibility. Aim to have cohesive pieces that are stylistically similar, be it in shapes, motifs, materials, or colors (and keep your tableware in mind when choosing the designs). Utilize trays for smooth transportation and cleanup, food domes to protect food from insects, and a chic caddy for easy access to napkins, flatware, and condiments.

Hydration station: Pitchers and carafes are perfect for premixed drinks, while a standing or rolling cooler is ideal for packaged beverages,

Home Game

Keep guests amused and busy with some fun and friendly competition. From oversize editions of indoor favorites like jumbling towers to old-school lawn games like croquet and bocce ball to cookout classics like cornhole, the options here are many, so to help you pick, think of which one you would most enjoy playing when it's just the two of you.

Sun-Kissed 197

as is a party-size ice bucket—and don't forget bottle openers and corkscrews. An outdoor bar cart can be useful but is not necessary; a small table or even a potting bench can be designated as your bar instead. Use a large beverage dispenser for water, and enhance it, if you'd like, with sliced cucumbers, lemons, or oranges; fresh mint (use glass pebbles at the bottom of the container to keep pulp from clogging the spigot); or a dash of rose water.

Grill zone: If you have a grill, a set of quality barbecue tools—with a turner, basting brush, meat fork, tongs, and any other preferred cooking utensils—is essential, of course, while optional accessories include a grilling basket, saucepot, burger press, cast-iron skillet, and Himalayan salt block. The grill master will also need a nearby tabletop for food preparation and plating, so if there isn't one built in, consider a movable barbecue prep cart. Extra trimmings to acquire include a set of bar towels (for easy grease cleanup), a butcher block (for on-site carving), and a heat-resistant chef's apron in leather or cotton canvas.

Other comforts: Make your guests even more comfortable by adding plush floor poufs for bohemian-style seating, citronella candles to stave off mosquitos, portable fans for when the sun is blazing, and a basket of cozy throw blankets for when it gets chilly. And if you find that you regularly need more seating for guests, it's worth investing in a set of attractive, comfortable folding patio chairs.

REGISTER THIS

Gear up to glamp in your own backyard.

Picnic basket: A handwoven gourmet picnic basket packed with plates, flatware, and napkins.

Thermoses: A pair of mine-and-yours thermoses or Yeti or Stanley insulated bottles.

Camp lantern: A vintage-inspired portable camp lantern to light the way.

DATE NIGHT

WRITTEN IN THE STARS

During the next clear summer night, one when you can afford to stay up late, why not forgo your usual indoor plans and instead cozy up under the moonlight?

Put on a few layers and gather throw blankets, a flashlight, and some beverages (hot chocolate in thermoses is always a great idea) and get nestled in on your lawn, balcony, or even rooftop (if it's accessible and safe). You can make the experience extra special by arranging a nighttime picnic—perhaps even surprising your partner by prepping and setting it up in advance. Just lay a couple of picnic blankets down and spruce up the site with plenty of cushions and dim lanterns or fairy lights. Keep the treats simple—a cheese board or popcorn and a bottle of wine will do just fine. Or, if you have a firepit, light it up and roast some marshmallows for s'mores.

If the sky is especially dark one night or there's an astronomical event like a meteor shower on the calendar, you can turn your romantic night picnic into an epic stargazing date. Bust out a telescope or a pair of binoculars and chart the stars together, or use your naked eye to take it all in. As you revel in the cosmos and the company of your spouse, you might lose track of time—the perfect opportunity to catch the sunrise.

Outside the Box

You've created a lovely backyard that suits your needs, and you find yourselves spending more and more time there. If you realize that you are the sort of couple that prefers being outside, it's time to up the ante and elevate your outdoor digs by incorporating some special features. A simple way of conjuring a clear vision is to ask yourselves to tap into the perfect summer day spent at home together. What can you picture? Are you soaking up rays with a pitcher of sparkling sangria? Are you hosting a festive barbecue with friends? Are you having an alfresco brunch for two? Ruminate on your ideal scenarios and brainstorm ways to amplify those experiences. Here are some ideas to consider for your upgraded open-air lifestyle.

A fire feature or two will warm up the environment. Heat lamps, chimineas, and firepits can add a luxe touch to the setting and help you extend the season.

Permanent high-fidelity outdoor speakers can wash your outdoor space with the soundtrack of your choice. Some styles are designed to mimic rocks or stones that blend into the landscape, and others are devised to be mounted to the exterior of the house.

An elegant outdoor shower can be a striking and convenient addition for those with a pool, as can luxury fabric pool floats.

Water structures, whose soothing sounds can infuse your backyard with a sense of tranquility, are available in a range of shapes and sizes. Look for cast-stone styles, in classical or contemporary designs, which will develop a beautiful patina over time.

A weatherproof TV can round out the ultimate entertaining hub—allowing for movie nights under the stars or epic Super Bowl parties.

A wood-fired pizza oven for grown-up pizza parties makes the perfect alternative—or addition—to a traditional barbecue setup.

Natural gas firepits are easy-to-use, permanent fixtures. Propane gas firepits with replaceable tanks are portable (and more budget-friendly) alternatives. Woodburning varieties are the most classic campfire option for those who are up for tending a fire.

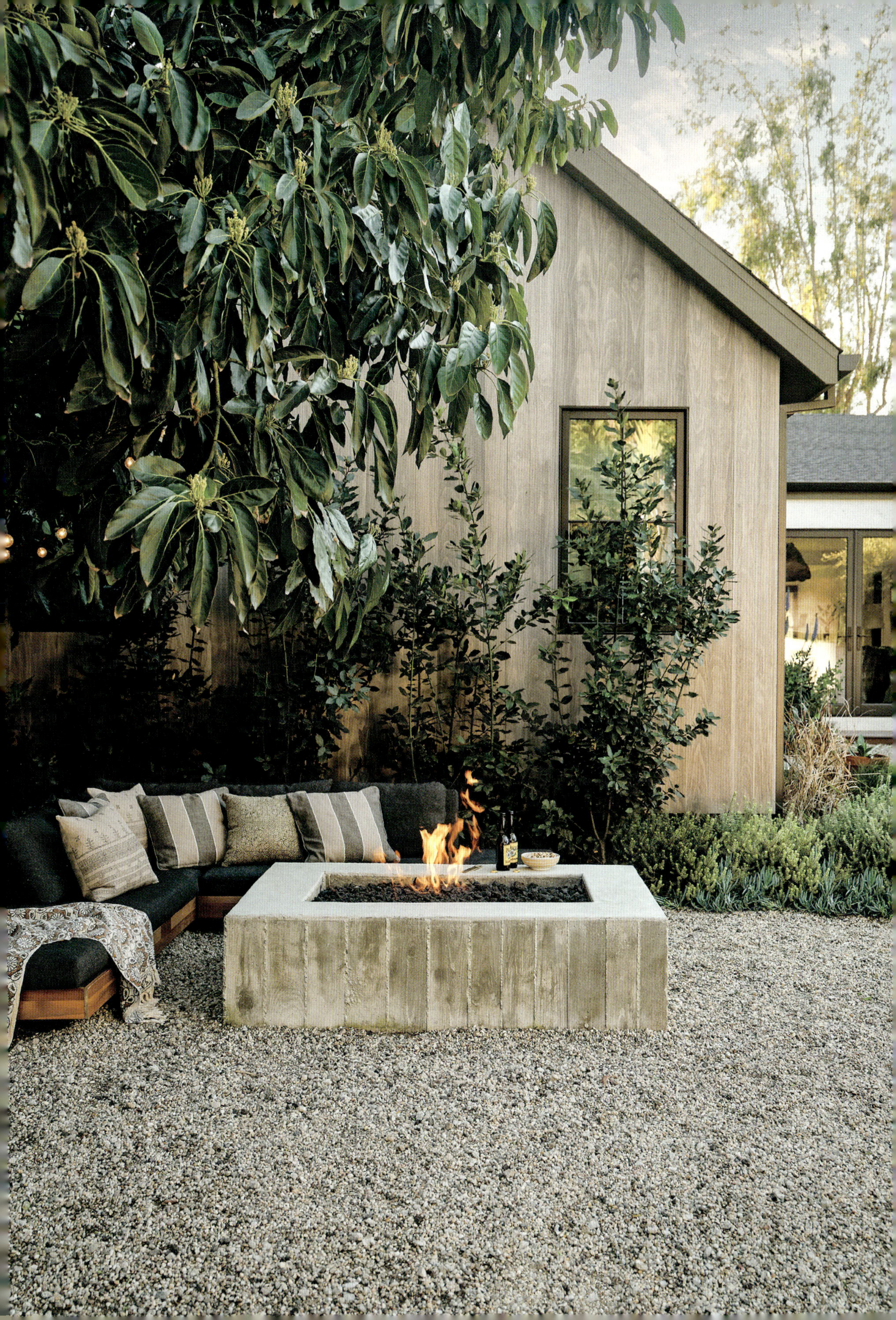

To Have and to Hold Onto

MERGING, EDITING, AND ORGANIZING

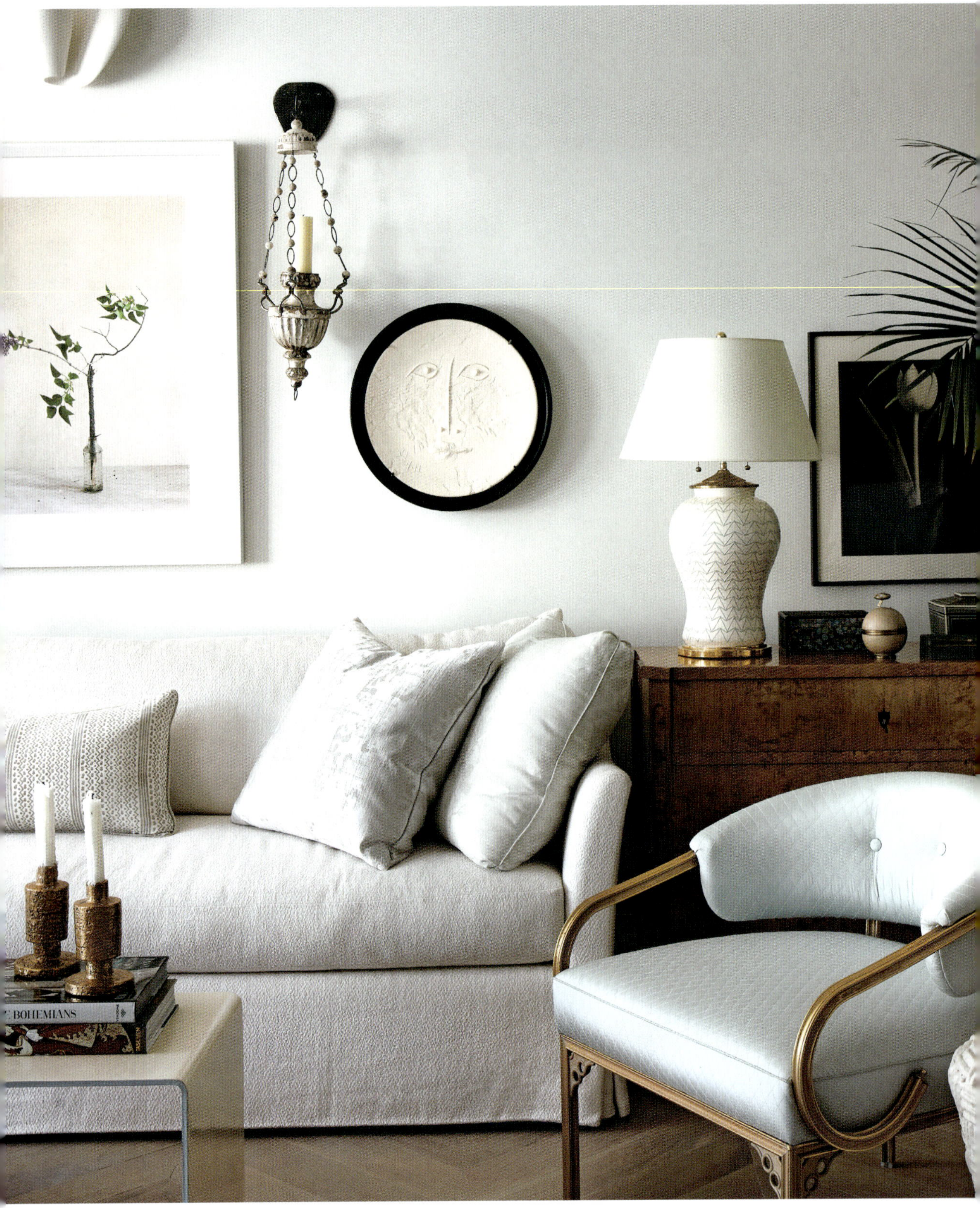
BOHEMIANS

In the end, the essence of a well-designed home is the love and attention that is put into the space. Your interiors don't have to meet some magazine-worthy standard—or, for that matter, anyone's standard but yours and your partner's—to be beautiful. When you are deliberate and caring with everything you bring into your home and the way in which you arrange and maintain it, that is when you are able to achieve a special, attractive, and comfortable abode that's designed for and around you.

This method of intentional curation starts not when you decide which new pieces to purchase but when you choose which things from your past you will each bring into your next phase. During this merging stage, it is so important to lead with compassion and reverence. Be kind to your partner and their belongings. You might really dislike something of theirs, but be mindful of how you express yourself. You never know how sentimental an item is for someone or how difficult it will be for them to part with it. Give your partner the courtesy of keeping things they can't let go of, and gently revisit the topic at a check-in date later on, like when you're spring-cleaning the home. In order to truly, meaningfully blend your lives and styles, you must never try to erase your partner's identity. Remember that it's both of you who will call your space home.

With a better grasp on what you will both be bringing to your new place, you can then open the door to what you still need—something old, something new, as it were—and turn the conversation to planning how you will organize your married life. The following are time-tested guidelines for merging, editing, and organizing your belongings to help you through these crucial initial steps. As you make headway, remember that not everything will be perfected on day one. Your home will evolve in tandem with your lives, and so it's only fair that you allow yourselves to rethink organizational systems, purge possessions regularly, or change your minds about certain features of your home. Your work at home is, in a way, never-ending, so if you wait for that definitive "at last I can sit back and enjoy it" moment, it may never come. Instead, cherish making a home together in all of its phases and practice gratitude whenever you can—toward both your home and your partner.

THE BIG EDIT

When two people come together, sometimes there is a lot of baggage—yes, actual baggage. Before you pack your things to move in, do the bulk of the legwork and independently cull your collections so that neither of you brings any unnecessary items to the new place. Use the flowchart opposite to help you edit your belongings and decide whether you should keep, mend, donate, sell, or toss an item, be it an article of clothing, a piece of furniture, a book, or kitchenware.

Use this same system to address any duplicate items between you once you merge your belongings. For furniture and décor, if both of your items are in keep-worthy shape, rely on your joint mood board (see page 15) and desired color palettes (see page 62) to help you choose which pieces fit best in your new shared home. For redundant equipment and appliances, do a closer side-by-side analysis to compare how old the items are, their conditions in relation to each other, and how well they would blend with the rest of your home (in size, colorways, and materials) to help you decide on the winner. Keep one, keep the other, or get a new replacement together, but avoid keeping both if there are no grounds for it. Take two televisions that are in similarly good condition, for example. If you realize you will benefit from having one in the living room and another in the "bonus" room, you can justify keeping both, but if you don't actually need that second TV, allow yourselves to let go of one to avoid stockpiling unnecessary belongings. This strategy will allow you to get off on the right foot with healthy habits (as clutter has been shown to have a negative effect on mental health) and start your new chapter in a streamlined new space.

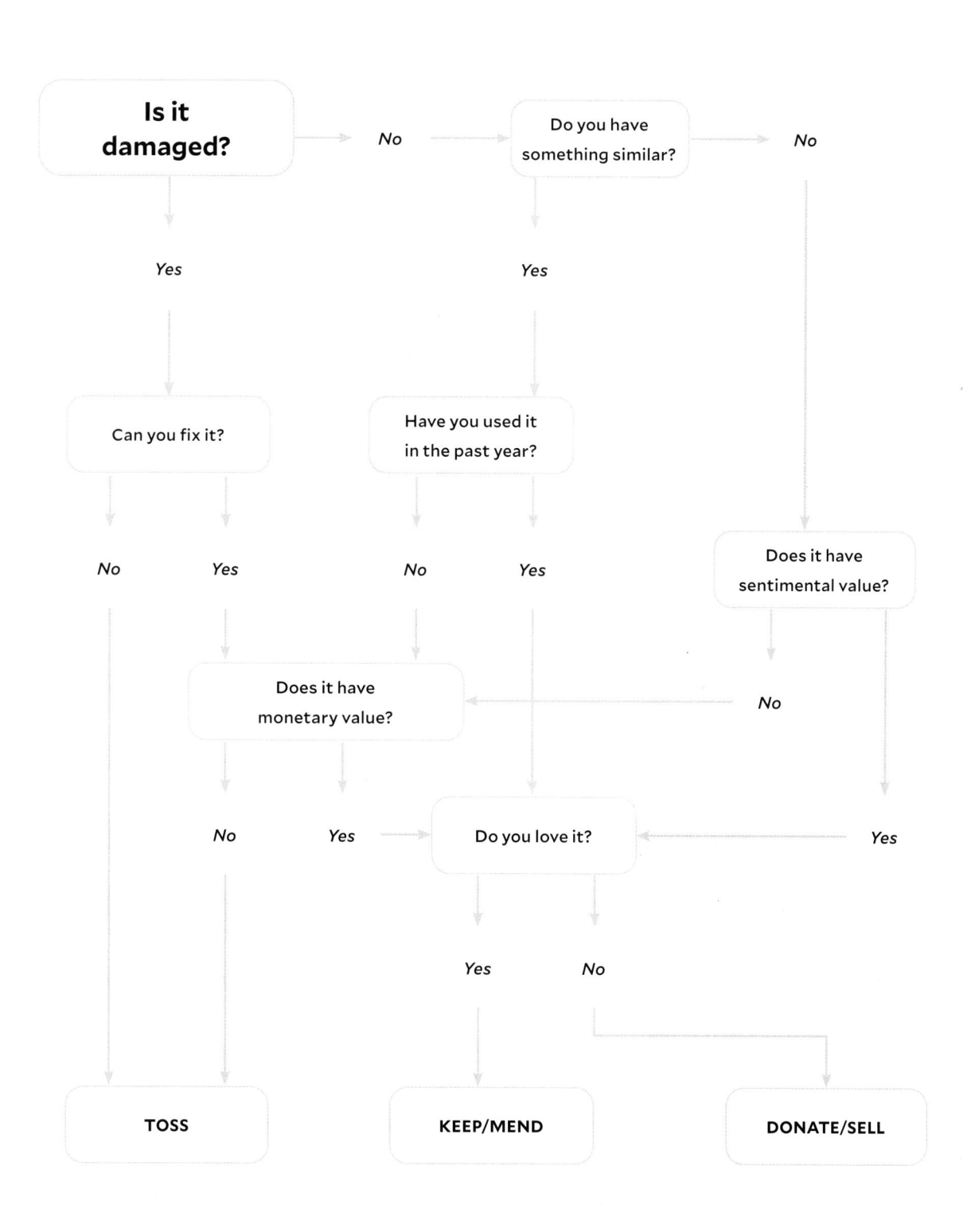

```
Is it damaged? ──No──▶ Do you have something similar? ──No──▶
     │                            │
     Yes                          Yes
     ▼                            ▼
Can you fix it?              Have you used it in the past year?
   │      │                        │        │
   No    Yes                       No       Yes
   │      │                        │        │
   │      ▼                        │        ▼
   │   Does it have monetary value? ◀───────┘
   │      │       │
   │      No     Yes
   │      │      │
   │      ▼      ▼
   │   Do you love it? ◀── Yes ── Does it have sentimental value?
   │      │     │                          │
   │     Yes    No                         No
   │      │     │                          │
   ▼      ▼     ▼                          ▼
 TOSS  KEEP/MEND  DONATE/SELL
```

To Have and to Hold Onto 207

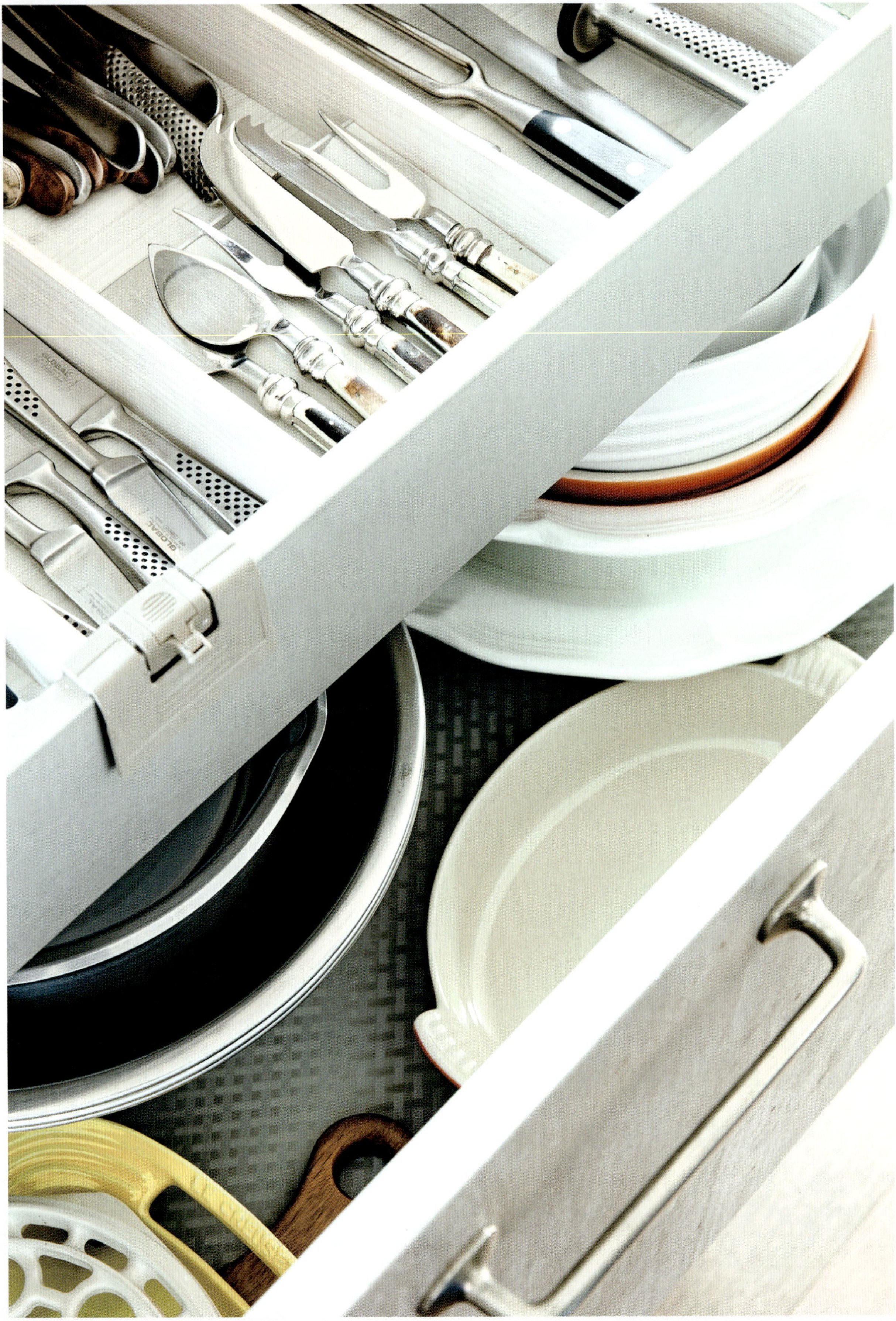
GLOBAL

ORGANIZING 101

The goal of organizing is not necessarily to make things look nice. Sure, that is a welcome side effect, but the true endgame is to make life easier, less stressful, and more peaceful for members of your household. A truly successful organizational system—be it for closets, drawers, cabinets, paperwork, shelves, sheds, or rooms themselves—is one that is intuitive and straightforwardly sustainable. There's no use in cleaning, categorizing, and tucking away items if you won't be able to remember where to find them or maintain that level of tidiness. So in order to get it right from the get-go, you must take into account how and by whom your systems will be used and come up with practices that are customized to you accordingly. Heed these key tenets of an organically well-organized space as you configure your home's unique solutions.

Everything should have its place. Designate a home for every single item, no matter how minute it seems—and be diligent about returning everything to its place. That way, you won't ever have to worry about not being able to find what you need.

Make essentials easily accessible. From the cleaning supplies under the kitchen sink to the skincare products in the bathroom medicine cabinet, keep the things that you need on a daily basis within arm's reach, and don't overcrowd any spaces, big or small.

Declutter often. Don't wait until things get out of hand to roll up your sleeves. Tidying and purging your home weekly (even daily) will allow you to maintain a comfortable lifestyle and avoid having to overhaul everything again and again.

Keep it simple. Not everyone thrives on detail-oriented features like printed labels and color-coding. If you do, then more power to you, but if you don't, that's totally okay. Find what level of commitment you and your partner can naturally sustain so that you aren't setting yourselves up for failure.

It's okay to change course. Like any other aspect of homelife, communication plays an important role in organization. If you're struggling to maintain the systems you've put in place, voice your dilemmas to your partner and work out the kinks together so you can get back on the same page.

Wedding Registry Checklist

KITCHEN AND COOKWARE

- ☐ Skillet
- ☐ Sauté pan
- ☐ Saucepan
- ☐ Roasting pan
- ☐ Stockpot
- ☐ Dutch oven
- ☐ Rondeau or braiser
- ☐ Bakeware (roasting pan, casserole dish, baking sheets, loaf pans, muffin tins, etc.)
- ☐ Salt and pepper shakers or mills
- ☐ Cooking knives (chef's knife, boning knife, paring knife, bread knife, etc.)
- ☐ Cutting boards
- ☐ Mixing bowl set
- ☐ Dish and tea towels
- ☐ Colander
- ☐ Cheese grater
- ☐ Measuring cups
- ☐ Cooking utensils set
- ☐ Food storage container set
- ☐ Stand mixer
- ☐ Stand mixer attachments (pasta roller and cutter, spiralizer, food grinder, etc.)
- ☐ Blender
- ☐ Food processor
- ☐ Rice cooker
- ☐ Toaster or toaster oven
- ☐ Air fryer
- ☐ Slow cooker
- ☐ Coffeemaker or espresso machine
- ☐ Teakettle

DINING AND ENTERTAINING

- ☐ Dinnerware sets
- ☐ Silverware sets
- ☐ Steak knives
- ☐ Water glasses
- ☐ Wineglasses
- ☐ Champagne flutes
- ☐ Mugs
- ☐ Espresso cups and saucers
- ☐ Teacups and saucers
- ☐ Teapot
- ☐ Creamer and sugar set
- ☐ Dessert plates
- ☐ Cereal bowls
- ☐ Cloth luncheon and/or dinner napkins
- ☐ Cloth cocktail napkins
- ☐ Coasters
- ☐ Napkin rings
- ☐ Place mats
- ☐ Chargers
- ☐ Centerpiece
- ☐ Tablecloths
- ☐ Table runners
- ☐ Place card holders
- ☐ Serving utensils
- ☐ Serving platters and trays
- ☐ Serving bowls
- ☐ Soup tureen
- ☐ Gravy boat
- ☐ Cake stand
- ☐ Trivets
- ☐ Cheese boards
- ☐ Cheese knives and spreaders
- ☐ Specialty barware and tools
- ☐ Decanters
- ☐ Wine chiller
- ☐ Ice trays
- ☐ Ice bucket and tongs
- ☐ Pitchers and carafes

BED AND BATH LINENS

- ☐ Sheet sets
- ☐ Comforter
- ☐ Duvet insert
- ☐ Duvet cover
- ☐ Blanket/quilt
- ☐ Sleeping pillows
- ☐ Decorative pillows
- ☐ Pillow shams
- ☐ Mattress topper
- ☐ Mattress pad
- ☐ Linen spray
- ☐ Towel sets
- ☐ Washcloths
- ☐ Bathrobes
- ☐ Shower curtain

HOME DÉCOR AND EXTRAS

- ☐ Picture frames
- ☐ Stationery
- ☐ Artworks
- ☐ Coffee-table books
- ☐ Bookends
- ☐ Lamps
- ☐ Throw blankets
- ☐ Throw pillows
- ☐ Candles
- ☐ Candleholders
- ☐ Decorative bowls and trays
- ☐ Bath accessories
- ☐ Hamper
- ☐ Storage baskets and bins
- ☐ Closet organizers
- ☐ Iron and ironing board
- ☐ Steamer
- ☐ Vacuum
- ☐ Air purifier
- ☐ Planters, plant pots, and saucers
- ☐ Vases
- ☐ Bar cart
- ☐ Unique collectibles
- ☐ Hobby and sports equipment
- ☐ Deluxe-edition board games
- ☐ Workout equipment
- ☐ Smart home devices
- ☐ Luggage and travel accessories
- ☐ Experiential tickets, passes, or memberships

OUTDOOR ENTERTAINING AND DÉCOR

- ☐ Outdoor tableware
- ☐ Outdoor serveware
- ☐ Outdoor speakers
- ☐ Bird feeders/birdhouses
- ☐ Planters/pots
- ☐ Wreaths
- ☐ Grill
- ☐ Grilling tools set
- ☐ Gardening tools set
- ☐ Pizza oven
- ☐ Picnic basket
- ☐ Thermoses
- ☐ Camp lantern
- ☐ Lawn games
- ☐ Firepit

Resources

FURNITURE, ART, AND DÉCOR

1stDibs
1stdibs.com

Anthropologie Home
anthropologie.com

The Artling
theartling.com

CB2
cb2.com

Chairish
chairish.com

Crate & Barrel
crateandbarrel.com

Design Within Reach
dwr.com

EstateSales.NET
estatesales.net

Etsy
etsy.com

Everything But The House
ebth.com

From the Bay
fromthebay.com

Garde
gardeshop.com

General Store
shop-generalstore.com

H&M Home
hm.com/home

HomeGoods
homegoods.com

JM Upholstery, Inc.
jmupholsteryinc.com

John Derian Company
johnderian.com

LiveAuctioneers
liveauctioneers.com

Lumens
lumens.com

March
marchsf.com

MG&Co.
us.matildagoad.com

Nickey Kehoe
nickeykehoe.com

Pierce & Ward
pierceandward.com

Pottery Barn
potterybarn.com

Prize
prizeantiques.com

Rejuvenation
rejuvenation.com

Room & Board
roomandboard.com

Ruby Lane
rubylane.com

Serena & Lily
serenaandlily.com

Shoppe Amber Interiors
shoppe.amberinteriordesign.com

Tappan Collective
tappancollective.com

West Elm
westelm.com

Zara Home
zarahome.com

COOKING AND DINING

All-Clad
all-clad.com

Breville
breville.com

Chemex
chemexcoffeemaker.com

Duralex
duralexusa.com

Emile Henry
emilehenryusa.com

Farmhouse Pottery
farmhousepottery.com

glassybaby
glassybaby.com

Heath Ceramics
heathceramics.com

Il Buco Vita
ilbucovita.com

Jono Pandolfi
jonopandolfi.com

Miyabi
zwilling.com

Sur La Table
surlatable.com

KitchenAid
kitchenaid.com

Nespresso
nespresso.com

Vermicular
vermicular.us

Libbey
shop.libbey.com

Our Place
fromourplace.com

Wedgwood
wedgwood.com

Le Creuset
lecreuset.com

Royal Copenhagen
royalcopenhagen.com

Williams Sonoma
williams-sonoma.com

Lodge
lodgecastiron.com

Shun
shun.kaiusa.com

Wüsthof
wusthof.com

LoQ
loq.us

SMEG
smeg.com

Year & Day
yearandday.com

Mauviel 1830
mauviel.com

Staub
staub-cookware.com

Zwilling
zwilling.com

BATH AND BEDDING

Bed Threads
bedthreads.com

Kassatex
kassatex.com

Quince
quince.com

Brooklinen
brooklinen.com

Matteo
matteola.com

Ralph Lauren Home
ralphlauren.com/home

The Company Store
thecompanystore.com

Parachute
parachutehome.com

Snowe
snowehome.com

Coyuchi
coyuchi.com

Peacock Alley
peacockalley.com

Garnet Hill
garnethill.com

Piglet in Bed
pigletinbed.com

TEXTILES, WALLPAPER, AND PAINT

Bed Threads
bedthreads.com

Bolé Road Textiles
boleroadtextiles.com

Claremont
claremontfurnishing.com

Benjamin Moore
benjaminmoore.com

Brook Perdigon Textiles
brookperdigontextiles.com

Dunn-Edwards
dunnedwards.com

Behr
behr.com

Chasing Paper
chasingpaper.com

Farrow & Ball
farrow-ball.com

Block Shop
blockshoptextiles.com

Clare
clare.com

House of Hackney
us.houseofhackney.com

Liberty
libertylondon.com

Little Greene
littlegreene.us

Lorena Canals
lorenacanals.com

Manuel Canovas
manuelcanovas.com

Natasha Baradaran
natashabaradaran.com

Nasiri Carpets
nasiricarpets.com

Perennials
perennialsfabrics.com

Portola Paints
portolapaints.com

Scalamandré
scalamandre.com

Schumacher
schumacher.com

Seema Krish
seemakrish.com

Serena Dugan Studio
serenadugan.com

Sherwin-Williams
sherwin-williams.com

St. Frank
stfrank.com

Tufenkian
tufenkian.com

The Wallpaper Company
thewallpapercompany.com

Zoffany
zoffany.sandersondesigngroup.com

PLANTS AND OUTDOOR FURNISHINGS

Bloomscape
bloomscape.com

Business & Pleasure Co.
businessandpleasureco.com

Garden Glory
gardenglory.com

Garden Goods Direct
gardengoodsdirect.com

Logee's
logees.com

Lulu and Georgia
luluandgeorgia.com

Oliver James Lilos
oliverjameslilos.com

Polywood
polywood.com

Roger's Gardens
rogersgardens.com

SarahCotta Plants
sarahcottaplants.com

Serena & Lily
serenaandlily.com

The Sill
thesill.com

Stone Yard, Inc.
stoneyardinc.com

Sutherland
sutherlandfurniture.com

Terrain
shopterrain.com

Yardbird
yardbird.com

FEATURED INTERIOR DESIGNERS AND ARCHITECTS

Alisa Bloom
alisab.com

A-List Interiors
alistinteriors.com

Allegra O. Eifler Design
allegraoeifler.com

Andrew Howard
andrewjhoward.com

Artistree Home
artistreehome.com

Ashe Leandro
asheleandro.com

Billy Cotton
billycotton.com

Brady Tolbert
bradytolbert.com

Butter Lutz Interior
butterlutz.com

Carly Waters Style
carlywatersstyle.com

Casamota
casamota.com

CAVdesign
cavdesign.com

Christopher Knight Interiors
christopherknightint@icloud.com

D.L. Rhein
dlrhein.com

Dana Ferraro of Molly Patton Design
mollypattondesign.com

De-spec
de-spec.com

De Sousa Hughes
desousahughes.com

Eliza Gran Studio
elizagranstudio.com

Ferguson & Shamamian
fergusonshamamian.com

Fragments Identity
fragmentsidentity.com

Frederick Tang Architecture
fredericktang.com

Hadley Wiggins
hadleywiggins.com

Heidi Caillier Design
heidicaillierdesign.com

Interiors by Patrick
patricktennantinteriors.com

Jamie Haller
jamiehaller.com

John De Bastiani Interiors
johndd.com

John Dittrick
johndittrickstyle.com

Julia Chasman Design
juliachasmandesign.com

Kati Curtis Design
katicurtisdesign.com

Kureck Jones LLC
kureckjones.com

Mark D. Sikes
markdsikes.com

Mercantile and Merchant
mercantileandmerchant.com

Nathan Turner
nathanturner.com

Nickey Kehoe
nickeykehoe.com

Raili CA Design
railicadesign.com

Robert Passal
robertpassal.com

Perella Architecture, Inc.
perellaarchitecture.com

Povero & Company
poandco.com

Ray Booth
raybooothdesign.com

Sarah Jacoby Architect
sarahjacobyarchitect.com

Simo Design
simodesign.com

Studio AK
studioakinteriors.com

Stephen Earle
stephenearledesign.com

Studio Mellone
studiomellone.com

Thomas Hamel & Associates
thomashamel.com

Tom Scheerer, Inc.
tomscheerer.com

Una Malan
unamalan.com

Photography Credits

Page 2: Photo by Joe Schmelzer/OTTO. Designed by Mercantile and Merchant.

Page 5: Photo by Lisa Romerein/OTTO. Home of Lee Rhodes.

Page 8: Photo by Noe DeWitt/OTTO. Designed by Jeffery Povero. Home of photographer Noe DeWitt.

Page 12: Photo by Stephen Kent Johnson/OTTO. Designed by Billy Cotton.

Page 14: Photo by Noe DeWitt/OTTO. Designed by homeowner Ariel Ashe.

Pages 16–17: Background by str33tcat/Shutterstock, Inc.

Page 18: Photo by Jenna Peffley/OTTO. Designed by Carly Waters.

Page 22: Photo by Tim Williams/Trunk Archive. Designed by Studio AK.

Page 24, left: Photo by Roger Davies/OTTO. Designed by homeowners Nathan Turner and Eric Hughes.

Page 24, right: Photo by Stephen Kent Johnson/OTTO. Designed by Christopher Knight.

Page 25, left: Photo by Eric Piasecki/OTTO. Designed by Kureck Jones.

Page 25, right: Photo by Kelly Marshall/OTTO.

Page 27, top: Photo by New Africa/Adobe Stock.

Page 27, bottom: Photo by Francesco Lagnese/OTTO. Designed by Tom Scheerer.

Page 28, top: Photo by Isabel Parra/OTTO. Designed by Alisa Bloom.

Page 28, bottom: Photo by David A. Land/OTTO. Designed by Frederick Tang Architecture.

Page 29, top: Photo by Eric Piasecki/OTTO. Designed by homeowner Anne Miller.

Page 29, bottom: Photo by Lisa Romerein/OTTO. Designed by homeowner Raili Clasen of Raili CA Design.

Page 33: Photo by David A. Land/OTTO. Designed by homeowner John Dittrick.

Page 35: Photo by Lisa Romerein/OTTO. Designed by Heidi Caillier.

Pages 36–37: Background by Efefne Design/Shutterstock, Inc.

Pages 38–39: Photo by Jenna Peffley/OTTO. Home of Shiza Shahid.

Page 42: Photo by Lisa Romerein/OTTO.

Page 44, top left: Photo by Liudmila/Adobe Stock.

Page 44, top right: Photo courtesy of Room & Board. Room & Board André sofa in Pelham Ink plain weave fabric with Charcoal Stain finish legs.

Page 44, bottom left: Photo courtesy of Crate & Barrel. Crate & Barrel Avondale sofa in Tessa fabric in Pebble.

Page 44, bottom right: Photo courtesy of Serena & Lily. Serena & Lily Miramar English Roll Arm sofa in Blush washed linen fabric with Earth leg color.

Page 47: Photo by BG Collection/Gallery Stock.

Page 48: Photo by Michael Grimm/Gallery Stock.

Page 50: Photo by BG Collection/Gallery Stock.

Page 52: Photo by Björn Wallander/OTTO. Designed by Carlos Mota.

Page 55: Photo by Liza Voloshin/Gallery Stock.

Page 56: Photo by Jenna Peffley/OTTO. Designed by Artistree Home.

Page 59: Photos by Shutterstock, Inc.

Page 61: Photo by Kelly Marshall/OTTO. Designed by CAVdesign.

Page 63: Photo by Tim Lenz/OTTO. Designed by Allegra O. Eifler Design.

Pages 64–65: Background by lovie/Shutterstock, Inc.

Pages 66–67: Photo by Jenna Peffley/OTTO. Designed by Jamie Haller.

Page 70: Photo by Jenna Peffley/OTTO. Designed by Julia Chasman Design.

Page 73: Photo by BG Collection/Gallery Stock.

Page 74: Photo by BG Collection/Gallery Stock.

Page 80, left: Photo by dolphy_tv/Adobe Stock.

Page 80, right: Photo by Peter Bagi/Gallery Stock.

Page 81, left: Photo by Christopher Testani/Gallery Stock.

Page 81, right: Photo by Александра Туркина/Adobe Stock.

Page 83: Photo by David Tsay/OTTO. Designed by homeowner Mary Emmerling.

Page 85: Photo by Esin Deniz/Adobe Stock.

Page 88: Photo by Trevor Tondro/OTTO. Designed by Heidi Caillier.

Pages 90–91: Background by Ana Krasavina/Shutterstock, Inc.

Pages 92–93: Photo by Jenna Peffley/OTTO. Home of Eliza Gran.

Page 97: Photo by Michael Turek/Gallery Stock.

Page 98: Photo by BG Collection/Gallery Stock.

Page 101: Photo by Matt Dutile/Gallery Stock.

Page 102: Photo by David Tsay/OTTO. Designed by homeowner Brady Tolbert.

Page 104, top left: Photo by Rawpixel.com/Adobe Stock.

Page 104, top right: Photo courtesy of Room & Board. Room & Board Glover round dining table with marbled white quartz top and oak with rye stain base.

Page 104, bottom left: Photo courtesy of Crate & Barrel. Crate & Barrel Ambrose Mappa Burl Wood dining table.

Page 104, bottom right: Photo courtesy of Serena & Lily. Serena & Lily Lake House expandable dining table in weathered oak.

Page 106: Photo by Ty Cole/OTTO. Designed by Sarah Jacoby Architect.

Page 113: Photo by Tim Lenz/OTTO. Designed by Dana Ferraro of Molly Patton Design.

Page 115: Photo by Brittany Ambridge/OTTO. Designed by A-List Interiors.

Page 116: Photos by Shutterstock, Inc.

Page 119: Photo by Svetlana Khutornaia/Adobe Stock.

Pages 120-121: Background by Amovitania/Shutterstock, Inc.

Pages 122-123: Photo by Jenna Peffley/OTTO. Designed by homeowner Natalie Saunders.

Page 126: Photo by okkijan2010/Adobe Stock.

Page 130, left: Photo by Stephen Kent Johnston/OTTO. Designed by Studio Mellone.

Page 130, right: Photo by Joe Schmelzer/OTTO. Designed by Una Malan.

Page 131, left: Photo by BG Collection/Gallery Stock.

Page 131, right: Photo by Douglas Friedman/Trunk Archive. Designed by Butter Lutz Interior.

Page 134: Photo by Jenna Peffley/OTTO. Designed by D.L. Rhein.

Page 137: Photo by BG Collection/Gallery Stock.

Page 138: Photo by BG Collection/Gallery Stock.

Page 141: Photo by Joe Schmelzer/OTTO. Designed by Patrick Tennant.

Page 142: Photo by Frank Oudeman/OTTO. Designed by De-spec.

Page 145: Photo by Paul Raeside/OTTO. Home of Keith McNally.

Pages 146-147: Background by Rodina Olena/Shutterstock, Inc.

Pages 148-149: Photo by Joe Schmelzer/OTTO. Designed by Simo Design.

Page 151: Photo by Roger Davies/OTTO. Designed by Nickey Kehoe.

Page 154: Photo by Lisa Romerein/OTTO. Designed by Ferguson & Shamamian.

Page 159: Photo by Jenna Peffley/OTTO.

Page 162: Photo by Eric Piasecki/OTTO. Designed by homeowner Andrew Howard.

Pages 164-165: Background by Faisal Dhany/Shutterstock, Inc.

Pages 166-167: Photo by Trevor Tondro/OTTO. Designed by Thomas Hamel.

Page 171: Photo by Brittany Ambridge/OTTO. Designed by Kati Curtis. Office of Kati Curtis Design.

Page 174, left: Photo by Trevor Tondro/OTTO.

Page 174, right: Photo by Kelly Marshall/OTTO.

Page 175, left: Photo by William Waldron/OTTO. Home of John Alexander.

Page 175, right: Photo by Eric Piasecki/OTTO. Designed by Stephen Earle.

Page 176: Photo by Roger Davies/OTTO. Designed by Nickey Kehoe.

Pages 180-181: Background by OlgaStock/Shutterstock, Inc.

Pages 182-183: Photo by Jenna Peffley/OTTO. Designed by D.L. Rhein.

Page 186: Photo by Joe Schmelzer/OTTO. Designed by homeowner Mark D. Sikes.

Page 188: Photo by Jenna Peffley/OTTO. Designed by Tammy Price of Fragments Identity. Home of Abigail Spencer.

Page 191: Photo by Eric Piasecki/OTTO. Designed by homeowner Ray Booth.

Page 192: Photo by Joe Schmelzer/OTTO. Designed by John De Bastiani Interiors.

Page 193, top left: Photo courtesy of Room & Board. Room & Board Palm sofa with right-arm chaise in Nevan Gray tweed fabric with Black legs.

Page 193, top right: Photo courtesy of Business & Pleasure. Business & Pleasure Al Fresco sun lounger in Rivie Green with Vintage Black frame.

Page 193, bottom left: Photo courtesy of POLYWOOD. POLYWOOD Long Island Adirondack two-piece set in POLYWOOD Heritage Green.

Page 193, bottom right: Photo courtesy of Serena & Lily. Serena & Lily Capistrano daybed in Driftwood finish and Chalk Perennials Performance basketweave fabric.

Page 195: Photo by David A. Land/OTTO. Designed by Hadley Wiggins-Marin.

Page 196: Photo by Jenna Peffley/OTTO. Home of Valerie Quant.

Page 201: Photo by Joe Schmelzer/OTTO. Designed by Ryan Perella. Home of Sam Donnelly.

Pages 202-203: Background by Zalevska/Shutterstock, Inc.

Pages 204-205: Photo by Stephen Kent Johnston/OTTO. Designed by Robert Passal.

Page 208: Photo by Joe Schmelzer/OTTO. Home of Ludo Lefebvre.

Acknowledgments

From the bottom of my heart, I'd like to express my unwavering gratitude to the following people, each of whom helped make this book possible:

My agent, Katherine Cowles. Thank you for taking a chance on me. I will never forget our very first conversation, which launched a new chapter in my life and left me feeling more inspired than ever before. Getting to write this book was a dream come true, and without you, I would not be here.

Melissa Goldstein, my friend and former colleague, who introduced me to Katherine. I can't thank you enough for not only thinking of me but believing in me. To be cheered on by an accomplished, talented writer and editor like yourself is a gift I truly cherish.

My brilliant editor, Bridget Monroe Itkin, to whom I owe my deepest gratitude. You have been a remarkable collaborator and guide, and I could not have asked for a better editor for my authorial debut. Thank you for trusting me with this wonderful project and allowing me to explore my ideas freely. Thank you, also, for your time, patience, insights, and perfect suggestions, and for shepherding *The Newlywed Home* so expertly and thoughtfully from beginning to end. This book is as much yours as it is mine.

The visionary creative director Suet Chong, who undertook the design of this special tome. Thank you for lending your expert eye to this project, and for making it look and feel exactly how I hoped it would.

And the rest of the mighty, world-class team at Artisan and Workman Publishing who had a role in the making of this book: publisher Lia Ronnen, production and managing editor Hillary Leary, copyeditor Sibylle Kazeroid, editorial assistant Julia Perry, typesetter Elissa Santos, production director Nancy Murray, production manager Donna Brown, associate publisher Zach Greenwald, and publicity/marketing mavens MacKenzie Collier and Amy Michelson. I sincerely thank you all for the tremendous amount of work you put in for *The Newlywed Home*. I am forever indebted to you for this rewarding experience.

Photo editor extraordinaire Lauren Schumacher White, who so generously signed on to help source and curate the photography: Though I must have thanked you a million times already for your assistance and hard work, I can thank you a million times more. You were instrumental in the making of this book, and I am beyond grateful for your dedication, time, and friendship.

My parents, Diana and Caruso Benliyan, and my parents-in-law, Noune and Artashes Kartalyan. My eternal gratitude goes to you for your unconditional, steadfast support, to say nothing of the incalculable amount of babysitting you graciously provided that enabled me to write this book in the first place. I am incredibly blessed to have such bright beacons in my life.

My brother, Filip Benliyan. Thank you for always checking in on me and my progress, and for rooting for me not just on this project but throughout my life. You were my first literary influence, inspiring me to read and write from an early age, and you taught me to trust my creative instinct and push myself past my comfort zone.

My tatik (grandmother) Manik Harmanjian and aunt Arshaluys Harmanjyan. Thank you for sharing your prized family recipes for this book and for spending all those painstaking hours in the kitchen with me as we perfected them.

My sister-friends Anna Mkhikian, Jacklin Maisyan, Mary Panosian, Anna Albaryan, and Katya Rosen. Thank you for holding my hand as I wrote this book—for always giving me a boost when I needed it, helping me find my footing when I lost it, and genuinely celebrating my achievements alongside me.

Special thanks to Sarah Bazik of SarahCotta Plants for lending your botanical expertise for this book—and for beautifying my home with the most exquisite flora.

To the teachers, editors, and mentors I've been lucky enough to have over the years, among them Dr. Carol M. Burke, Amy DePaul, Barry Siegel, Eric Mercado, Bruce Wallin, Michalene Busico, Jenny Murray, and Lesley McKenzie: You helped me find my voice at different stages of my career, and I am so honored and grateful to have crossed paths with each of you. And to the late, great Andrea B. Stanford, my first interior design editor, whose enduring style continues to inspire me today and whose kind words of support still ring in my ears. I miss you dearly.

Most of all, I'd like to thank the love of my life, my husband, Ashot Kartalyan. No one knows the amount of work that went into writing this book more than you, and no one was more monumental in helping me cross the finish line. Thank you for being my person—for tolerating my late nights; brainstorming with me; proofreading my drafts; providing strength, motivation, and comfort around the clock; and devotedly supporting me in every way. I could not have done this without you, and I love you more than you will ever know.

Finally, my darling little boy, Roman Kartalyan, who was barely six months old when I began working on this project. The period it took me to complete this book is one that I will treasure forever. It was my first time being a mother and my first time authoring a book—and I couldn't be prouder of bringing them up together.

Index

Page numbers in *italic* indicate photos.

A

accent lighting, 49, 108
Adirondack chairs, *193*
air quality, 57, 133
ambient lighting, 49
appliances
   for hybrid kitchen, 75
   for minimalist kitchen, 72
   registering for, 210
   replacing, 76
   specialty, 80, *80,* 81, *81*
art
   bathroom, *154*
   bedroom, 136, *137*
   "bonus" room, 172, 179
   creative studio for, 173
   entryway, 19, 32, *33*
   hallway, 34
   kitchen, 71
   living room, 54
   in outdoor spaces, *194,* 195
   registering for, 210
   stairway gallery, 34, *35*
authenticity, 10, 123. *See also* personalization

B

backyards. *See* outdoor spaces
balconies, 189. *See also* outdoor spaces
bar carts, 114, *115*
bars
   in "bonus" room, 173
   in dining room, 114, *115, 116,* 117
   outdoor, 197–198
bath for two, 160–161
bathrobes, 158
bathrooms, *148–149,* 149
   guest, *162,* 163
   organizing, 156–157
   personalizing, 158, *159*
   registering for items, 158, 210
   sharing, 150–152, *151*
   updating, 153, *154,* 155
bathtubs, *154,* 155, 160
bed frames, 129

bedding, 132, *134,* 134–135, 144, 210
bedrooms, *8, 122–123,* 123
   art above bed, 136, *137*
   bedding, 132, *134,* 134–135, 144, 210
   beds, *130,* 130–131, *131,* 144, *145*
   best practices for, 132–133
   clothes storage in, *142,* 143
   guest rooms, 144, *145*
   sleeping issues, 124–125
   mattresses, *126,* 127–129
   nightstands, *138,* 138–139
   recreating resort luxuries in, 140, *141*
   registering for items, 135, 210
   sleeping issues, 124–125
   window coverings, 133
beds, *130,* 130–131, *131,* 144, *145*
belongings, 10
   editing, 206–207
   merging, 205, 206
   organizing, 209
benches, 23, 107, 187
big-ticket items/projects
   for "bonus" room, 170
   couches, 43–45, *44*
   dining tables, 103–105, *104*
   kitchen renovation, 76–77
   mattresses, *126,* 127–129
   painting exterior of house, 187
   patio sets, 190, *191–193,* 193
board games, 100, 173
"bonus" rooms, *166–167,* 167
   collaborating on use of, 168–169
   designing, 170, *171*
   as home office, *176,* 176–177
   possible vignettes for, 172–175
   registering for items, 170
   separating stations in, *174,* 174–175, *175*
   sharing space in, 177
   style for, 179
bookends, 51
books/libraries, *50,* 50–51, 89, 172
box spring beds, 130, *130*
box springs, 129

C

cabinets
   bar, 114
   bathroom, 156
   curio, 53
   entryway, 23, 28, *28*
   kitchen, 71, *73,* 76
   living room, 53
camp lanterns, 198
ceiling light fixtures, 49
centerpieces, 100
chairs
   "bonus" room, 175, *175*
   dining room, *106,* 107
   entryway, 23
   as nightstands, *138*
   outdoor, 187, 189
   patio sets, 190, *191–193,* 193
chaises, 44, *188,* 189, *193*
chandeliers, 108
chargers, 96
chef's knife, 79
Cherry Stem Cordial, 118, *119*
chesterfield couch, *44*
chimineas, 200
closets
   bedroom, *142,* 143
   entryway, 28
   guest room, 144
   as home offices, 176
   storage, 29
clothes storage, 28, *28,* 132, *142,* 143
cocktail napkins, 100
cocktail station, *116,* 117
cocktail table, 46
cocktails, signature, 114
coffee table, 41, 46, *47*
coffee-table books, 51
collages, creating, 15
colors
   bathroom, 155
   bedroom, 132
   curtain, 133
   dinnerware, 99
   exterior of house, 187
   kitchen, 71, 72, *73*
   living room, 62, *63*
   outdoor spaces, 193, 194

communication/conversations, 11
  collaborating on "bonus" room use, 168–169
  establishing "house rules," 20–21
  finding kitchen style, 68–69
  functions of living rooms, 40–41
  fundamentals of, 11
  gardens, 184–185
  hosting as a couple, 94–95
  setting the tone for your home, 13, *112*
  sharing a bathroom, 150–152, *151*
consoles, 23, 32
cookware, 78, 79, 210
copper sauté pan, 79
couches, 25, *25*, 43–45, *44,* 144
creative studio, 169, 173. *See also* "bonus" rooms
culling belongings, 206–207
curb appeal, *186,* 187
curio cabinets, 53
curtains, 133

D

date night
  bath for two, 160–161
  game nights, 112, *113*
  moonlight cozying, 199
  mystery box for, 31
  Nostalgia Theater, 60, *61*
  in outdoor spaces, 199
  preparing meals together, 82, *83*
  recreating resort luxuries in bedroom, 140, *141*
  sharing new pursuits together, 178
daybed, *193*
décor and details. *See also* art; personalization
  bathroom, 157, 158
  bedroom, 136, *137,* 138–139
  "bonus" room, 86
  coffee table, 46, *47*
  cozy kitchen spot, 86
  entryway, 19, 24, 30, 32, *33*
  guest bathroom, *162,* 163
  guest bedroom, 144, *145*
  hallways, 34
  kitchen, *70,* 72, 75, 76, *88,* 89
  living room, *52,* 53
  outdoor spaces, 187, 194

registering for, 210
design, 205. *See also* décor and details; *individual spaces*
  bedroom, 123
  "bonus" room, 170, *171,* 179
  creating shared vision for, 15
  dining room, 107, 108
  entryway, 23
  guest bathroom, 163
  living room, 40, 43–46
  outdoor spaces, 183, 189, 190, 193–194, *195*
  plants in, 57, 58
  in setting tone of home, 13
  as teammates, 10
dining rooms, *92,* 93
  bar cart/cabinet, 114, *115, 116,* 117
  dining table, 103–105, *104*
  dinner parties, 94–96, *97, 98,* 99, 100, *101*
  lighting, 108
  registering for items, 96, 99, 100, 210
  seating, *106,* 107
  table setting, 110, *110–111*
dining tables, 103–105, *104,* 189
dinner napkins, *98,* 99
dinner parties, 94–96, *97, 98,* 99, 100, *101*
dinnerware, 96, *97,* 99, 100, *110–111*
dividing rooms/areas
  "bonus" room, 168, *174,* 174–175, *175*
  dining areas, 105
  entryway, 24, *24*
  outdoor, 189
drapes, 133
Dutch oven, 79
duvets, 134, 135

E

English roll arm couch, *44*
entertaining, 109
  dinner parties, 94–96, *97, 98,* 99, 100, *101*
  in living room, 39, 41
  in outdoor spaces, 189, *196,* 197–198
  pre-entertaining tasks, 109
  registering for items, 210
entryway, *18–19,* 19
  composition of, *22,* 23

defining, 24–25, *24–25*
detail components, 30, 32, *33*
first impression made by, 19
guest book in, 30
party favors in, 30
registering for items, 32
storage in, 19, 23, 26–29, *27–29*
étagères, 175, *175*
expectations of partners, 10
experiences, registering for, 170

F

firepits, 199, 200, *201*
fireplaces, 54, *55*
first impressions
  from entryway, 19
  from exterior of house, *186,* 187
flatware, 96, 99, 100, *110–111, 196,* 197
floor coverings, 25, *25,* 34, 89, 194
flooring, bathroom, 155
footboards, 131, *131*
furnishing a home. *See also individual spaces*
  combining/editing personal belongings in, 205–207
  organization system for, 209
  personal standards for, *204–205,* 205

G

game nights, 112, *113*
game room, 173
games, board, 100
gardens, 184–185
glassware, 96, 99, 100, *110–111, 196*
grills, outdoor, 198
guest bathrooms, *162,* 163
guest bedrooms, 144, *145*
guest book, 30

H

half baths, *162,* 163
hall trees, 23, 28, *28*
hallways, 23, 34
headboards, 131, *131*
heat lamps, 200
hobbies. *See also* leisure activities
  in "bonus" room, 167 (*See also* "bonus" rooms)
  living room spaces for, 41
  sharing, 178
  stored in entryway, 29, *29*

Index 221

home
  creating a, 9–11
  establishing "house rules" for, 20–21
  personal standards for, *204–205*, 205
  setting the tone for your, *12*, 13
  shared vision for, *14*, 15
home office, 169, *176*, 176–177. *See also* "bonus" rooms
home recording studio, 173
"house rules," 20–21
hutches, 53
hybrid kitchen, *74*, 75

I
"invisible work," 87

K
key storage, 27, *27*
kitchen, *66–67*, 67–69
  cookware and tools, 78–79, 210
  creating cozy spot in, 86
  everyday function of, 67
  finding style for, 68–69
  finishing touches for, *88*, 89
  hybrid, *74*, 75
  maximalist, *70*, 71
  minimalist, 72, *73*
  outdoor, 189
  registering for items, 79, 210
  renovating, 76–77
  sharing workload in, 87
  specialty equipment for, 80, *80*, 81, *81*
knives, 78, 79

L
lamps
  bedroom, 132–133, 139
  dining room, 108
  guest room, 144
  home office, 176, 179
  kitchen, 75, 86
  living room, *48*, 49, 51
  outdoor, 194
laundry hamper, 132
Lawson couch, *44*
leisure activities. *See also* entertaining; hobbies
  in "bonus" room, 167 (*See also* "bonus" rooms)
  equipment for, in entryway, 29, *29*

gardening, 184–185
living room spaces for, 41
sharing, 178
lighting
  bathroom, 153
  bedroom, 132–133, 136, *137*
  "bonus" room, 172
  cozy kitchen spot, 86
  dining room, 108
  entryway, 32
  hallways, 34
  kitchen, 76
  lamps, 49, 51, 108, 132–133, 139, 194
  layered, 49
  living room, *48*, 49
  outdoor, 187, 194
linens
  bedding, *134*, 134–135, 144, 210
  dining room, 99
  guest room, 144
  kitchen, 89
  napkins, *98*, 99, 100, *110–111*
  for outdoor entertaining, *196*
  registering for, 210
  tablecloths, 96
  towels and washcloths, 158
living rooms, *38–39*, 39
  book collections, *50*, 50–51
  coffee table, 41, 46, *47*
  color palette, 62, *63*
  couches, 43–45, *44*
  fireplace, 54, *55*
  functions of, 40–41
  lighting, *48*, 49
  plants, *56*, 57–58, *59*
  registering for items, 51
  storage, *52*, 53

M
mail holders, 27, *27*
mantelshelf, 54, *55*
mattresses, 125, *126*, 127–129
maximalist kitchen, *70*, 71
meals. *See also* recipes
  creating cozy spot for, 86
  dinner parties, 94–96, *97, 98*, 99, 100, *101*
  preparing, 82, *83*
Mediterranean-Style Dolmades, 84–85, *85*
merging belongings, 205, 206
mid-century couch, *44*

minimalism
  in bedroom, 132
  in guest rooms, 144, *145*
  in kitchen, 72, *73*
mirrors
  above mantlepiece, 54
  bathroom, 153
  entryway, *22*, 23, 32
Mix-and-Match Bath Soak, 161
mood boards, 15
movie nights, 60, *61*
movie theater, mini, 172
music studio, 173
mystery box, 31

N
napkins, *98*, 99, 100, *110–111*
nightstands, *138*, 138–139, 144, *145*
Nostalgia Theater, 60, *61*

O
organization, 209
  bathroom, 156–157
  books and libraries, 51
  entryway, 26–28, *27, 28*
  kitchen, 71, 72
ottomans, 23, 44, 132
outdoor spaces, *182*, 183
  continuity between indoor spaces and, 194, *195*
  curb appeal, *186*, 187
  date night in, 199
  entertaining in, *196*, 197–198
  gardens, 184–185
  living areas in, *188*, 189
  patio sets, 190, *191–193*, 193
  registering for items, 198, 210
  special features for, 200, *201*

P
party favors, 30
patio sets, *188*, 190, *191–193*, 193
patios, 189. *See also* outdoor spaces
pedestal tables, *104*
personalization. *See also* décor and details
  bathroom, 149, 158, *159*
  bedroom, 123
  "bonus" room, 179
  dining room, 103, 107, 114
  entryway, 30, 32, *33*
  hallways, 34
  kitchen, *88*, 89
  outdoor spaces, 183, 187

222 Index

pet accoutrements, 29, *29*
pets, in the bedroom, 124
picnic, nighttime, 199
picnic basket, 198
pillow shams, 135
pillows, 134, *134*, 135, 198
pizza oven, 200
place card holders, 99
place mats, 99
planters/pots, *56*, 57, 75, 184, 194
plants
   in "bonus" room, 174, *174*
   gardens, 184–185
   houseplants, *56*, 57–58, *59*
   in kitchen, 71, 75, 89
   for outdoor living spaces, 194
platform beds, 130, *130*

R
reading lamps, 51
reading nook, 172
recipes
   Cherry Stem Cordial, 118, *119*
   Mediterranean-Style Dolmades, 84–85, *85*
   Mix-and-Match Bath Soak, 161
recreation room, 169. *See also* "bonus" rooms
remodeling, 77
renovations, 76–77, 153. *See also* updating
resort luxuries, in bedroom, 140, *141*
room dividers, 174, *174*

S
sconces, 108, 153
seating
   benches, 23, 107, 187
   "bonus" room, 175, *175*
   chairs, 23, *106*, 107, *138*, 175, *175*
   couches, 25, *25*, 43–45, *44*, 144
   dining room, *106*, 107
   entryway, 23
   living room, 40
   outdoor, 187, *188*, 189, 190, *191–193*, 193
serveware, 96, 99, 100, 197
shared vision, *14*, 15
sheets, 134, 135
shelves
   bathroom, 156
   bedroom closets, 143

"bonus" room, 172, 175, *175*
entryway, 23
étagères, 175, *175*
kitchen, 71, 72, *74*
living room, 50, *50*, 53
mantelshelf, 54, *55*
shoe storage, 28, *28*
showers, outdoor, 200
signature cocktails, 114
60-30-10 color ratio, 62
sleep, 124–125, 132
sofas, 43–45, *44*
speakers, outdoor, 200
staircases, 34, *35*
storage
   bathroom, 151, 156–157
   bedroom, 132
   "bonus" room, 175, *175*
   entryway, 19, 23, 26–29, *27–29*
   guest bathroom, *162*, 163
   guest room, 144
   kitchen, 71, 72, *74*, 75
   living room, *52*, 53
style(s). *See also* décor and details
   bedroom, 123
   "bonus" room, 179
   couches, 43–45, *44*
   dining room, 103–105, *104, 106, 107*
   garden, 184–185
   kitchen, 68–69
   merging, 15
   outdoor spaces, 193–194, *195*
   previewed by exterior of house, 187
sweet talk. *See* communication/conversations
swing, outdoor, 187

T
table settings, 96, *97*, 110, *110–111*
tablecloths, 96
tables
   cocktail table, 46
   coffee table, 46, 47
   in defining entryway, 25, *25*
   dining room, 103–105, *104*
   entryway, 19, 23, 32
   kitchen worktable, 75
   living room, 41
   outdoor, 189
   patio sets, 190, *191–193*, 193

tableware, *74, 196,* 197
task lights, *48*
televisions, 41, 125, 172, 200
thermoses, 198
toiletries, 149, 151, 156, 157, 163
toilets, 153, 155
tone for your home, setting, *12,* 13
towels, 158
track lighting, 49
traffic flow, 23, 25, *25,* 34
trestle tables, *104*

U
updating
   bathroom, 153, *154,* 155
   kitchen, 76

V
vanities, bathroom, 153, 155, 157
vases, 96
video gaming setup, 173

W
walk-in closet, *142,* 143
wall space
   above bed, 136, *137*
   above fireplaces, 54, *55*
   above kitchen cabinets, 71
   for fitness equipment, 29, *29*
   maximizing, 24, *24*
washcloths, 158
water structures, 200
wedding registry checklist, 210–211
   bathrobes, 158
   bathroom linens, 158
   bedding, 135
   "bonus" room items, 170
   dining room items, 96, 99, 100
   entryway items, 32
   kitchen essentials, 79
   living room items, 51
   for outdoor spaces, 198
welcome basket, 144
window treatments, 76, 133, 155
word art, 179
workday patterns/styles, 177
workout equipment, 170, 172
worktables, kitchen, 75

PHOTOGRAPH BY JESSICA SAMPLE

ANUSH J. BENLIYAN is a design and lifestyle journalist and magazine editor whose work has been featured in national and regional print publications including *C Magazine*, *Luxe Interiors + Design*, *Santa Barbara Magazine*, the *Robb Report*, *Los Angeles* magazine, *Pasadena Magazine*, and *The Agency* magazine, and in international editions of *Elle Decor*. She has spent her career interviewing and celebrating interior designers, architects, artisans, artists, chefs, and other creative visionaries. An Armenian American born and raised in Los Angeles, she currently resides in Pasadena, California, with her musician husband, their young son, and their adopted dachshund.